JOE FRANKLIN'S
Great
Entertainment
TRIVIA
GAME

SQUAREONE
PUBLISHERS

To my wife, Lois; my son, Brad;
my grandchildren, Billy and Sarah—
without me, you would not be on this page . . .
and without you, I wouldn't be me.

COVER DESIGNER: Phaedra Mastrocola
COVER PHOTOS COURTESY OF: Joe Franklin
RESEARCH ASSISTANTS: Evan Schwartz and Anthony Pomes
EDITORS: Marie Caratozzolo and Joanne Abrams
TYPESETTER: Gary A. Rosenberg

Square One Publishers
Garden City Park, New York 11040
www.squareonepublishers.com

CONTENTS

ACKNOWLEDGMENTS

I have a lot of people to thank:

First, my publisher Rudy Shur, who spent all those hours watching two-reel silent movies on my TV show when he was a kid; my tried and trusted research assistants Evan Schwartz and Anthony Pomes, whose passion and enthusiasm for all the persons, places, and things in the world of entertainment give me hope for the future; my editors Marie Caratozzolo and Joanne Abrams, who made sure all the t's were dotted and the i's were crossed . . . well, now you see why I need 'em; my longtime radio producer and friend Richie Ornstein; my friend Peter Muller, for his advice and counsel over the years; Steven Garrin of VideoActive Productions and VoiceWorks Sound Studios, who has worked with me on a number of important projects with talent, smarts, and good old-fashioned gusto; all the wonderful people at my Memory Lane restaurant in New York City, who have helped make it a memorable place for all who come to dine with us; and Ron Simon of the Museum of Television & Radio, for his expert curatorial assistance in helping me check on the veracity of some of the book's questions.

I'd also like to give thanks to performers like Eddie Cantor, Jimmy Durante, Kate Smith, Buster Keaton, and so many others who have lined the hallways of my life with moments of purest show-business gossamer. (I've been waiting to use that word somewhere, so . . . .) Lastly, I must thank you, the reader. Your deep-rooted love of movies, TV, and music helps keep the world of entertainment growing and flourishing.

My name's Joe—it's nice to meet you.

HOW TO PLAY THE GAMES

Welcome, my friends. Are you ready to put your knowledge of entertainment facts and details to the test? My trivia book is guaranteed to challenge, while providing endless hours of fun and enjoyment. The games in this book have been designed in a way that allows you, the reader, to play either alone or with others. When looking up the answer to a question in most trivia books, the reader is able to see the answers to other questions at the same time. This book doesn't allow that to happen, but you must first understand how to play the games. Ready?

THE BASICS

There are eighty games in this book, each with a dozen questions. Every game is numbered and has been given a title that reflects the basic category of its questions, such as Game Shows, War Movies, and Leading Ladies. You'll also find a number of games titled "Memory Lane Grab Bag"; these include a potpourri of questions from a variety of categories.

THE PAGE SETUP

Each page holds four frames that are situated from the top of the page to the bottom (as seen in the sample on the next page). Each frame is divided in half with a left side and a right. The box on the left contains a question. The box on the right contains the answer to the question from the previous page. In other words, the answer to the question in the top frame of page 1 is found on the right side of the top frame of page 2. (It sounds more complicated than it actually is.) Stay with me . . .

Typical Page Layout

Questions will always be found on the left side of each frame. Answers to questions (from the previous page) will be found on the right side of the frame.

TOP FRAME

SECOND FRAME

THIRD FRAME

BOTTOM FRAME

PLAYING THE GAMES

The most important point is that the questions for each game are not read from the top of each page to the bottom. Rather, the twelve game questions are found on the same frame level on consecutively numbered pages. I know this sounds a little confusing, so let me help make this clear with an example and an accompanying graphic.

Let's start with Game #1, which begins in the top frame of page 1. Here, you will find the number and name of the game you are about to play. Turn to page 2 (the next right-hand page) for the game's first question, which is located on the left half of the top frame. As explained above, for the answer to this question, you should turn to page 3 (the next right-hand page) and look at the right half of the top frame. This game's second question is found on the left half of the top frame. And that's how you continue, turning the page for each new question (**Q**), and finding its answer (**A**) on the page that follows. (See the graphic on the next page.)

Questions are always found on the left-hand side of each frame, and answers are always found on the right.

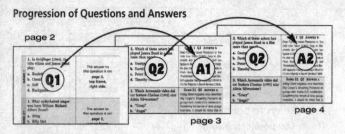

Individual games are always played on the same frame level.

By this time, you've probably noticed that the pages are not numbered in the traditional manner. The right-hand pages are numbered consecutively from 1 to 140. This was done to help make it easier for you to follow the sequence of games and their questions. Beginning with the top frame (and staying in that top frame), play the games, which flow from one right-hand page to the next until you have reached the last page. Then make a U-turn and continue playing the games in the top frame from the back of the book to the front. While going in this direction, you'll be answering the questions on the consecutive left-hand pages, which are numbered from 141 to 280, from the back of the book to the front.

Now what? Well, once you've completed the games in the top frame from the front of the book to the back, and then from the back to the front, you'll once again find yourself on page 1. Simply drop down one level to the next frame and begin playing the games found on this new frame level.

THE PROMISE

Friends, I can promise you this. If you play the first few games as I've described, you'll quickly understand how to play all of the games—front to back and back to front. And, best of all, you will be entertained, amused, and maybe even enlightened by the challenging questions and their informative answers.

GAME 1

"The Name Is Bond, James Bond."

How Well Do You Know Secret Agent 007?

These games allow you to play alone or with others. However, because the book's format is different from other trivia books, be sure to read "How to Play the Games" on page vi.

Turn to page 2 for the first question.

GAME 21

Rockin' and Rollin'

Songs, Albums, and Performers

Turn to page 2 for the first question.

GAME 41

Taking Up "Space"

Star Treks, Trials, and Other Sci-Fi "Tribble"-ations

Turn to page 2 for the first question.

GAME 61

Chicken or the Egg

Which Came First?

Turn to page 2 for the first question.

Game 21 begins on page 1, second frame, with its first question on page 2.	**GAME 20 Q12 ANSWER a** According to Heston, he made $1.25 an hour posing for these classes (in 1946, that was halfway decent money). In 1967's *Planet of the Apes*, all of America got to see Heston in a loincloth in full Panavision glory for just $1.50 a ticket. Inflation . . .
Game 41 begins on page 1, third frame, with its first question on page 2.	**GAME 40 Q12 ANSWER c** Although Chicago has released all of its albums in Roman numeral sequence, the titles do not always state the number. However, any album to feature numerals always takes into account the albums that came before. To date, the band is up to album twenty-seven (I mean, XXVII) with the latest: *The Very Best of Chicago: Only the Beginning*.
Game 61 begins on page 1, bottom frame, with its first question on page 2.	**GAME 60 Q12 ANSWER c** Hunting (played by Matt Damon) is a rebellious twenty-year-old janitor with a brilliant mathematical mind. Damon collaborated with Ben Affleck on the script for *Good Will Hunting* during their college days at Harvard. This well-received 1997 film won the Oscar for Best Screenplay Written Directly for the Screen.
I hope you enjoyed taking this walk with me down Memory Lane. And as they say in the movies, "The End."	**GAME 80 Q12 ANSWER c** Diane Keaton's performance won her the Best Actress award, and although co-star Woody Allen won Oscars as well, they were for Best Director and Best Original Screenplay (shared with co-writer Marshall Brickman). The movie also won the Best Picture award.

GAME 1	**1.** In *Goldfinger* (1964), the title villain and James Bond play: **a.** Roulette **b.** Chemin de fer **c.** Golf **d.** Backgammon	The answer to this question is on: **page 3, top frame, right side.**
GAME 21	**1.** What spiky-haired singer was born William Michael Albert Broad? **a.** Sting **b.** Billy Idol **c.** Rod Stewart **d.** Sid Vicious	The answer to this question is on: **page 3, second frame, right side.**
GAME 41	**1.** In which science fiction TV show were the Cylons the bad guys? **a.** *Space: 1999* **b.** *Dr. Who* **c.** *Battlestar Galactica* **d.** *ALF*	The answer to this question is on: **page 3, third frame, right side.**
GAME 61	**1.** Which Elliott Gould movie came first? **a.** *M*A*S*H* **b.** *Bob & Carol & Ted & Alice* **c.** *California Split* **d.** *The Long Goodbye*	The answer to this question is on: **page 3, bottom frame, right side.**

12. What did Charlton Heston do to earn money while in college?

a. Posed in a loincloth for art classes

b. Played chess

c. Delivered furniture

d. Did radio voiceovers

GAME 20 Q11 ANSWER c

Alice was played by Pert Kelton in 1951, Audrey Meadows (the best-known Alice) from 1954 to 1956, Sue Ann Langdon in 1962, and Sheila MacRae in 1971. Because he thought she was too pretty, Gleason almost didn't hire Meadows for the role.

---

12. Which pop group has named all of its album titles in numerical order?

a. Genesis

b. Led Zeppelin

c. Chicago

d. Van Halen

GAME 40 Q11 ANSWER d

Densmore plays an audio engineer who records Morrison (Val Kilmer) reading his poetry. Much of Stone's film was based on Densmore's memoir *Riders on the Storm.* The film also features cameos by The Doors' record producer Paul Rothchild, and Morrison's girlfriend Patricia Kennealy.

---

12. In the Gus Van Sant film *Good Will Hunting,* what is Will Hunting's job at MIT?

a. Messenger

b. Groundskeeper

c. Janitor

d. Electrician

GAME 60 Q11 ANSWER b

In the words of Cher, who played the Italian widow, "It was bad luck!" Cher's love interest is Ronnie Cammareri (Nicolas Cage), whose character loses his hand in a slicer when talking with his brother Johnny (Danny Aiello). The accident results in some "bad blood" between the brothers. Mamma mia!

---

12. Which film did *not* receive Oscars for both Best Actress and Best Actor?

a. *The Silence of the Lambs* (1991)

b. *One Flew Over the Cuckoo's Nest* (1975)

c. *Annie Hall* (1977)

d. *Coming Home* (1978)

GAME 80 Q11 ANSWER a

Considering it an act of mercy, Stewart's character euthanized his wife, who had been suffering from a terminal illness. The movie was the 1952 Oscar winner for Best Picture, and also boasted a strong performance from relative newcomer Charlton Heston.

---

2. Which actor did *not* play Blofeld to Sean Connery's James Bond?

a. Donald Pleasence
b. Telly Savalas
c. Charles Gray
d. Max von Sydow

GAME 1 Q1 ANSWER c
Auric Goldfinger (Gert Fröbe) loses when Bond catches him trying to cheat. Fröbe, whose birth name was Karl-Gerhart Froeber, was born in Saxony, Germany. He couldn't speak English well, so the producers had a British actor overdub his lines in post-production.

2. Which band cooked up the double album *Mellon Collie and the Infinite Sadness*?

a. Red Hot Chili Peppers
b. Strawberry Alarm Clock
c. Smashing Pumpkins
d. Blind Melon

GAME 21 Q1 ANSWER b
Best known for '80s hits "White Wedding" and "Rebel Yell," Idol was born November 30, 1955. He had a featured part in the 1998 Adam Sandler back-to-the-eighties comedy *The Wedding Singer*, which co-starred Drew Barrymore.

2. Which actor from the TV show *Night Court* appeared as a Klingon in the film *Star Trek III: The Search for Spock*?

a. Markie Post
b. Harry Anderson
c. John Larroquette
d. Richard Moll

GAME 41 Q1 ANSWER c
Commander Adama (Lorne Greene) and the crew of the Battlestar Galactica fight the cybernetic Cylons during the show's run from 1978 to 1980. This show was the first weekly series to have a budget of over $1 million an episode—an expense resulting from its post-*Star Wars* visual effects.

2. By release date, not alphabetically, which of the following movies came first?

a. *M*
b. *Q*
c. *X*
d. *Z*

GAME 61 Q1 ANSWER b
Gould played Ted in the 1969 Paul Mazursky film. The other three films were directed by Robert Altman, whom Gould tried to get fired from *M*A*S*H* (1970). Altman also directed Gould (playing himself) in both *Nashville* and *The Player*.

11. How many actresses have played "Alice Kramden" on *The Honeymooners*?

a. Two
b. Three
c. Four
d. Five

GAME 20 Q10 ANSWER c
Debuting on ABC a year after the film's theatrical release, *Delta House* happened to co-star a pretty actress named Michelle Pfeiffer. She would go on to co-star with Tony Danza in *The Hollywood Knights* (1980) and then play a Pink Lady in 1982's *Grease 2* before hitting the big time as Al Pacino's wife in *Scarface* (1983).

11. Which member of The Doors plays a character in Oliver Stone's *The Doors* (1991)?

a. Jim Morrison
b. Robbie Krieger
c. Ray Manzarek
d. John Densmore

GAME 40 Q10 ANSWER d
Crispin Glover played the mysterious Pop Art icon in Oliver Stone's rock epic *The Doors* (1991), while David Bowie played Warhol in the acclaimed independent film *Basquiat* (1993). Jared Harris drew raves for his portrayal of the artist in the film *I Shot Andy Warhol* (1996), based on the life of Warhol's would-be assassin Valerie Solanas.

11. In the movie *Moonstruck*, how did Loretta Castorini's (Cher's) first husband die?

a. Struck by lightning
b. Hit by a bus
c. Slipped off a subway platform
d. Fell off a ladder

GAME 60 Q10 ANSWER b
In addition to "Ferret Face," Major Burns (played by Larry Linville) was also "affectionately" referred to as the "Lipless Wonder."

11. In *The Greatest Show on Earth*, Jimmy Stewart plays a clown who is hiding from the police for:

a. Killing his wife
b. A string of burglaries
c. Arson
d. Counterfeiting

GAME 80 Q10 ANSWER d
For his role in *The Goodbye Girl*, Dreyfuss won the award at age twenty-nine. To date, he has received one other nomination—for *Mr. Holland's Opus*, which he lost to Al Pacino for *Scent of a Woman*. Nominations for Best Supporting Role were received by Haley Joel Osment (*The Sixth Sense*) and River Phoenix (*Running on Empty*).

3. Which of these actors has played James Bond in a film more than once?

a. George Lazenby
b. David Niven
c. Peter Sellers
d. Timothy Dalton

GAME 1 Q2 ANSWER b
Sean Connery faced Pleasence in *You Only Live Twice* (1967), Gray in *Diamonds Are Forever* (1971), and von Sydow in *Never Say Never Again* (1983). He also met with uncredited Blofelds in *From Russia With Love* (1963) and *Thunderball* (1965). Savalas played Blofeld opposite George Lazenby's Bond in *On Her Majesty's Secret Service* (1969).

---

3. Which Aerosmith video did *not* feature *Clueless* (1995) star Alicia Silverstone?

a. "Crazy"
b. "Angel"
c. "Cryin'"
d. "Amazing"

GAME 21 Q2 ANSWER c
Rolling Stone magazine once described Billy Corgan's Smashing Pumpkins as grunge-rock-meets-ELO-melodicism. Considering the demise of other grunge musicians, it should be noted that in 1996, the band fired drummer Jimmy Chamberlain for continued drug abuse.

---

3. From which planet was *ALF*?

a. Mars
b. Ork
c. Melmac
d. France

GAME 41 Q2 ANSWER c
Larroquette was a loyal and dutiful Klingon to his master, played by fellow NBC-TV star Christopher Lloyd (well known as the burnout Reverend Jim on *Taxi*). From 1993 to 1996, Larroquette starred on the NBC sitcom *The John Larroquette Show*.

---

3. What was the first full-length live-action Technicolor feature film?

a. *Flowers and Trees*
b. *Becky Sharp*
c. *Snow White and the Seven Dwarfs*
d. *Gone With the Wind*

GAME 61 Q2 ANSWER a
Peter Lorre is unforgettable in *M*, Fritz Lang's riveting 1931 German thriller about a child murderer; *Q* (1982) was about a prehistoric Aztec flying serpent; *X* (1963) was one of Roger Corman's well-regarded thrillers, with Ray Milland as the "Dr. with X-Ray eyes"; and *Z* (1969) starred Yves Montand and won the Oscar for best foreign film.

10. Which TV show was based on *National Lampoon's Animal House* (1978)?

a. *Food Fight*

b. *Brothers and Sisters*

c. *Delta House*

d. *Coed Fever*

GAME 20 Q9 ANSWER a
Brando played the role of a Nazi in this mini-series sequel, for which he won an Outstanding Supporting Actor Emmy.

---

10. Which of the following actors has *not* played Andy Warhol?

a. Crispin Glover

b. David Bowie

c. Jared Harris

d. Mick Jagger

GAME 40 Q9 ANSWER b
Gere played his trumpet parts in Francis Ford Coppola's *The Cotton Club* (1985). In Martin Scorsese's *New York, New York* (1977), DeNiro learned to mimic his sax parts. So did Forest Whitaker as Charlie Parker in *Bird* (1988), and Sean Penn on guitar in Woody Allen's *Sweet and Lowdown* (1999).

---

10. What was Major Frank Burns' nickname on *M*A*S*H*?

a. Hot Pants

b. Ferret Face

c. Coochie-Coo

d. Funny Man

GAME 60 Q9 ANSWER d
It was always war when the *Cheers* gang faced off against the crowd from Gary's Olde Towne Tavern. The rivalry between the two bars began when Cheers beat the Tavern in bowling, setting off a war of practical jokes. The multiple award-winning *Cheers* ran on NBC from 1982 to 1993.

---

10. Who is the youngest male to win an Oscar for Best Actor in a Leading Role?

a. Haley Joel Osment

b. Ricky Schroeder

c. River Phoenix

d. Richard Dreyfuss

GAME 80 Q9 ANSWER a
In addition to this achievement, Cher was nominated for Best Actress for her incredible role in *Mask*, and for Best Supporting Actress for her role in *Silkwood*. Since that time, however, Cher has acted in only a few films (*Mermaids* in 1990, *Faithful* in 1996, and *Tea With Mussolini* in 1999).

4. All of these actresses were partners of *Avenger* John Steed and appeared in James Bond films except:

a. Honor Blackman

b. Joanna Lumley

c. Maud Adams

d. Diana Rigg

GAME 1 Q3 ANSWER d
Dalton has played Agent 007 in *The Living Daylights* (1987) and *Licence to Kill* (1989). Niven, Sellers, and even Woody Allen played Sir James, James, and Jimmy Bond, respectively, in the 1967 spoof *Casino Royale*—a predecessor to the Mike Myers *Austin Powers* comedies. Lazenby appeared once as Bond in *On Her Majesty's Secret Service*.

---

4. "Blue Suede Shoes" was written by:

a. Elvis Presley

b. Jerry Leiber and Mike Stoller

c. Carl Perkins

d. Fats Domino

GAME 21 Q3 ANSWER b
The group's "Angel" video features an anonymous beauty who floats above Steven Tyler's supine body as he sings. In Aerosmith's "Crazy" video, Alicia Silverstone appears with Tyler's daughter Liv.

---

4. Which character was *not* an Enterprise crew member during *Star Trek's* first season?

a. Lt. Uhura

b. Mr. Sulu

c. Ensign Chekov

d. Bones McCoy

GAME 41 Q3 ANSWER c
ALF (Alien Life Form) was a fur-covered, 229-year-old alien, whose spaceship crashlanded in Willie Tanner's (Max Wright's) garage. Mork was from Ork. The Coneheads claimed to be from France. Last time I checked, the Martians were from Mars.

---

4. Which was Pink Floyd's first album?

a. *Wish You Were Here*

b. *Piper at the Gates of Dawn*

c. *Saucerful of Secrets*

d. *Dark Side of the Moon*

GAME 61 Q3 ANSWER b
This 1935 adaptation of Thackeray's *Vanity Fair* was directed by Rouben Mamoulian and starred Miriam Hopkins, who garnered an Academy Award nomination for the title role. The first commercial Technicolor film was *Flowers and Trees* (1932), one of Disney's "Silly Symphony" cartoon shorts.

9. Which Oscar-winning actor appeared in the 1979 mini-series *Roots: The New Generation*?

a. Marlon Brando

b. Gregory Peck

c. Karl Malden

d. Sidney Poitier

GAME 20 Q8 ANSWER c
After leaving her job as an editor for Pendent Publishing, Elaine worked for J. Peterman, the clothing catalog egomaniac. Vandalay is the name that George Costanza used for the many fictional enterprises in which he was involved.

9. Which actor actually played an instrument in one of his films?

a. Robert DeNiro

b. Richard Gere

c. Sean Penn

d. Forest Whitaker

GAME 40 Q8 ANSWER c
Although its first two albums were named *Van Halen* (1978) and *Van Halen II* (1979), the band didn't return to numerical titles until 1997. That's when Gary Cherone became Van Halen's third lead vocalist (after David Lee Roth and Sammy Hagar). Cherone lasted for one album and tour before he was dropped from the band.

9. Which bar always played practical jokes on the gang at *Cheers*?

a. Gary's Down Home Tavern

b. Gary's Good Time Tavern

c. Gary's Olde Time Tavern

d. Gary's Olde Towne Tavern

GAME 60 Q8 ANSWER d
In this 1967 war drama, Clint Walker, Jim Brown, and Charles Bronson played three of the dozen criminals recruited for a World War II suicide mission. George Kennedy played an officer—Major Max Armbruster.

9. For which of the following movies did Cher receive the Oscar for Best Actress?

a. *Moonstruck* (1987)

b. *Silkwood* (1983)

c. *Mask* (1985)

d. *The Witches of Eastwick* (1987)

GAME 80 Q8 ANSWER b
Actually, Prince Rogers Nelson (a.k.a. The Artist Formerly Known as Prince) has also co-written hit songs for singers such as Stevie Nicks ("Stand Back") and written for Cyndi Lauper ("When You Were Mine"). When I'm ready to record my album of great hits, I know who I need to get in touch with.

5. Horror film icon Christopher Lee appeared as which Bond villain in *The Man With the Golden Gun* (1974)?

a. Scaramanga

b. Nick Nack

c. Jaws

d. Blofeld

GAME 1 Q4 ANSWER c
Honor Blackman, who played Pussy Galore in *Goldfinger* (1964), was replaced in the original *Avengers* by Diana Rigg. Rigg appeared in *On Her Majesty's Secret Service* (1969) as Contessa Tracy di Vincenzo. Joanna Lumley, who had a bit part in the same Bond film, also appeared in the *New Avengers*.

5. Which 1985 concert event featured performances by Bob Dylan, Billy Joel, Tom Petty, and Foreigner?

a. Band Aid

b. USA for Africa

c. Live Aid

d. Farm Aid

GAME 21 Q4 ANSWER c
Perkins was also the original singer of this 1956 rockabilly song, which was a #2 hit. It made Perkins the first white country artist to cross over to R&B. Elvis's recording of the song reached only #20 on the pop charts.

5. Who played Mork's son on *Mork & Mindy*?

a. Tom Posten

b. Robin Williams

c. Ray Walston

d. Jonathan Winters

GAME 41 Q4 ANSWER c
The ship's navigator and junior science officer Pavel Chekov (Walter Koenig) was added in the show's second season by creator Gene Roddenberry. Koenig was picked to play Chekov because he resembled Davey Jones from the popular TV show *The Monkees*. That's why Chekov is seen wearing that moptop wig in his first few episodes.

5. Which was Bill Cosby's first big-screen comedy?

a. *Let's Do It Again*

b. *A Piece of the Action*

c. *Uptown Saturday Night*

d. *Ghost Dad*

GAME 61 Q4 ANSWER b
Pink Floyd recorded its 1967 album in the same studio at the same time The Beatles were working on tracks for *Sgt. Pepper's Lonely Hearts Club Band*. Drummer Nick Mason called it a "most humbling" introduction to recording.

8. On *Seinfeld,* Elaine worked for which of the following publishers?

a. Square One Publishers
b. Vandalay House
c. Pendent Publishing
d. Peterman Press

GAME 20 Q7 ANSWER a
Burghoff played Walter "Radar" O'Reilly, who received the nickname because of his uncanny knack of knowing what was going to happen right before it actually did. He would state, "Incoming . . ." and within ten seconds, the sound of incoming helicopters would be audible.

8. *Van Halen III* is the band's album number:

a. Three
b. Twelve
c. Thirteen
d. Fifteen

GAME 40 Q7 ANSWER b
This still-popular sitcom debuted on ABC-TV September 26, 1969. By April of 1970, the Bradys had found their way to *TV Guide,* and would eventually find their way into the recording studio to make three albums in two years and to undertake a summer concert tour in 1972. The final new episode of *The Brady Bunch* aired on March 8, 1974.

8. Which of the following actors was not one of *The Dirty Dozen*?

a. Clint Walker
b. Jim Brown
c. Charles Bronson
d. George Kennedy

GAME 60 Q7 ANSWER a
Although Lee Marvin played the part of Reisman, John Wayne was offered the role first. Instead, Wayne chose to star in and direct *The Green Berets,* another war film.

8. Which pop music star wrote Sinead O'Connor's hit "Nothing Compares 2 U"?

a. Michael Jackson
b. Prince
c. Madonna
d. Cyndi Lauper

GAME 80 Q7 ANSWER b
The Simpsons first aired on *The Tracey Ullman Show* in 1987. In 1989, Matt Groening's little cartoon was given its own half-hour spot on FOX-TV.

6. James Bond author, Ian Fleming, has a cameo in which Bond film?

a. *Thunderball* (1965)

b. *Dr. No* (1962)

c. *From Russia With Love* (1963)

d. *Goldfinger* (1964)

GAME 1 Q5 ANSWER a

"Love is required, whenever he's hired. It comes just before the kill," according to the theme song. Francisco Scaramanga, the deranged former KGB agent, kills with a golden gun and a 23-carat gold bullet.

6. Which of the following is *not* a Troggs song?

a. "Wild Thing"

b. "Love Is All Around"

c. "Summer in the City"

d. "With a Girl Like You"

GAME 21 Q5 ANSWER d

The idea for Farm Aid came at the Live Aid Concert in July 1985, when Bob Dylan said on stage, "Wouldn't it be great if we did something for our own farmers right here in America?" Farm Aid raised more than $7 million for America's family farmers.

6. On *Star Trek*, how long was the original mission of the U.S.S. Enterprise supposed to last?

a. Four years

b. Five years

c. Six years

d. Ten years

GAME 41 Q5 ANSWER d

Jonathan Winters played Mearth for the show's final season. On Mork's planet, Ork, children are hatched full grown from giant eggs, and then they get younger. Winters and Williams, both improvisational geniuses, often ad-libbed their material on the show.

6. Of the following "rock-and-roll" songs, which came first?

a. "Rock and Roll Band"

b. "I'm Just a Singer (In a Rock and Roll Band)"

c. "It's Only Rock & Roll (But I Like It)"

d. "I Love Rock and Roll"

GAME 61 Q5 ANSWER c

The 1974 chase for a stolen lottery ticket followed Cosby's earlier dramatic turns as a frontiersman in *Man and Boy* and a private eye in the crime drama *Hickey & Boggs* (both 1972). The latter co-starred *I Spy*'s Robert Culp, who also directed the film.

GAME 20

7. Which of the following actors was in both *M*A*S*H* the movie and the TV series?

a. Gary Burghoff
b. Wayne Rogers
c. Loretta Swit
d. Larry Linville

GAME 20 Q6 ANSWER b
Scorsese wanted to cast George Memmoli from his earlier film *Mean Streets* in this part, but the actor died before shooting started on the picture. Peter Boyle, Albert Brooks, and Harvey Keitel all have supporting roles in *Taxi Driver*.

GAME 40

7. Which year did *The Brady Bunch* first appear on the cover of *TV Guide*?

a. 1969
b. 1970
c. 1971
d. 1972

GAME 40 Q6 ANSWER c
This disaster epic boasted a script co-written by *Godfather* author Mario Puzo, and was presented in movie theaters with the new "Sensurround" sound system that caused theaters to vibrate during the earthquake sequences. Here's a bit of trivia—in the credits, Walter Matthau is listed under his real name, Walter Matuschanskavasky.

GAME 60

7. Who played the role of Major John Reisman, leader of *The Dirty Dozen*?

a. Lee Marvin
b. John Wayne
c. Robert Ryan
d. Robert Mitchum

GAME 60 Q6 ANSWER b
After Hanks' plane crashes, he is marooned on an island along with a number of FedEx packages, many of which he uses in his efforts to survive.

GAME 80

7. On which variety show did *The Simpsons* make its debut?

a. *The Carol Burnett Show*
b. *The Tracey Ullman Show*
c. *The Garry Shandling Show*
d. *In Living Color*

GAME 80 Q6 ANSWER a
Running from September 1964 to June 1969, *Peyton Place* has the unique distinction of being television's first prime-time soap opera. In the cast were a very young Mia Farrow (before becoming "Mrs. Sinatra" and having *Rosemary's Baby* in 1968) and Ryan O'Neal (who became the star of a very touching *Love Story* opposite Ali McGraw in 1970).

Mr. Franklin Is Ready
for His Close-Up . . .

People always ask me who the *real* Joe Franklin is. Damned if I know. It would be hard for me to tell you exactly *who* I am. The Greek philosopher Plato once wrote, "I think, therefore I am." Applied to myself, I would say "I collect, therefore I am." No big mystery, really. I wake up each day, head to my office, go to the radio station to do a show, visit my restaurant, call my wife and son, eat a meal here and there, stop by a flea market in search of rare collectibles, come home at night, relax with a Rudy Vallee record and a 16mm print of a Lillian Gish silent, go to sleep, wake up the next day, and do it all over again. I'm just me, pure and simple. Still, people want to capture the true essence of Joe Franklin.

Over the years, I've appeared in some very notable big-time movies as (guess who?) myself. I made an appearance in two Woody Allen movies—the first time, you can hear my TV show playing on a small TV set in the background of a scene between Woody and Mariel Hemingway in *Manhattan* (1979). More prominently, my show and I were featured in *Broadway Danny Rose* (1984), Woody's nostalgic film about theatrical talent agents. There, I was called upon to play myself and to interview an Italian singer—portrayed wonderfully by Nick Apollo Forte—who was trying for a comeback.

In a case of art imitating life, in the mid-1970s, I interviewed a real-life Italian singer named Nick DiMauro—a trained opera singer who was making a go at pop music with an album called *Being Alive*. As it turns out, both of his sons went on to become talented musicians and still recall with pride the time their dad appeared on my show. It makes me feel good to know how I've touched the lives of so many different performers through the years.

In 1984, I again appeared as myself in Ivan Reitman's smash hit comedy, *Ghostbusters*. You will see me in the film interviewing Dan Aykroyd's character and asking him that most paranormal of questions, "How is Elvis and have you seen him lately?" Soon after the film's release, in another case of life imitating art, Dan Aykroyd appeared on my show to have a chat and promote the film.

In 1991, I made yet another appearance as myself (who else?) in the wonderful George Gallo comedy, *29th Street*. Starring Danny Aiello and Anthony LaPaglia, it's the true story of Frank Pesce, the first person to win the New York State Lottery back in 1976. I play a pivotal role in the film, because I am the person who reads out the winner of the lottery, setting the film's plot in motion. I had great fun improvising all of my lines, and did my best to prolong the moment before reading out the winner's name. You can even hear one of the audience members shouting at me to hurry it up and cut the suspense (but not in those words!). The power of the microphone can be a wonderful thing sometimes.

In addition to these high-profile cameos, I've also appeared in a bunch of pictures by the late director Harry Hurwitz. One of these films was *That's Adequate*, which had a big, big cast including Tony Randall, James Coco, and a relative newcomer named Bruce Willis.

If any of you budding filmmakers out there would like to feature me in a film, I am almost always available. However, I'm looking to branch out—perhaps play a tall, debonair leading man who is a martial arts master and beguiles, charms, and seduces a bevy of beautiful, buxom women who quiver at my touch. That's the *real* Joe Franklin!

7. *Never Say Never Again* (1983) is basically a remake of which earlier Bond film?

a. *Diamonds Are Forever* (1971)

b. *Thunderball* (1965)

c. *You Only Live Twice* (1967)

d. *Dr. No* (1962)

GAME 1 Q6 ANSWER c
In the second film of the Bond series, *From Russia With Love*, Fleming appears briefly standing at the window of a train, wearing grey trousers and a white sweater. Fleming died a year later in 1964.

---

7. How many of Bruce Springsteen's singles have hit #1?

a. Seven

b. Three

c. One

d. None

GAME 21 Q6 ANSWER c
"Summer in the City" was a hit for the Lovin' Spoonful. The Troggs, considered by many to be the first British punk band, is probably best remembered for "Wild Thing," which hit #1 in 1966. The band still has two of its original members, including lead singer Reg Presley. In 1992, the group performed at Sting's wedding.

---

7. Who played Mr. Sulu on *Star Trek*?

a. James Doohan

b. George Takei

c. Walter Koenig

d. DeForest Kelly

GAME 41 Q6 ANSWER b
The Enterprise was to search the final frontier for five years, boldly going "where no man has gone before." Of course, the mission has continued for over thirty-five years thanks to the continued interest of Trekkies, Trekkers, and other fans of the films and television shows.

---

7. *Mystic Pizza* included the first film performance credited for which actor?

a. Julia Roberts

b. Vincent D'Onofrio

c. Matt Damon

d. Edward Norton

GAME 61 Q6 ANSWER b
The Moody Blues explained "I'm Just A Singer (In A Rock and Roll Band)" in 1973. The Rolling Stones convinced us "It's Only Rock & Roll (But I Like It)" in 1974. Boston was the "Rock and Roll Band" of the moment in 1976; and Joan Jett told us "I Love Rock and Roll" in 1982.

6. In *Taxi Driver* (1976), the angry passenger who tells Robert DeNiro how he plans to kill his wife is played by:

a. Peter Boyle

b. Martin Scorsese

c. Albert Brooks

d. Harvey Keitel

GAME 20 Q5 ANSWER b
Lolita was about 150 minutes long, and *Eyes Wide Shut* ran 155 minutes (although some naysayers have sworn the film was far longer). *Barry Lyndon* is often thought to be the longest Kubrick film at 183 minutes, but *Spartacus* is, in fact, the winner at 196 minutes.

---

6. In the 1974 disaster picture *Earthquake*, Charlton Heston's wife is played by:

a. Rita Hayworth

b. Trish Van Devere

c. Ava Gardner

d. Kim Novak

GAME 40 Q5 ANSWER b
ABBA is from Sweden, and had several huge disco hits in the late 1970s, including "Take a Chance on Me" and "Dancing Queen." In 2001, bandleaders Björn Ulvaeus and Benny Andersson scored a huge hit on Broadway with *Mamma Mia!*, the musical based on ABBA's music.

---

6. For which courier service does Tom Hanks work in *Cast Away*?

a. UPS

b. FedEx

c. Airborne

d. DHL

GAME 60 Q5 ANSWER d
Written by Neil Simon, this film was remade in 1999 with Steve Martin and Goldie Hawn as the midwestern couple for whom everything goes awry on a trip to New York City. I don't know why they remade it—the original is a classic.

---

6. Which of the following TV soap operas aired at night during prime time?

a. *Peyton Place*

b. *Ryan's Hope*

c. *Loving*

d. *The Edge of Night*

GAME 80 Q5 ANSWER c
Eight-year-old Wesley was played by Brice Beckham. Arnold was the name of Gary Coleman's character who always wanted to know "What you talkin' 'bout?" on *Diff'rent Strokes*, while Rickie was played by Rickie Schroeder on *Silver Spoons*. Jonathan was the name of Judith Light's son on *Who's the Boss?*

8. The character "Jaws" appears in *The Spy Who Loved Me* (1977) and what other James Bond film?

a. *Octopussy* (1983)

b. *For Your Eyes Only* (1981)

c. *The Living Daylights* (1987)

d. *Moonraker* (1979)

GAME 1 Q7 ANSWER b
Screenwriter Kevin McClory was a co-writer and producer of *Thunderball,* and had the rights to make his own Bond film based on his story. McClory hoped to start a second series of Bond films, but *Never Say Never Again* was the only film he made. Somebody must have said, "Never again," I guess.

---

8. The Heartbreakers are the backup band for which performer?

a. Huey Lewis

b. Tom Petty

c. Elvis Costello

d. Joan Jett

GAME 21 Q7 ANSWER d
A number of Springsteen's *albums* went to #1, but the closest he got himself to the top with a single was in 1984, when "Dancing in the Dark" climbed to #2. It was beaten out by Kenny Loggins' "Footloose."

---

8. Yoda the Jedi Master does *not* appear in which "Star Wars" film?

a. *Return of the Jedi*

b. *The Phantom Menace*

c. *A New Hope*

d. *The Empire Strikes Back*

GAME 41 Q7 ANSWER b
The Japanese-American actor got his start in film during his college years, when he was hired to dub Japanese dialogue into English for the 1956 sci-fi classic *Rodan.* Takei voiced eight characters in this flim, which is about a prehistoric creature terrorizing Tokyo.

---

8. Which film did George Lucas direct first?

a. *Star Wars*

b. *THX 1138*

c. *American Graffiti*

d. *Dementia 13*

GAME 61 Q7 ANSWER c
Matt Damon has one line in this story of sisters working at a Connecticut pizza parlor. He plays Steamer, the younger brother of the rich boy who is dating Julia Roberts' character.

5. Which Stanley Kubrick movie has the longest running time?

a. *Lolita* (1962)

b. *Spartacus* (1960)

c. *Eyes Wide Shut* (1999)

d. *Barry Lyndon* (1975)

GAME 20 Q4 ANSWER d
Once a show as popular as fellow NBC sitcom *Seinfeld*, Paul Reiser's *Mad About You* saddened and disappointed many of the show's fans when the last episode showed the couple getting a divorce.

---

5. Which of the following pop bands is *not* from Australia?

a. Men at Work

b. ABBA

c. Air Supply

d. Bee Gees

GAME 40 Q4 ANSWER d
Nancy Reagan agreed to appear on the program to help publicize her "Just Say No" anti-drug campaign. Ironically, some of the show's cast members battled drug addiction in real life.

---

5. Who played opposite Jack Lemmon in the 1970 film *The Out of Towners*?

a. Sandy Duncan

b. Lee Remick

c. Shirley MacLaine

d. Sandy Dennis

GAME 60 Q4 ANSWER b
Kellerman's was typical of the Catskill Mountain (Borscht Belt) resorts that were popular family vacation getaway spots during the 1950s and 1960s. My wife Lois and I went to the Catskills on our honeymoon. I remember seeing Jackie Mason perform at our resort—I nearly fell over from laughing so much. Funny man—still is.

---

5. In the 1980s TV sitcom *Mr. Belvedere*, who was the family's annoying son?

a. Arnold

b. Rickie

c. Wesley

d. Jonathan

GAME 80 Q4 ANSWER a
Sixteen contestants—eight men and eight women—were marooned on this tropical island in the South China Sea. In order to survive, they banded together, but each week, they also voted one person off the island. The last one standing won $1 million. Sounds a lot like working in broadcasting . . .

GAME 1

9. Which one-name Bond girl was *not* a reformed Bond villain?

a. Domino

b. Solitaire

c. Octopussy

d. Mayday

GAME 1 Q8 ANSWER d
The 7'4" tall actor Richard Kiel reprised his metal-toothed role in a cameo in the 1999 live-action cartoon film *Inspector Gadget*. Previously seen in the prison football film *The Longest Yard* (1974), Kiel was set to play TV's *Incredible Hulk*, but producers wanted someone with more bulk, so Lou Ferrigno got the part.

GAME 21

9. Who recorded the song "True Colors"?

a. Madonna

b. Cyndi Lauper

c. Spandau Ballet

d. Buddy Holly

GAME 21 Q8 ANSWER b
When Petty was eleven, he met Elvis Presley on a Florida movie set for the film *Follow That Dream*. A few years later, Petty decided to follow his own dream with fellow musicians from Mudcrunch, his high school band.

GAME 41

9. Which *Star Trek* cast member appeared in movies with both Cary Grant and John Wayne?

a. George Takei

b. Leonard Nimoy

c. William Shatner

d. James Doohan

GAME 41 Q8 ANSWER c
Yoda (the voice of Frank "Fozzie the Bear" Oz), first appeared in *The Empire Strikes Back*, died in *Return of the Jedi*, and reappeared in *The Phantom Menace*—the first of the "Star Wars" prequels.

GAME 61

9. Which is the first album released by '60s rock group Cream?

a. *Disraeli Gears*

b. *Goodbye Cream*

c. *Fresh Cream*

d. *Wheels of Fire*

GAME 61 Q8 ANSWER b
THX 1138 (1971) was based on Lucas's film short of the same name that he made while still a film student in 1967. It bombed at the box office, but this first film remained important to Lucas—look for the letters "THX 138" on John Milner's license plate in Lucas's second film, *American Graffiti* (1973).

11

4. What was Paul and Jamie's wedding song in *Mad About You*?

a. "In My Life"

b. "You've Got a Friend"

c. "Moon River"

d. "What the World Needs Now"

GAME 20 Q3 ANSWER a
A fantastic humorist, writer, and class-act musician, Steve Allen accompanied the enigmatic Kerouac on piano. He also had Kerouac on his talk show in 1959.

---

4. On which NBC-TV sitcom did First Lady Nancy Reagan make a cameo appearance?

a. *Silver Spoons*

b. *ALF*

c. *The Facts of Life*

d. *Diff'rent Strokes*

GAME 40 Q3 ANSWER c
Holbrook appeared occasionally on wife Carter's sitcom. On *Diff'rent Strokes*, Carter was married to Bein's character Phillip Drummond. Gerald McRaney is married to *Designing Women* co-star Delta Burke. British actor Edward Woodward starred on his own show, *The Equalizer,* from 1985 to 1989.

---

4. What is the name of the resort hotel in *Dirty Dancing*?

a. Hellerman's

b. Kellerman's

c. Feldman's

d. Hellman's

GAME 60 Q3 ANSWER c
Based upon true events, this 1975 movie received a number of Academy Award nominations, including Best Picture, Best Director (Sidney Lumet), Best Actor in a Leading Role (Al Pacino), and Best Actor in a Supporting Role (Chris Sarandon). Frank Pierson won the Oscar for Best Original Screenplay.

---

4. Where did "reality" TV's first *Survivor* series take place?

a. Pulau Tiga

b. Marquesas

c. Fiji

d. Bora Bora

GAME 80 Q3 ANSWER d
This 1966 film, based on Edward Albee's play, was the first to be directed by Mike Nichols. All four actors in this film—Elizabeth Taylor, Richard Burton, Sandy Dennis, and George Segal—were nominated for Academy Awards. Elizabeth Taylor and Sandy Dennis won for Best Actress and Best Supporting Actress, respectively.

10. Who is the only actor to play Felix Leiter in more than one Bond film?

a. Jack Lord

b. David Hedison

c. Bernie Casey

d. Norman Burton

GAME 1 Q9 ANSWER d
Grace Jones played Mayday, the genetically engineered fighting machine, in *A View to a Kill* (1985), Roger Moore's last outing as Bond. *Charlie's Angels* star Tanya Roberts was the other Bond girl in this film.

10. Which performer was treated for rabies after biting the head off a bat onstage?

a. Alice Cooper

b. Marilyn Manson

c. Ozzy Osbourne

d. Jimi Hendrix

GAME 21 Q9 ANSWER b
The title track of Lauper's 1986 album has since been adapted by a well-known film company as its unofficial theme. Madonna sang "True Blue" the same year. Spandau Ballet recorded "True" in 1983. Finally, Buddy Holly's "True Love Ways" was on the 1957 *Chirping Crickets* album.

10. How many times did Kirstie Alley play the female Vulcan Federation officer Lt. Saavik in the *Star Trek* movies?

a. One

b. Two

c. Three

d. None

GAME 41 Q9 ANSWER a
Takei appeared with Wayne in the 1968 film *The Green Berets*. In 1966, he was cast in Grant's final film, *Walk, Don't Run*. Speaking of running, Takei carried the Olympic Flame in the 1984 Los Angeles Torch Relay and has completed five marathons.

10. Which Woody Allen film featured Sylvester Stallone's first Hollywood appearance?

a. *Love and Death* (1975)

b. *Sleeper* (1973)

c. *Take the Money and Run* (1969)

d. *Bananas* (1971)

GAME 61 Q9 ANSWER c
Featuring Eric Clapton on guitar, Jack Bruce on bass, and Ginger Baker on drums, Cream was one of the first "supergroups" of the late '60s. The group's hit songs include "I Feel Free," "Strange Brew," "White Room," and "Sunshine of Your Love," a song that Jimi Hendrix often played live in concert.

3. Which TV talk show host recorded a poetry album with Beat Generation writer Jack Kerouac? (Hint: it wasn't me)

a. Steve Allen

b. Jack Paar

c. Johnny Carson

d. David Frost

GAME 20 Q2 ANSWER a

As his musical ideas began to branch into stranger and more interesting realms, Zappa soon shortened the band name by dropping "Mothers of Invention" and leaving it simply "Frank Zappa." *Lumpy Gravy* was the first album in Zappa's name alone.

3. Who is *Designing Women's* Dixie Carter married to in real life?

a. Conrad Bein

b. Gerald McRaney

c. Hal Holbrook

d. Edward Woodward

GAME 40 Q2 ANSWER d

π marked the brilliant directorial debut of filmmaker Darren Aronofsky in 1998. Shot on a small budget with a cast of unknowns, this black-and-white film grabbed the attention of the film community. Aronofsky's second film, *Requiem for a Dream* (2000), boasts a powerhouse Oscar-nominated performance by Oscar-winner Ellen Burstyn.

3. In *Dog Day Afternoon*, why does Al Pacino's character Sonny try to rob a bank?

a. To pay his mortgage

b. To pay off a loan shark

c. To pay for his male lover's sex change operation

d. To buy a restaurant

GAME 60 Q2 ANSWER a

Martin Scorsese's film *GoodFellas* tells the story of real-life mobster Henry Hill and his more than thirty years in the world of organized crime. It was nominated for six Oscars but took home only one for Best Supporting Actor Joe Pesci. In 1995, Scorsese directed another mob film based on a Nicholas Pileggi book called *Casino*.

3. Which of the following small-cast films got Oscar nominations for all the actors?

a. *American Buffalo*

b. *Death and the Maiden*

c. *Deathtrap*

d. *Who's Afraid of Virginia Woolf?*

GAME 80 Q2 ANSWER b

Some say that Petey's real name was Jiggs (a.k.a. General Grant) and he is buried in the Aspin Hill Pet Cemetery in Silver Spring, Maryland. Others contend that Petey rests in the Pet Memorial Cemetery in Calabasas, California. I had a dog once. I brought him into my office one day—nine years later, I still can't find him.

11. Who played the first Bond girl?

a. Honor Blackman

b. Mie Hama

c. Ursula Andress

d. Maud Adams

GAME 1 Q10 ANSWER b
CIA agent Felix Leiter has appeared in eight James Bond films, beginning with the first, *Dr. No* (1962), which featured Jack Lord in the role. David Hedison portrayed the character twice, in *Live and Let Die* (1973) and *Licence to Kill* (1989). To date, the character has been played by six different actors, while Bond has been played by five.

11. "I Want You to Want Me" was a hit for:

a. The Beatles

b. Peter Frampton

c. Bread

d. Cheap Trick

GAME 21 Q10 ANSWER c
This incident, which occurred in Des Moines, Iowa, in 1982, is just one example of the wild antics for which Ozzy was famous. He and his family became unexpected television stars in 2002 with the debut of the MTV "reality sitcom" *The Osbournes.*

11. To date, which actor has *not* directed a *Star Trek* movie?

a. William Shatner

b. Jonathan Frakes

c. Patrick Stewart

d. Leonard Nimoy

GAME 41 Q10 ANSWER a
Alley played Saavik in *Star Trek II: The Wrath of Khan.* Although the Saavik character appeared in *Star Trek III: The Search for Spock* and *Star Trek IV: The Voyage Home,* actress Robin Curtis played the part.

11. Who was the first African-American to win the Best New Artist Grammy?

a. Stevie Wonder

b. Aretha Franklin

c. Natalie Cole

d. Whitney Houston

GAME 61 Q10 ANSWER d
In *Bananas,* Stallone and a fellow hoodlum threatened and chased Allen on a subway train. Stallone played another thug in Neil Simon's *The Prisoner of Second Avenue* (1975), starring Jack Lemmon and Anne Bancroft. Gee, it's a good thing Sly finally played a nice guy in *Rocky*—even if he did pound raw meat in the film!

2. What is the title of the first album by Frank Zappa and the Mothers of Invention?

a. *Freak Out*
b. *Absolutely Free*
c. *We're Only In It for the Money*
d. *Lumpy Gravy*

GAME 20 Q1 ANSWER d
Robert Altman's 1971 anti-Western brought Christie and Beatty together on-screen for the first time. Though Beatty and Altman allegedly despised each other by the end of the shoot and have not worked together since, Christie found her way into another Altman film, *Nashville* (1975), in which she played herself.

---

2. Which math symbol is also a movie title?

a. +
b. <
c. ⊤
d. π

GAME 40 Q1 ANSWER c
Seinfeld played Frankie, the governor's joke writer, during the show's 1980/81 season. Michael Keaton also got his start playing a joke writer for the president on *All's Fair*. *Benson* was a spinoff of *Soap*, which was where my good friend Billy Crystal had his television debut—*not* playing a joke writer.

---

2. *GoodFellas*, the 1990 mob movie, is based on a Nicholas Pileggi book titled:

a. *Wiseguy*
b. *GoodFellas*
c. *Henry Hill*
d. *City Hall*

GAME 60 Q1 ANSWER b
Caught in an afterlife in which you must defend your life choices, Brooks' character is a well-meaning coward who falls for the fearless and radiant Streep. Brooks also wrote and directed this 1991 romantic comedy.

---

2. What was the name of The Little Rascals' dog?

a. Spike
b. Petey
c. Fido
d. Rover

GAME 80 Q1 ANSWER a
A Clockwork Orange caused a huge controversy in Britain when it was released in January of 1972. A rash of copycat crimes based on the violence of the film led Kubrick to withdraw the film from distribution in Britain a year later. At one point, Kubrick considered casting Mick Jagger as Alex and the rest of The Rolling Stones as his droogs.

GAME 1

12. Who played Agent 007 in the most consecutive James Bond releases?

a. Sean Connery

b. Roger Moore

c. Timothy Dalton

d. Pierce Brosnan

GAME 21

12. Cleveland's funk-rock trio, The James Gang, walked onto the charts with:

a. "Walk This Way"

b. "Walk of Life"

c. "I'm Walkin'"

d. "Walk Away"

GAME 41

12. In the 1967 *Planet of the Apes*, how many astronauts are with Taylor (Charlton Heston) when their spaceship crashes?

a. One

b. Two

c. Three

d. None

GAME 61

12. Who was first offered the part of Masha opposite Robert DeNiro in *The King of Comedy*?

a. Meryl Streep

b. Jessica Lange

c. Sally Field

d. Tuesday Weld

GAME 1 Q11 ANSWER c
Ursula Andress played Honey Ryder in *Dr. No* (1962). She was also in the 1967 Bond spoof *Casino Royale*. Maud Adams appeared in both *The Man With the Golden Gun* (1974) and as the title character in *Octopussy* (1983). Honor Blackman played Pussy Galore in *Goldfinger* (1964), while Mie Hama played Kissy Suzuki in *You Only Live Twice* (1966).

GAME 21 Q11 ANSWER d
Although this song was originally recorded in 1977 for the band's *In Color* album, it was the live version from its 1979 *Live at Budokan* that reached #7. *Live at Budokan* eventually went triple platinum.

GAME 41 Q11 ANSWER c
Shatner directed *Star Trek V: The Final Frontier*. Nimoy directed *Star Trek III: The Search for Spock* and *Star Trek IV: The Voyage Home*. Frakes directed *Star Trek 8: First Contact* and *Star Trek 9: Insurrection*. Stewart directed episodes of *Star Trek: The Next Generation* for television.

GAME 61 Q11 ANSWER c
Hailed as the next Aretha Franklin, the second of Nat "King" Cole's children won the Best New Artist award in 1975 for her album *Inseparable*. The album included the #1 R&B tune "This Will Be."

GAME 20 **1.** Which film first paired off-screen lovers Warren Beatty and Julie Christie? **a.** *Heaven Can Wait* **b.** *Shampoo* **c.** *Darling* **d.** *McCabe & Mrs. Miller*	The answer to this question is on: **page 268,** **top frame,** **right side.**
GAME 40 **1.** On which sitcom did Jerry Seinfeld get his start? **a.** *Soap* **b.** *Bosom Buddies* **c.** *Benson* **d.** *All's Fair*	The answer to this question is on: **page 268,** **second frame,** **right side.**
GAME 60 **1.** What movie pairs Albert Brooks with Meryl Streep? **a.** *Lost in America* (1985) **b.** *Defending Your Life* (1991) **c.** *The Muse* (1999) **d.** *Unfaithfully Yours* (1984)	The answer to this question is on: **page 268,** **third frame,** **right side.**
GAME 80 **1.** What are the names of Alex's "three droogs" in Stanley Kubrick's *A Clockwork Orange* (1971)? **a.** Pete, Georgy, and Dim **b.** Paul, George, and Ringo **c.** Barry, Robin, and Maurice **d.** Tom, Dick, and Harry	The answer to this question is on: **page 268,** **bottom frame,** **right side.**

GAME 2

And the Answer Is . . .

"I'll Take Game Show Trivia for 100, Alex."

Turn to page 16 for the first question.

GAME 1 Q12 ANSWER b

Connery and Moore both played Bond seven times. Connery's streak of four films was upset in 1969 by George Lazenby in *On Her Majesty's Secret Service*. Moore's sixth consecutive film was Octopussy (1983). Connery returned that same year in *Never Say Never Again*—an unofficial Bond film, but Connery made it feel like the real thing.

GAME 22

Music to Your Eyes

Some General Music Trivia

Turn to page 16 for the first question.

GAME 21 Q12 ANSWER d

"Walk Away" is from the group's third album, *Thirds* (1971). The band's star attraction, Joe Walsh, left the band shortly after to pursue a solo career. In 1976, he joined The Eagles, but continued his solo work. He has played with or produced hits for Dan Fogelberg, ELP, Diana Ross, Steve Winwood, Ringo Starr, and Who bassist, John Entwistle.

GAME 42

Family Affairs

Keeping Afloat in the Entertainment Gene Pool

Turn to page 16 for the first question.

GAME 41 Q12 ANSWER c

Lieutenants Dodge, Landon, and Stewart are with Taylor as he traverses through space. Stewart, the only female in the team, suffocates due to an air leak in her hibernation chamber, while Dodge is shot and stuffed as part of a natural museum exhibit. Landon is lobotomized.

GAME 62

Thanks for the Memories

The Final Curtain

Turn to page 16 for the first question.

GAME 61 Q12 ANSWER a

DeNiro and Streep first worked together in the 1978 film *The Deer Hunter*. DeNiro thought they might also work well together on *The King of Comedy* (1983), but the part wound up being played by Sandra Bernhard. DeNiro and Streep later worked together again in 1984's *Falling in Love* and 1996's *Marvin's Room*.

GAME 20

Memory Lane Grab Bag

Turn to page 267 for the first question.

GAME 19 Q12 ANSWER a
This likeable film involves a bunch of kids, a pirate's treasure map, and a family of thieves led by Anne "*Throw Momma From the Train*" Ramsey. It has been described as Steven Spielberg's homage to *The Little Rascals*.

GAME 40

Memory Lane Grab Bag

Turn to page 267 for the first question.

GAME 39 Q12 ANSWER d
The Motels, led by singer and head lyricist Martha Davis, began in 1971 as The Warfield Foxes. This hit song came from the group's 1982 album, *All Four One*. When I think of a song called "Only the Lonely," I always think of either Frank Sinatra's tender 1958 ballad or Roy Orbison's early 1960s classic.

GAME 60

Memory Lane Grab Bag

Turn to page 267 for the first question.

GAME 59 Q12 ANSWER a
By 1977, the forty-two-year-old Elvis had gained a significant amount of weight—in his last TV special, he was just over 300 pounds. In the end, however, he still had a wonderful singing voice, and this is what the world has chosen to remember. Elvis, if you're still out there somewhere . . . come see me at my radio show.

GAME 80

Memory Lane Grab Bag

Turn to page 267 for the first question.

GAME 79 Q12 ANSWER c
Ginsberg appears twice—first in the film's prologue set to the tune of "Subterranean Homesick Blues" (with Dylan calmly turning cards over with bits of lyric written on them), and later before Dylan first plays the Royal Albert Hall. By the way, the filmmaker left the apostrophe out of "Don't" in the movie title on purpose!

1. The first game show produced by Chuck Barris was:

a. *The Dating Game*

b. *The Newlywed Game*

c. *The Gong Show*

d. *The $1.98 Beauty Pageant*

The answer to this question is on:

page 17, top frame, right side.

---

1. Which boy band was knocked from the #1 spot in album sales by The Beatles in 2001?

a. Backstreet Boys

b. Hanson

c. ☆NSYNC

d. Boyz II Men

The answer to this question is on:

page 17, second frame, right side.

---

1. Which Hollywood family has had the most Academy Award nominations?

a. The Barrymore family

b. The Fonda family

c. The Beatty/MacLaine family

d. The Huston family

The answer to this question is on:

page 17, third frame, right side.

---

1. Which *M*A*S*H* character was killed in a helicopter crash?

a. Trapper John McIntyre

b. Lt. Colonel Henry Blake

c. Nurse Bigelow

d. Captain Tuttle

The answer to this question is on:

page 17, bottom frame, right side.

12. *The Goonies* (1985) was written and directed by all of the following directors *except:*

a. Joel Schumacher

b. Steven Spielberg

c. Richard Donner

d. Chris Columbus

GAME 19 Q11 ANSWER c

Reynolds stars in this stunt-filled comedy that is actually one long car chase. Field plays his girl, and Williams is cast as Little Enos Burdett. In addition to *Smokey and the Bandit,* Reynolds' real-life girlfriend Sally Field appeared with him in *Hooper* (1978), *The End* (1978), and *Smokey and the Bandit II* (1980) before they called it quits.

12. Who wrote and recorded the 1982 Top 10 hit "Only the Lonely"?

a. Cyndi Lauper

b. Quarterflash

c. Scandal

d. The Motels

GAME 39 Q11 ANSWER b

One of the more promising New Wave bands to come from the UK in the early '80s, Modern English was an early favorite on MTV. The video's success no doubt helped push "I'll Melt With You" to the top of the charts. The song enjoyed renewed attention in the late 1990s, when a fast-food franchise used it in its TV and radio commercials.

12. Where was Elvis scheduled to perform on August 16, 1977—the day he died in Memphis, Tennessee?

a. Portland, Maine

b. Portland, Oregon

c. Las Vegas, Nevada

d. Honolulu, Hawaii

GAME 59 Q11 ANSWER b

The two superstars stood side-by-side and sang each other's songs in a medley format, with Sinatra singing "Love Me Tender" and Presley singing "Witchcraft." Though Sinatra was initially dismissive of Presley's musical style, he seemed to warm up to the King over the years . . . so long as Sinatra continued to be Chairman of the Board . . .

12. Which Beat poet appears alongside Bob Dylan in the documentary film *Dont Look Back* (1967)?

a. Lawrence Ferlinghetti

b. Michael McClure

c. Allen Ginsberg

d. Gary Snyder

GAME 79 Q11 ANSWER a

Peter, Paul & Mary's recording of "Blowin' in the Wind" reached #2 in July 1963 on the *Billboard* chart. The Byrds later reached #1 in June 1965 with their electric version of Dylan's "Mr. Tambourine Man." The Jimi Hendrix Experience had a hit in 1968 with Dylan's "All Along the Watchtower."

2. Who was *not* a host of *Concentration*?

a. Hugh Downs

b. Jack Narz

c. Wink Martindale

d. Bob Clayton

GAME 2 Q1 ANSWER a

The Dating Game premiered in 1965. Before becoming a television producer, Barris was known as the composer of "Palisades Park," a Top 10 hit for Freddy Cannon in 1962.

---

2. Which of these performers holds the record for most consecutive #1 singles?

a. Elvis Presley

b. The Beatles

c. Michael Jackson

d. Whitney Houston

GAME 22 Q1 ANSWER a

In what seemed like déjà vu, The Beatles crept to the top of the album charts all over again in 2001 with a greatest hits collection simply called *1*. Ironically, the name of the dethroned Backstreet Boys' album was *Black & Blue*.

---

2. Which John Huston movie won the most Oscars?

a. *The African Queen* (1951)

b. *The Treasure of the Sierra Madre* (1948)

c. *The Dead* (1987)

d. *Prizzi's Honor* (1985)

GAME 42 Q1 ANSWER d

Patriarch Walter Huston was nominated four times. Son John received fourteen nominations (eight for writing, five for directing, one for acting). Daughter Angelica was nominated three times, and her brother Tony has one, for a family total of twenty-two nominations (with four wins).

---

2. Which star of John Huston's 1961 film *The Misfits* died first?

a. Marilyn Monroe

b. Clark Gable

c. Montgomery Clift

d. Thelma Ritter

GAME 62 Q1 ANSWER b

McLean Stevenson, who played Lt. Colonel Henry Blake in the TV series, left at the end of the third season to pursue another TV project. Unfortunately, *The McLean Stevenson Show* was short-lived, but since the writers had killed off his character, Stevenson could not return to *M*A*S*H*.

11. Who was *not* in the cast of *Smokey and the Bandit* (1977)?

a. Sally Field
b. Burt Reynolds
c. Charles Durning
d. Paul Williams

Woody's first film appearance was in *What's New, Pussycat?* (1964). Other performers who had cameos in *Around the World* include George Raft, Red Buttons, Andy Devine, Noel Coward, John Carradine, Charles Boyer, and Marlene Dietrich.

---

11. Name the pop group that had its one big hit in 1982 with "I'll Melt With You"?

a. A Flock of Seagulls
b. Modern English
c. Wang Chung
d. Loverboy

Brothers Fred and Richard Fairbrass made quite a splash on MTV and the charts with this instant hit. It was even used in the 1993 Jack Lemmon-Walter Matthau comedy *Grumpy Old Men*. Following this single with the albums *Up* (1992) and *Smashing* (1996) didn't do much for the brothers, who were soon too sexy to be noticed.

---

11. Which fellow entertainer threw Elvis a "Welcome Home" TV special when he returned from the U.S. Army in 1960?

a. Jackie Gleason
b. Frank Sinatra
c. Steve Allen
d. Ed Sullivan

Shot in black and white, 1956's *Love Me Tender* is actually quite a good film. In fact, Elvis's death scene at the end of the film was said to make his mother cry at the movie premiere. His last film, 1969's *Change of Habit*, ended a career of more than thirty feature films.

---

11. Which of the following acts was the first to have a chart-topping hit with a song written by Bob Dylan?

a. Peter, Paul & Mary
b. Jimi Hendrix
c. Joan Baez
d. The Byrds

Critics and fans alike considered this 1997 album to be Dylan's very best album since 1974's *Blood on the Tracks*. *Time Out of Mind* won three Grammys in 1998, and Dylan then won an Oscar in 2000 for Best Featured Song in a Motion Picture ("Things Have Changed") from the Michael Douglas film *Wonder Boys*.

3. Which of these actors was never one of the bachelors on *The Dating Game*?

a. Jim Carrey

b. Tom Selleck

c. Andy Kaufman

d. Ted Danson

GAME 2 Q2 ANSWER c
Former deejay Martindale hosted the late '70s/early '80s version of *Tic Tac Dough*. Bob Clayton was *Concentration's* announcer from 1963 to 1969, when he took over hosting duties after Ed McMahon's six-month stint. Clayton hosted until 1973.

---

3. Which singer has the world record for the Best-Selling Solo Country Album?

a. Shania Twain

b. Garth Brooks

c. Faith Hill

d. Willie Nelson

GAME 22 Q2 ANSWER d
Whitney had seven in a row, starting with "Saving All My Love for You" in 1985, followed by "How Will I Know?," "Greatest Love of All," "I Wanna Dance with Somebody (Who Loves Me)," "Didn't We Almost Have It All?," "So Emotional," and "Where Do Broken Hearts Go?" in 1988.

---

3. Which member of the Coppola family has *not* yet won an Oscar?

a. Talia Shire

b. Carmine Coppola

c. Nicholas Cage

d. Francis Ford Coppola

GAME 42 Q2 ANSWER b
The Treasure of the Sierra Madre won three Oscars. *African Queen* and *Prizzi's Honor* each received one, and *The Dead* didn't win any. Only John Huston has directed a parent and child to Academy Award wins. His father, Walter, won Supporting Actor for *Treasure . . .* and daughter Angelica won Supporting Actress for *Prizzi's Honor.*

---

3. In the final episode of *The Fresh Prince of Bel-Air*, the family's home is sold to characters from:

a. *Diff'rent Strokes*

b. *The Jeffersons*

c. *Good Times*

d. *227*

GAME 62 Q2 ANSWER b
Gable died of a heart attack only days after filming wrapped. He was fifty-nine. Monroe died at age thirty-six of a drug overdose in 1962—a little over a year after the movie was released. Clift died in 1966 at age forty-five, and Ritter died in 1969 at age sixty-four.

10. *Around the World in Eighty Days* (1956) featured cameos by all of these actors *except:*

a. Joe E. Brown
b. Woody Allen
c. Buster Keaton
d. Frank Sinatra

GAME 19 Q9 ANSWER c
Other films that came out of Robert Redford's Sundance Film Festival include Quentin Tarantino's *Reservoir Dogs* (1992), Kevin Smith's *Clerks* (1994), and Reginald Hudlin's *House Party* (1990).

---

10. Which of the following groups had its one big hit in 1991 with "I'm Too Sexy"?

a. Frankie Goes to Hollywood
b. Depeche Mode
c. Kajagoogoo
d. Right Said Fred

GAME 39 Q9 ANSWER a
David Gates wrote and performed "The Goodbye Girl" for the film. He also founded the Los Angeles group Bread, which formed in 1969 and had a big hit with its song "Make It With You." The group broke up in 1973, came back together in 1976, and then broke up again in 1977. In need of some bread, Bread again reformed in 1997 for a brief tour.

---

10. Which film was Elvis Presley's first?

a. *King Creole*
b. *Jailhouse Rock*
c. *Loving You*
d. *Love Me Tender*

GAME 59 Q9 ANSWER a
Elvis was born in Tupelo, Mississippi in 1935 to parents Vernon and Gladys. According to historical records, Elvis had a twin brother, Jesse Garon, who died the day they were born.

---

10. Which of the following Bob Dylan albums won a Grammy?

a. *Bringing It All Back Home*
b. *Blonde on Blonde*
c. *Blood on the Tracks*
d. *Time Out of Mind*

GAME 79 Q9 ANSWER c
Tom Cruise's character in this film mirrors writer/director Cameron Crowe, whose real-life exploits as the youngest reporter for *Rolling Stone* magazine were captured in *Almost Famous* (2000). In addition to the Dylan album cover, a love scene between Cruise and Cruz is accompanied by a rare live acoustic performance of Dylan's "4th Time Around."

4. Which prime time TV game show appeared first?

a. *The $64,000 Question*
b. *Twenty-One*
c. *Dotto*
d. *The $64,000 Challenge*

GAME 2 Q3 ANSWER d
Andy Kaufman appeared on the show as his "Foreign Man" character before he made it famous on *Taxi*. Tom Selleck made two appearances, and wasn't picked either time.

4. What was Sting's first solo album?

a. *Bring on the Night*
b. *Ten Summoner's Tales*
c. *Dream of the Blue Turtles*
d. *Soul Cages*

GAME 22 Q3 ANSWER a
To date, Twain's album *Come On Over* has sold over 19 million copies in the United States alone, with total sales of 36 million worldwide. It was still in the Top 30 of *Billboard's* Top 200 after 122 weeks.

4. Which of these families has won the most acting Oscars?

a. Henry, Jane, and Peter Fonda
b. Kirk, Michael, and Eric Douglas
c. Eric and Julia Roberts
d. Warren Beatty and Shirley MacLaine

GAME 42 Q3 ANSWER a
Although she received two acting nominations (for *Rocky* and *Godfather Part II*), Shire has yet to win an Oscar. Carmine Coppola, the father of Shire and five-time Oscar winner Francis Ford, won his Oscar for Best Dramatic Score for *The Godfather Part II*. His grandson Nicholas Cage won Best Actor for *Leaving Las Vegas*.

4. Which girl group went "Head Over Heels" just before disbanding?

a. The Go-Gos
b. The Bangles
c. Bananarama
d. The Supremes

GAME 62 Q3 ANSWER b
On *The Fresh Prince of Bel-Air's* finale, George and Louise Jefferson (Sherman Hemsley and Isabel Sanford) move on up one more time, buying the Banks estate from Will's Uncle Phillip.

9. Which film was *not* first a hit at the Sundance Film Festival?

a. *You Can Count on Me*

b. *The Brothers McMullen*

c. *Pulp Fiction*

d. *Blood Simple*

GAME 19 Q8 ANSWER b
Gable and Colbert won their only Oscars for performances in *It Happened One Night*, which also won Oscars for writing, direction, and best picture. Colbert was nominated again the following year for *Private Worlds* (1935).

9. Which singer/songwriter had a solo hit in 1977 with his song from *The Goodbye Girl*?

a. David Gates

b. John Sebastian

c. Gordon Lightfoot

d. Willie Nelson

GAME 39 Q8 ANSWER b
At a time when The Eagles were bringing country sounds into the pop realm, Michael Murphy was a for-real cowboy. Equestrian ballads, however, never really caught on, and cowboys went back to singing about cowgirls. Michael has often been confused with the film actor Michael Murphy, so he now goes by his full name, Michael Martin Murphy.

9. What was Elvis Presley's middle name?

a. Aaron

b. Charles

c. Medger

d. Garon

GAME 59 Q8 ANSWER c
Cage is one of the most die-hard celebrity Elvis fans ever. He even sings an Elvis song to co-star Laura Dern in David Lynch's film *Wild at Heart*. And in 2002, he married the King's daughter, Lisa Marie Presley. If Elvis really is still alive, I'm sure he's a Nicolas Cage fan . . .

9. In *Vanilla Sky* (2001), Tom Cruise and Penelope Cruz mimic the cover of which Dylan album?

a. *Highway 61 Revisited*

b. *Desire*

c. *The Freewheelin' Bob Dylan*

d. *Blood on the Tracks*

GAME 79 Q8 ANSWER b
Simply named *Bob Dylan*, the first album was recorded quickly after Dylan signed a recording contract. The album lacked the essence of Dylan's music as he performed it live in coffeehouses. His second album, *The Freewheelin' Bob Dylan* (1963), put him in the national spotlight with the instant classic "Blowin' in the Wind."

5. Who was *not* a host of
Wheel of Fortune?

a. Chuck Woolery

b. Rolf Bernishke

c. Tom Kennedy

d. Pat Sajak

GAME 2 Q4 ANSWER a
The $64,000 Question debuted in 1955.
It was based on radio's *Take It or Leave
It*, which had a top prize of $64.

---

5. Who has won the most
Grammys as a solo artist?

a. Paul McCartney

b. Michael Jackson

c. Stevie Wonder

d. Elvis Presley

GAME 22 Q4 ANSWER c
Sting's 1985 album was released two
years after *Synchronicity* by his former
group, The Police. *Dream of the Blue
Turtles* includes the hits "Fortress
Around Your Heart," "Love Is the Seventh
Wave," and "If You Love Somebody, Set
Them Free."

---

5. Which actress is Goldie
Hawn's daughter?

a. Sarah Michelle Gellar

b. Kate Hudson

c. Reese Witherspoon

d. Mena Suvari

GAME 42 Q4 ANSWER a
The Fondas have won three Academy
Awards for acting. Jane won for *Klute*
and *Coming Home,* and Henry won for
On Golden Pond. MacLaine won for
Terms of Endearment. The Roberts sib-
lings' only win is for Julia's performance
in *Erin Brockovich*. Michael Douglas won
for *Wall Street*. Both Henry Fonda and
Kirk Douglas received honorary Oscars.

---

5. The last film Peter Sellers
made was:

a. *Revenge of the Pink Panther*

b. *Being There*

c. *The Fiendish Plot of Dr.
Fu Manchu*

d. *Murder by Death*

GAME 62 Q4 ANSWER a
Not long after "Head Over Heels" peaked
in 1984, group members Jane Weidlin
and Belinda Carlisle pursued solo careers. Meanwhile, Bananarama's hit
"Cool Summer" became popular again
from the movie *Blue Crush* (2002), and
The Bangles ultimately regrouped and
wrote a new song for *Austin Powers in
Goldmember* (2002).

8. Clark Gable won the Best Actor Oscar in 1934. Who won as Best Actress?

a. Shirley Temple

b. Claudette Colbert

c. Katherine Hepburn

d. Norma Shearer

GAME 19 Q7 ANSWER c
Supporting actor nods went to Red for *Sayonara* (1957) and Whoopi for *Ghost,* (1990). Mel Brooks got his Oscar for the screenplay of his 1968 debut, *The Producers.* Incidentally, his Broadway musical adaptation of the film swept the 2000 Tonys. Wilder, nominated twice for Mel Brooks's films, has not yet won an Oscar.

8. What was the big 1975 hit for singer/songwriter Michael Murphy?

a. "Heart of Gold"

b. "Wildfire"

c. "Desperado"

d. "Horse With No Name"

GAME 39 Q7 ANSWER c
Larson's recording of this song quickly became a Top 10 hit in late 1979. Soon after, she made a move from pop to country and won the Best New Vocalist Award from the Academy of Country Music in 1984. She died in 1997 at the age of forty-five.

8. In which movie does Nicolas Cage skydive while dressed in an Elvis Presley jumpsuit?

a. *Leaving Las Vegas* (1995)

b. *Wild at Heart* (1990)

c. *Honeymoon in Vegas* (1992)

d. *Birdy* (1984)

GAME 59 Q7 ANSWER b
On this show, Elvis proved he could still shake, rattle, and roll with the best of them. He also wore a tight black leather suit in response to and in order to compete with the look of younger rock stars like Rolling Stones' frontman Mick Jagger and The Doors' enigmatic singer, Jim Morrison.

8. What year was Bob Dylan's first album released?

a. 1961

b. 1962

c. 1963

d. 1964

GAME 79 Q7 ANSWER a
Dylan was born in May 1941 as Robert Allen Zimmerman. When he was still a little boy, the family moved to Hibbing, which is where Robert Zimmerman lived until he changed his name to Bob Dylan and went to New York City to seek his fortune as a singer/songwriter.

6. Which was the first game show implicated in the 1958 "quiz show scandals"?

a. *The $64,000 Question*

b. *Twenty-One*

c. *Dotto*

d. *The $64,000 Challenge*

GAME 2 Q5 ANSWER c
Tom Kennedy hosted the syndicated version of *The Price is Right* from 1985 to 1986, but is most recognized for hosting *Name That Tune*. His brother is veteran game show host Jack Narz, and they are brothers-in-law with perennial game show host Bill Cullen, who emceed the earlier incarnation of *Name That Tune* from 1954 to 1955.

---

6. The artist Prince first reached the top of the pop charts with what song?

a. "Little Red Corvette"

b. "When Doves Cry"

c. "1999"

d. "Purple Rain"

GAME 22 Q5 ANSWER c
Stevie Wonder has won nineteen Grammys as a solo artist, including six for Best Male R&B Performance. Michael Jackson comes in second with fourteen. Presley received only three Grammy Awards. The Beatles were awarded ten Grammys, but McCartney has received only one on his own—the Lifetime Achievement Award in 1990.

---

6. Bob Dylan's son Jakob is the lead for which band?

a. The Wallflowers

b. The Traveling Willoughbys

c. Blues Traveler

d. The Honeydrippers

GAME 42 Q5 ANSWER b
Hudson won acclaim and an Academy Award nomination for her role as Penny Lane in *Almost Famous* (2000). She was originally cast as William Miller's sister, but auditioned for Penny Lane when Sarah Polley gave up the role.

---

6. What was John Wayne's last picture?

a. *Brannigan*

b. *Rooster Cogburn*

c. *The Shootist*

d. *McQ*

GAME 62 Q5 ANSWER c
The Fiendish Plot of Dr. Fu Manchu was completed not long before Sellers died of a heart attack in 1980. Previously cut scenes of Sellers as Inspector Jacques Clouseau later wound up in Blake Edwards' *Trail of the Pink Panther* (1982).

7. Which of these Oscar-nominated funny people did *not* win an Academy Award?

a. Mel Brooks
b. Red Buttons
c. Gene Wilder
d. Whoopi Goldberg

GAME 19 Q6 ANSWER c
Some producers would be happy if a movie takes in $11 million internationally, but not when it took $100 million to make. This 1995 Renny Harlin box office flop starred his then-wife, Geena Davis, Matthew Modine, and Frank Langella. By comparison, *Heaven's Gate* grossed only $1.5 million, but it cost only $44 million to make.

7. Which singer/songwriter wrote Nicolette Larson's one big hit, "Lotta Love"?

a. Carole King
b. Joni Mitchell
c. Neil Young
d. Harry Nilsson

GAME 39 Q6 ANSWER b
Edwin Starr was one of Motown's most unique-sounding soul singers. In the mid-1980s, "War" was sung live and released as a hit single by Bruce Springsteen and the E Street Band. In the 1990s, Elaine's character repopularized it in a *Seinfeld* episode.

7. In what year was Elvis Presley's popular TV comeback special aired?

a. 1967
b. 1968
c. 1969
d. 1970

GAME 59 Q6 ANSWER d
Believe it or not, Elvis first appeared on my show in late 1955, after Colonel Tom Parker had just become his manager. The soon-to-be King sang a rendition of "Shortnin' Bread" during the appearance. In early 1956, he did the Berle and Dorsey Brothers shows, and then Ed Sullivan that September.

7. Where was Bob Dylan born?

a. Duluth, Minnesota
b. Erie, Pennsylvania
c. Sedona, Arizona
d. St. Louis, Missouri

GAME 79 Q6 ANSWER c
This is a John Lennon song from 1974. Lennon and Dylan were aware of each other as songwriters. In late 1964, Lennon wrote a Dylanesque song called "You've Got to Hide Your Love Away." In 1965, Dylan wrote "4th Time Around" as an alleged parody of "Norwegian Wood (This Bird Has Flown)." I guess love *isn't* all you need.

Chaplin & Other Silent Film Funnymen

In my career, I've been blessed with the ability to meet and interview some of the greatest comedy stars of the silent film era. I first met Charlie Chaplin at the Lincoln Center Honorarium Party, where he was given a Lifetime Achievement Award in 1972. He was in a wheelchair at the time, but he was very charming and friendly. I interviewed him for the TV show, and he gave me some souvenirs. I've always asked all my guests for souvenirs throughout the years, and Chaplin didn't disappoint. He gave me one of his bowler hats and one of the canes he used while acting as the Little Tramp. (It's on display at my restaurant in Times Square, New York City.) Chaplin was a beautiful man. Though he did experience some political problems in this country, I still feel that Chaplin was one of our warmest and most sincere film artists. His films almost always make me laugh *and* cry.

I also met Harold Lloyd. He used to call me whenever he was in New York, and we became close. He gave me some great props from his films. He would sit in my office and answer the phone for me—back when more than one person could actually sit in my office at the same time.

One silent film star that I always wanted to meet was Harry Langdon. A great comedian. *The Strong Man* is one of my favorite silent-film comedies. Langdon was one of those actors who was at his best when directed by somebody else, though. Frank Capra directed most of his best early films, including *The Strong Man.* But Langdon let stardom go to his head. He thought he could direct himself. Sadly, the films that he directed himself were not that great and his career soon went into a landslide. Yet, he was still working on films at the time of his death in 1944.

Eddie Cantor's Sweet & Poignant Story

Eddie Cantor told me this story back in the old days. There was once a child star in Hollywood—I never found out which star it was—who eventually outgrew his popularity. Times were tough back then, and the money made in the actor's youth did not last into his adulthood. He was in debt, had bills to pay, and needed a job desperately. Since he couldn't even get arrested on any of the Hollywood studio lots, he went to a department store around Christmas time and applied for a job playing Santa Claus. During the job interview, the store manager recognized the actor and said, "You can't be serious about wanting this job." The actor said, "Not only am I serious—I'm hungry!" So the store gave the actor the job as Santa Claus.

The actor was listening to all the kids' holiday gift wishes, and along came one very nice kid with a list of toys he wanted for Christmas. The actor said in his Santa voice, "Yes, little boy, I'll bring you all of these things." The kid then turned to his mother, who was standing on the line, and said, "Mommy, can we make sure Santa gets our address so he knows where to bring my presents on Christmas Eve?" The mother walked up and looked at Santa. Suddenly, the actor realized that he was facing his ex-wife.

The actor felt embarrassed and hoped she wouldn't recognize him through all the makeup and white beard. She wrote the address on an envelope and handed it to Santa. Mother and child walked away. Later on, the actor looked at the envelope and saw, in his ex-wife's handwriting, "You are still the world's greatest actor." I always thought that was such a sweet and poignant story. Memory Lane is filled with many such tales.

7. Who has hosted more TV game shows?

a. Alex Trebek
b. Gene Rayburn
c. Bill Cullen
d. Peter Marshall

GAME 2 Q6 ANSWER c
Dotto, which began airing in prime time early in 1958, was the first program implicated in the quiz show scandals. The allegations of rigged games caused the cancellation of all four of these quiz shows in the fall of 1958.

---

7. Elvis Costello and Jimmy Cliff sang together on which "weekend" song?

a. "Working for the Weekend"
b. "Seven-Day Weekend"
c. "Weekend in New England"
d. "Here Comes the Weekend"

GAME 22 Q6 ANSWER b
When his movie *Purple Rain* was released in 1984, Prince rocketed to superstardom. Although "Little Red Corvette" (1983) reached #10, it was "When Doves Cry" and "Let's Go Crazy" from the film's soundtrack that made him "royalty."

---

7. Jennifer Jason Leigh is the daughter of which actor?

a. Tony Curtis
b. Jason Robards
c. Vic Morrow
d. Laurence Olivier

GAME 42 Q6 ANSWER a
In 1996, The Wallflowers struck platinum five times over with the album *Bringing Down the Horse,* which also spawned two hit singles and won two Grammys. Father Bob wrote a song called "Wallflower," recorded in 1971, during the time when his songwriting muse turned to the sounds of country music.

---

7. Which *Three's Company* character was the last to leave the apartment in the last episode?

a. Jack
b. Terry
c. Janet
d. Mr. Furley

GAME 62 Q6 ANSWER c
The 1976 film, co-starring Lauren Bacall, Jimmy Stewart, and Ron Howard, was about an aging gunfighter, dying of cancer, who is looking to live out his last few months in peace. Wayne died three years later of lung and stomach cancer.

6. To date, which movie is in the *Guinness Book of World Records* as having the largest box office loss?

a. *Hudson Hawk* (1991)

b. *Howard the Duck* (1986)

c. *Cutthroat Island* (1995)

d. *Heaven's Gate* (1980)

GAME 19 Q5 ANSWER c
Costing $200 million to make, *Titanic* is the first film in history to take in more than $1 billion in worldwide gross receipts. That's a helluva lotta loot for a sinking ship!

6. What year did Edwin Starr go to #1 with his strident anti-war hit "War"?

a. 1969

b. 1970

c. 1971

d. 1972

GAME 39 Q5 ANSWER c
Although his song reached #1 on the charts the same year Bob Dylan's "Like a Rolling Stone" reached #2, Barry McGuire's singing style and songwriting were considered very derivative of Dylan's. He did beat Dylan, however, by finding Jesus and becoming a born-again Christian a full five years before Dylan did the same in 1978.

6. On which television show did Elvis Presley make his first network appearance?

a. *The Ed Sullivan Show*

b. *The Milton Berle Show*

c. *Stage Show with Tommy and Jimmy Dorsey*

d. *The Joe Franklin Show*

GAME 59 Q5 ANSWER b
In this film, Moore plays a nun who assists "Doctor" Elvis in cleaning up the surrounding ghetto. Because Moore doesn't wear a habit, Elvis doesn't realize she's a nun—until he falls for her. *Change of Habit* was Elvis's last film. Colonel Parker chose it for him over *Midnight Cowboy*.

6. Which of the following is *not* a Bob Dylan song?

a. "Rainy Day Women #12 & 35"

b. "4th Time Around"

c. "No. 9 Dream"

d. "Bob Dylan's 115th Dream"

GAME 79 Q5 ANSWER d
In this classic 1977 movie, Woody finds himself taking a young woman (Shelley Duvall) to see the Maharishi at Madison Square Garden. While on line, she recalls seeing Bob Dylan in concert and gives a hilariously self-conscious reading of the lyrics from the chorus in "Just Like a Woman."

8. Who was *not* a host of *The $10,000* (or *$20,000*) *Pyramid*?

a. Dick Clark

b. Bill Cullen

c. John Davidson

d. Jim Lange

8. Which was the first female African-American act to perform at the Grand Ole Opry?

a. Whitney Houston

b. The Pointer Sisters

c. Donna Summer

d. The Ronettes

8. Which actor had his wife, ex-girlfriend, and daughter appear with him in a film?

a. Frank Sinatra

b. Clint Eastwood

c. Tony Curtis

d. Ronald Reagan

8. What year did TV's *The Fugitive* finally "stop running"?

a. 1969

b. 1968

c. 1967

d. 1966

GAME 2 Q7 ANSWER c
Groucho Marx called him "the second-wittiest man on the air." Starting with *Winner Take All* in 1952 until his last taping of *The Joker's Wild* in 1986, Cullen hosted over twenty game shows and was a panelist on a half-dozen more. He was the host of the original *The Price is Right* from 1956 until 1964.

GAME 22 Q7 ANSWER b
The duo took its reggae "Seven-Day Weekend" in 1984. Loverboy was "Working for the Weekend" in 1981; Barry Manilow took his "Weekend in New England" in 1977; and Dave Edmunds told us "Here Comes the Weekend" in 1976.

GAME 42 Q7 ANSWER c
Leigh (born Jennifer Lee Morrow) is the daughter of late actor Vic Morrow and screenwriter Barbara Turner. Her first major film role was in the 1982 teen classic *Fast Times at Ridgemont High.* Her father was killed that same year, during the filming of *Twilight Zone: The Movie* (1983).

GAME 62 Q7 ANSWER b
In a poignant way, it made perfect sense that Terry (Priscilla Barnes) would be the last to look into the apartment—by the show's end, both Janet and Jack had found mates, but Terry hadn't. Audiences were left with the image of a single person closing the door on one life in search of another.

GAME 19

5. To date, what is the highest-grossing film of all time?

a. *Star Wars* (1977)

b. *The Wizard of Oz* (1939)

c. *Titanic* (1997)

d. *Gone With the Wind* (1939)

GAME 19 Q4 ANSWER c

In *Punchline*, Hanks, a medical school dropout, and Field, a housewife, are both struggling stand-up comedians. Hanks plays Field's mentor. Some say Field's character is based loosely on Roseanne Barr. Interestingly, John Goodman played Field's husband in this movie and Barr's husband on the TV series *Roseanne*.

GAME 39

5. What is the name of Barry McGuire's 1965 antiwar single and his one big hit?

a. "Where Have All the Good Times Gone?"

b. "In the Year 2525"

c. "Eve of Destruction"

d. "Hey World"

GAME 39 Q4 ANSWER a

The first time this song was a one-time hit was when Phil Phillips recorded it in 1957 and it went to #2, selling over 2 million copies that year. Since then, the song has also been a hit for Del Shannon in 1982, and again in 1984 for The Honeydrippers. It was also featured prominently throughout the 1989 Al Pacino thriller named (aptly) *Sea of Love*.

GAME 59

5. In which Elvis Presley movie did he star opposite Mary Tyler Moore?

a. *Live a Little, Love a Little* (1968)

b. *Change of Habit* (1969)

c. *The Trouble With Girls* (1969)

d. *Kissin' Cousins* (1964)

GAME 59 Q4 ANSWER d

The *Girls!* that Elvis was torn over were Stella Stevens and Laurel Goodwin, who had a short acting career in the early 1960s.

GAME 79

5. Which Bob Dylan song is satirized in Woody Allen's *Annie Hall*?

a. "I Shall Be Released"

b. "Blowin' in the Wind"

c. "Like a Rolling Stone"

d. "Just Like a Woman"

GAME 79 Q4 ANSWER c

Dylan was asked to write a song for this film about the seamier side of New York City starring Jon Voight, Dustin Hoffman, and my good friend Sylvia Miles. But because he did not have the song finished in time for the film, director John Schlesinger went instead with Fred Neil's song "Everybody's Talkin'" as sung by Harry Nilsson.

9. Which celebrity won the big prize on *The $64,000 Question* for knowledge of Shakespeare?

a. Dr. Joyce Brothers

b. Geoffrey Holder

c. Jack Benny

d. Barbara Feldon

GAME 2 Q8 ANSWER d
Jim Lange is best known for being the host of *The Dating Game* for fifteen years from 1965 to 1980. He also hosted *Name That Tune* in 1984 and *The New Newlywed Game* in 1985.

---

9. Who was the first U.S. artist to record for The Beatles' Apple Records label?

a. Ronnie Spector

b. Michael Jackson

c. Hoyt Axton

d. James Taylor

GAME 22 Q8 ANSWER b
In 1974, the group's country song "Fairytale," reached #13 on the Country & Western charts. That same year, the Pointers performed at the Grand Ole Opry. In 1975, the group won its first Grammy for "Fairytale" (Best Country Performance by a Duo or Group). Elvis Presley recorded the hit in 1975.

---

9. Who is the only Oscar winner to have parents who both received Oscars?

a. Angelina Jolie

b. Liza Minnelli

c. Michael Douglas, Jr.

d. Mira Sorvino

GAME 42 Q8 ANSWER b
Eastwood directed them all in the 1999 film *True Crime*. His former girlfriend Frances Fisher played a district attorney; their daughter, Francesca Ruth Eastwood, played his daughter; and wife Dina Ruiz Eastwood appeared as a TV reporter.

---

9. What was the title of Nirvana's last studio album before frontman Kurt Cobain's untimely death in 1993?

a. *In Utero*

b. *Nevermind*

c. *Incesticide*

d. *Bleach*

GAME 62 Q8 ANSWER c
David Janssen starred as Dr. Richard Kimble—the man falsely accused of killing his wife. The show's final episode in 1967 was one of the summer's biggest events. In 1994, *The Fugitive* was released as a movie starring Harrison Ford. The TV show reappeared for one season in 2000 with Tim Daly as the good doctor.

GAME 19

4. In *Forrest Gump* (1994), Sally Field plays Tom Hanks's mother. In what other movie do the two star?

a. *Soapdish* (1991)
b. *Every Time We Say Goodbye* (1986)
c. *Punchline* (1988)
d. *Volunteers* (1985)

GAME 19 Q3 ANSWER c
This low-budget John Sayles film is about seven friends who get together ten years after being arrested on the way to a protest. The idea of a group of friends reuniting was revisited by writer/director Lawrence Kasdan in his wonderful 1983 film *The Big Chill*.

GAME 39

4. Which singer had a big hit in 1957 with "Sea of Love"?

a. Phil Phillips
b. Cliff Richard
c. Fabian
d. Eddie Fisher

GAME 39 Q3 ANSWER c
Big Country was considered one of the very best bands of the early '80s. "In a Big Country" became a Top 20 hit in 1983 and was an MTV favorite.

GAME 59

4. Shelley Fabares appeared in all of these Elvis Presley movies *except:*

a. *Girl Happy* (1965)
b. *Spinout* (1966)
c. *Clambake* (1967)
d. *Girls! Girls! Girls!* (1962)

GAME 59 Q3 ANSWER a
Mae Axton, one of Colonel Tom's P.R. people (and Hoyt Axton's mother), and Tommy Durden co-wrote the song when Tommy showed her an article about a suicide. The suicide note read, "I walk a lonely street." Durden suggested putting a heartbreak hotel at the end of that street, and they wrote and recorded the demo in twenty-two minutes.

GAME 79

4. For which film did Bob Dylan write "Lay, Lady, Lay"?

a. *The Wild Bunch* (1969)
b. *Cool Hand Luke* (1967)
c. *Midnight Cowboy* (1969)
d. *They Shoot Horses, Don't They?* (1969)

GAME 79 Q3 ANSWER d
This mid-1980s supergroup was comprised of Dylan, Petty, George Harrison, Roy Orbison, and ELO's Jeff Lynne. For many music fans, Tom Petty is seen as carrying on in the tradition of Dylan. Petty's group The Heartbreakers was even Dylan's backing group for a while in the mid-1980s.

10. Monty Hall co-created and hosted *Let's Make a Deal* beginning in what year?

a. 1957

b. 1960

c. 1963

d. 1966

GAME 2 Q9 ANSWER d
Feldon won in 1957, two years after graduating from Carnegie-Mellon. Dr. Brothers was the second top prizewinner in the show's history, and also competed in the spinoff for *Question* alumni, *The $64,000 Challenge.* "Uncola man" Holder won $16,000. Jack Benny appeared in one episode, but quit after winning just $1.

10. How many Grammy awards did Meat Loaf win for the 1977 smash *Bat Out Of Hell*?

a. Five

b. Three

c. One

d. None

GAME 22 Q9 ANSWER d
When The Beatles started Apple Records in 1968, Peter Asher (of Peter & Gordon fame) was put in charge of signing new groups to the label—Taylor was the first artist he signed. Taylor's first album, named simply *James Taylor*, included the hit "Carolina In My Mind."

10. What was the name of Mallory Keaton's rebellious boyfriend and eventual husband on the sitcom *Family Ties*?

a. Eddie

b. Jimmy

c. Nick

d. Tom

GAME 42 Q9 ANSWER b
In 1972, Liza Minnelli won the Best Actress award for her performance in *Cabaret*. Her father, Vincente Minnelli, won as Best Director for *Gigi* in 1958, while her mother, Judy Garland, received a special Juvenile Award—a miniature Oscar—in 1939 for her performance in *The Wizard of Oz*.

10. Which of the following directors died before his final film was released?

a. Charlie Chaplin

b. Stanley Kubrick

c. Alan J. Pakula

d. Alfred Hitchcock

GAME 62 Q9 ANSWER a
Signed by David Geffen, Nirvana was the leading group of the new sound in the '90s. They were also the decade's most chaotic and unpredictable group, giving alternately good and bad performances wherever they went. Cobain's wife, Courtney Love, found fame following his alleged suicide, as her group Hole's album *Live Through This* began to climb the charts.

3. Which of these "seven" movies reportedly cost under $70,000 to make?

a. *Seven* (1979)

b. *The Magnificent Seven* (1960)

c. *Return of the Secaucus Seven* (1980)

d. *The Seven-Ups* (1973)

GAME 19 Q2 ANSWER d
The 1984 version of the George Orwell classic starred John Hurt and featured Richard Burton in his last film role. Bertolucci's *1900* was released in 1976; Spielberg's star-studded turkey *1941* came out in 1979; and *1969*, starring Robert Downey, Jr. and Keifer Sutherland as high school buddies, was released in 1988.

---

3. Which Scottish rock band had its one big hit with the song "In a Big Country"?

a. Men at Work

b. The Rubble Rousers

c. Big Country

d. The Haggis Hounds

GAME 39 Q2 ANSWER d
This all-white soul group featured three singers (Kenny Jeremiah and brothers Charlie and Richard Ingui). Its one hit, which reached #1 in 1967, was really the brainchild of the group's Philadelphia-based producers Kenny Gamble and Leon Huff, who wrote the song.

---

3. Which of these Elvis Presley hits is from the 1950s?

a. "Heartbreak Hotel"

b. "Return to Sender"

c. "Are You Lonesome Tonight?"

d. "Can't Help Falling in Love"

GAME 59 Q2 ANSWER c
Elvis requested and received a meeting with President Nixon with the intent of getting a special FBI narcotics agent badge to detain wrongdoers at will—as well as turning The Beatles (especially John Lennon) in on drug charges. Don't be cruel, Elvis . . .

---

3. Which of the following rock musicians was a member of The Traveling Wilburys along with Bob Dylan?

a. Keith Richards

b. Pete Townshend

c. Ron Wood

d. Tom Petty

GAME 79 Q2 ANSWER b
Dylan first met Johnny Cash in 1964 at the annual Newport Folk Festival. His friendship with Cash was the only thing that convinced Dylan to perform on TV, which he had avoided after his appearance on *The Steve Allen Show* in 1964.

GAME 2

11. What game show host was a member of the cast of *Rowan & Martin's Laugh-In*?

a. Gene Rayburn

b. Peter Marshall

c. Richard Dawson

d. Chuck Barris

GAME 2 Q10 ANSWER c

"Will you take the box or go for what's behind door number 1, door number 2, or door number 3?" *Let's Make a Deal* aired at different times on all three major networks between 1963 and 1986 (it was off between 1977 and 1980 and from 1981 to 1984).

GAME 22

11. Which band released the album (*Untitled*)?

a. The Beatles

b. The Byrds

c. Derek and the Dominoes

d. Nirvana

GAME 22 Q10 ANSWER d

Bat Out of Hell is listed in the *Guinness Book of World Records* as having the longest run on the British charts (over 400 weeks!). Its hit song "Two Out of Three Ain't Bad" reached #11 in the States, and went on to become a classic (in spite of not winning a Grammy).

GAME 42

11. Who tried to seduce Steven Keaton away from his wife, Elise, in *Family Ties*?

a. Judith Light

b. Morgan Fairchild

c. Markie Post

d. Geena Davis

GAME 42 Q10 ANSWER c

Nick Moore, played by Scott Valentine, was made to look and sound very much like Sylvester Stallone at the height of his *Rambo* days.

GAME 62

11. How did Bob Newhart's 1980s sitcom *Newhart* end?

a. Bob opens a bookstore

b. Bob becomes a monk

c. Bob wakes up in bed next to Suzanne Pleshette

d. Bob marries Don Rickles

GAME 62 Q10 ANSWER b

Kubrick died in his sleep the day after he finished editing 1999's *Eyes Wide Shut*. Chaplin's last film was 1966's *A Countess From Hong Kong;* he died in 1977 at his Switzerland home. Pakula's last movie was *The Devil's Own* in 1997; he died a year later in a freak accident. Hitchcock died in 1980—his last film was *Family Plot* (1976).

2. Which movie was released in its title year?

a. *1900*

b. *1941*

c. *1969*

d. *1984*

The 1915 epic told a lengthier, more complex story than had ever before been attempted in film. The movie's controversial retelling of the Civil War and its aftermath still causes many to bristle, especially the scenes depicting the assassination of Lincoln and the rise of the Ku Klux Klan.

---

2. Which group had a single hit with the groovy song "Expressway to Your Heart"?

a. The Rascals

b. The Lovin' Spoonful

c. The Chambers Brothers

d. The Soul Survivors

This Norwegian band had its moment in the chartbusting sun with this 1985 hit. It also made a big splash with MTV viewers, as the video for this song won as Best Concept Video at the 1996 MTV Video Music Awards.

---

2. In 1970, what did President Nixon present to Elvis at the White House?

a. A hug and kiss

b. A porcelain hound dog

c. An FBI special narcotics agent badge

d. An album for Elvis to sign

This Jerry Leiber-Mike Stoller song topped the R&B charts for Thornton in 1953, three years before Elvis released the hit single. Presley's "Hound Dog" was backed with "Don't Be Cruel" and was the #1 single of the year in 1956.

---

2. On which country star's TV show did the normally reclusive Bob Dylan appear in May 1969?

a. Chet Atkins

b. Johnny Cash

c. Loretta Lynn

d. Roy Clark

Written shortly after Dylan's infamous performance at the Newport Folk Festival in July 1965, this song was released as a single following "Like a Rolling Stone," which reached #2 in *Billboard* in August of that year. It reached #7 on the charts, and was later available on an album as part of *Bob Dylan's Greatest Hits*.

12. Which future president appeared as a guest and later as a panelist on *What's My Line?*

a. Gerald Ford
b. Jimmy Carter
c. Ronald Reagan
d. George H. Bush

GAME 2 Q11 ANSWER c
Dawson and fellow *Hogan's Heroes* actor Larry Hovis appeared on *Laugh-In* on a recurring basis. Dawson later became the kiss-friendly host of *Family Feud*.

12. What is the only Grateful Dead single to make it to the Top 10?

a. "Truckin"
b. "Uncle John's Band"
c. "Touch of Grey"
d. "Casey Jones"

GAME 22 Q11 ANSWER b
Apparently, this title was the result of a company in a rush to release the album. When asked about it by a Columbia Records exec, Byrds manager Terry Melcher casually answered that the album was "as yet untitled."

12. Which of the following musicians does *not* have a child who also became a recording artist?

a. Ringo Starr
b. John Lennon
c. John Bonham
d. Jimmy Page

GAME 42 Q11 ANSWER a
Judith Light, who began her career on the ABC daytime soap opera *One Life to Live*, went on to star opposite Tony Danza on the popular sitcom *Who's the Boss?* Morgan Fairchild starred on *Knots Landing*, while Markie Post kept watch over *Night Court*. Geena Davis appeared twice on *Family Ties* in 1984.

12. Which Huxtable graduates college in the final episode of *The Cosby Show*?

a. Theo
b. Rudy
c. Vanessa
d. Denise

GAME 62 Q11 ANSWER c
At the end of *Newhart's* last episode, Bob wakes up in bed next to Suzanne Pleshette, his wife from *The Bob Newhart Show*. This suggested that all of *Newhart* had been a dream inside another sitcom. *Dallas* used a similar trick to bring Bobby Ewing (Patrick Duffy) back from the dead.

GAME 19

1. What was D.W. Griffith's epic film about the South?

a. *Gone With the Wind*

b. *Song of the South*

c. *Birth of a Nation*

d. *Fried Green Tomatoes*

The answer to this question is on:

page 254, top frame, right side.

GAME 39

1. The '80s pop group Aha had its one hit with which of the following songs?

a. "Say You, Say Me"

b. "Do You Really Want to Hurt Me?"

c. "Take on Me"

d. "Hangin' Tough"

The answer to this question is on:

page 254, second frame, right side.

GAME 59

1. Which Elvis Presley hit was originally written for Willie Mae "Big Mama" Thornton?

a. "Blue Suede Shoes"

b. "Heartbreak Hotel"

c. "Hound Dog"

d. "Don't Be Cruel"

The answer to this question is on:

page 254, third frame, right side.

GAME 79

1. Which Bob Dylan song was first released as a single, *not* part of an album?

a. "The Times They Are a-Changin'"

b. "It Ain't Me, Babe"

c. "Positively 4th Street"

d. "Mr. Tambourine Man"

The answer to this question is on:

page 254, bottom frame, right side.

GAME 3

The '70s

Break Out the Polyester and the Platform Shoes

*Turn to page 30
for the first question.*

Turn to page 30
for the first question.

GAME 2 Q12 ANSWER c
Reagan was a mystery guest during the show's initial run in 1953. Carter was a contestant during the show's syndicated run in the early 1970s, appearing when he was governor of Georgia.

GAME 23

Cartoon Fun

The World of Animation

*Turn to page 30
for the first question.*

Turn to page 30
for the first question.

GAME 22 Q12 ANSWER c
Formed in 1965, the Grateful Dead waited twenty-two years for one of its songs to reach the Top 10. When "Touch of Grey" reached #9 in 1987, the late Jerry Garcia allegedly was "appalled" to learn the group had a hit.

GAME 43

"YO!"

You're in the Stallone Zone

*Turn to page 30
for the first question.*

Turn to page 30
for the first question.

GAME 42 Q12 ANSWER d
Ringo Starr's son, Zack Starkey, is also a drummer and has toured with The Who. John Bonham's son, Jason, has toured as live drummer with his father's bandmates Robert Plant and Jimmy Page; he also heads The Jason Bonham Band. Both Julian and Sean Lennon are recording artists in the tradition of their father.

GAME 63

Bands on the Run

Chords and Discords in the Music Biz

*Turn to page 30
for the first question.*

Turn to page 30
for the first question.

GAME 62 Q12 ANSWER a
Theo (Malcolm Jamal-Warner) was the only son of the family, and often the one who pushed many of father Cliff's buttons. The joy with which Cosby embraced his sitcom son in this last episode mirrored the sorrow with which he had to bury his real-life son Ennis, who was murdered in 1997.

GAME 19

The Silver Screen

Fun for Film Fanatics

*Turn to page 253
for the first question.*

GAME 18 Q12 ANSWER b
Springsteen's only other album of the '80s, *Live 1975–1985*, which was released in 1986, also reached #1. *Nebraska*, an album of folky demos that Bruce recorded at home, got as far as #3.

GAME 39

One-Hit Wonders

Who Sang That Song?

*Turn to page 253
for the first question.*

GAME 38 Q12 ANSWER d
Bette Davis remains forever one of Hollywood's greatest and most courageous actresses. In *All About Eve,* she threw her star power around with the likes of George Sanders, Anne Baxter, Celeste Holm, and a little-known actress named Marilyn Monroe.

GAME 59

"The King" and His Court

All About Elvis

*Turn to page 253
for the first question.*

GAME 58 Q12 ANSWER c
Quint's boat proved inspirational to both the *Jaws* franchise and another film production: *Jaws II* used the *Orca* as the setting of the film's first underwater scene and subsequent shark attack. Meanwhile, a movie about a killer whale was released in 1977. The film's name? *Orca.*

GAME 79

"The Answer, My Friends . . ."

Mr. Zimmerman and Other Dylanisms

*Turn to page 253
for the first question.*

GAME 78 Q12 ANSWER c
Despite the seemingly autobiographical parallels to his own life, Woody Allen has said in several interviews that he based his character Harry Block not on himself, but on *Portnoy's Complaint* novelist Phillip Roth. Allen originally wanted either Dennis Hopper or Elliott Gould to play the lead part. When neither one was available, he took the role himself.

GAME 3

1. *Lady Sings the Blues* (1972) is the story of:

a. Lena Horne
b. Billie Holiday
c. Nina Simone
d. Bessie Smith

The answer to this question is on:

page 31, top frame, right side.

GAME 23

1. What was the first animated movie ever to be rated X by the MPAA?

a. *Fritz the Cat*
b. *Heavy Traffic*
c. *Cool World*
d. *American Pop*

The answer to this question is on:

page 31, second frame, right side.

GAME 43

1. What was the name of Rocky Balboa's dog?

a. Moby Dick
b. Butkus
c. Cuff
d. Jelly

The answer to this question is on:

page 31, third frame, right side.

GAME 63

1. Which musician was *not* one of the original members of The Eagles?

a. Don Henley
b. Glenn Frey
c. Joe Walsh
d. Randy Meisner

The answer to this question is on:

page 31, bottom frame, right side.

12. Which of Bruce Spring-steen's albums of the 1980s did *not* go to #1 on *Billboard's* album chart?

a. *The River* (1980)

b. *Nebraska* (1982)

c. *Born in the U.S.A.* (1984)

d. *Tunnel of Love* (1987)

GAME 18 Q11 ANSWER b

"Tush" comes from their fourth album, *Fandango*, released in 1975. Formed in 1970 by bearded bandmembers Dusty Hill and Billy Gibbons, and beardless drummer Frank Beard, ZZ Top is the only rock-and-roll group still around after three decades with all of its original members.

12. Bette Davis says, "Fasten your seatbelts. It's going to be a bumpy night!" in:

a. *What Ever Happened to Baby Jane?* (1962)

b. *The Little Foxes* (1941)

c. *Dark Victory* (1939)

d. *All About Eve* (1950)

GAME 38 Q11 ANSWER c

Olivier, who plays a former Nazi SS dentist, continually asks this question of Dustin Hoffman, whom he believes has info about a diamond-smuggling ring. In one chilling scene, Olivier asks the question while drilling a hole in Hoffman's front tooth (without Novocain, of course). This scene alone explains my fear of dentists . . .

12. What was the name of Quint's fishing boat in *Jaws*?

a. *Lorna Doone*

b. *Thresher*

c. *Orca*

d. *Neptune*

GAME 58 Q11 ANSWER b

In a way, Tim Burton's film of Pee-wee's quest to reclaim his bike is both a parody of and an homage to Vittorio de Sica's classic Italian film *The Bicycle Thief*. Be sure to look at this film for the rock group Twisted Sister in a small cameo. Pee-wee again graced the silver screen in a 1988 sequel called *Big Top Pee-wee*.

12. Which Woody Allen film is about a novelist with a severe case of writer's block?

a. *Shadows and Fog* (1992)

b. *Stardust Memories* (1980)

c. *Deconstructing Harry* (1997)

d. *Manhattan* (1979)

GAME 78 Q11 ANSWER b

Searching for the right sentence to reflect writer Jack Torrence's psychotic state of mind, Kubrick and co-screenwriter Diane Johnson finally settled on this sentence above several others, including "A stitch in time." For the record, midway through the film, Jack does tell his son Danny that he wishes they could stay in the Overlook Hotel forever.

2. "All the Young Dudes"
was a 1972 hit for:

a. David Bowie

b. Mott the Hoople

c. T. Rex

d. Iggy Pop

GAME 3 Q1 ANSWER b
Lady Sings the Blues, starring Diana Ross, was the first film produced by Motown Records. For her portrayal of Holiday, the former Supreme received an Academy Award nomination for Best Actress.

---

2. Who was *not* one of
Donald Duck's nephews?

a. Dewey

b. Chewie

c. Huey

d. Louie

GAME 23 Q1 ANSWER a
Ralph Bakshi directed *Fritz the Cat* in 1972. Its 1973 follow-up, *Heavy Traffic,* was a mixture of live action and animation. After directing the fully-animated classic *American Pop* in 1981, he returned to the live-action/animation mix in 1992's *Cool World.*

---

2. In how many "Rocky" films
did Burgess Meredith act?

a. Two

b. Three

c. Four

d. Five

GAME 43 Q1 ANSWER b
Butkus was actually Stallone's pet, and appeared in the first two "Rocky" films. In *Rocky,* he even appears in the credits as Butkus Stallone: Dog. Incidentally, Rocky's two turtles in that movie were named Cuff and Link.

---

2. Which James appears
on the front of the Wings
album *Band on the Run*?

a. James Coburn

b. James Mason

c. James Caan

d. James Garner

GAME 63 Q1 ANSWER c
The Eagles self-titled first album was released in 1972. Joe Walsh, formerly of the James Gang, joined the band in 1976 for the album *Hotel California.* In later years, Walsh continued recording solo albums and performed live many times with Beatles drummer Ringo Starr's tour band.

11. Which song was *not* on ZZ Top's 1983 smash album *Eliminator*?

a. "Gimme All Your Lovin"

b. "Tush"

c. "Sharp Dressed Man"

d. "Legs"

GAME 18 Q10 ANSWER b

The platinum-haired punk rocker, born William Broad, had a string of hits in the 1980s, including a remake of "Mony Mony," which went to #1. "Goody Two Shoes" (1982) was the first solo effort by Adam Ant.

---

11. "Is it safe?" In which film does Sir Laurence Olivier ask this question over and over?

a. *The Boys from Brazil* (1978)

b. *Dracula* (1979)

c. *Marathon Man* (1976)

d. *Spartacus* (1960)

GAME 38 Q10 ANSWER b

When Roy Scheider said this line to sea captain Quint (played with gusto by Robert Shaw), audiences throughout the world knew exactly what he meant. I am happy to report that I have never once been to the beach. If this film is any indication of the entertainment available there, I will gladly remain in the city, thank you very much . . .

---

11. Which vehicle is stolen from Pee-wee Herman (Paul Reubens) in 1985's *Pee-wee's Big Adventure*?

a. His golf cart

b. His bicycle

c. His skateboard

d. His private airplane

GAME 58 Q10 ANSWER a

In this exciting James Bond film, Roger Moore drives underwater in his submarine car with Bond girl Barbara Bach, who later went on to marry Beatles drummer Ringo Starr—who, interestingly, sang the group's #1 hit, "Yellow Submarine."

---

11. What sentence does Jack Nicholson type over and over again in *The Shining* (1980)?

a. "Wendy and Danny will die."

b. "All work and no play makes Jack a dull boy."

c. "For ever and ever and ever."

d. "Help, I'm trapped!"

GAME 78 Q10 ANSWER c

O'Rourke is a former editor-in-chief of *National Lampoon*. It makes sense that he would contribute to the one comedy in the list. Pretty *easy*, huh? The 1983 film starred Rodney Dangerfield, Joe Pesci, and Jennifer Jason Leigh.

3. Who was *not* featured in the movie *Sgt. Pepper's Lonely Hearts Club Band* (1978)?

a. Andy Gibb

b. Peter Frampton

c. George Burns

d. Steve Martin

GAME 3 Q2 ANSWER b
The '70s glam-rock group Mott the Hoople had a friend in Mr. "Ziggy Stardust" himself, David Bowie. He both wrote the song "All the Young Dudes" and produced Mott the Hoople's album of the same name. The musical partnership represented a high point in glitter rock reccrdings.

3. On which crossover radio/TV show did Alan Reed, the voice of Fred Flintstone, get his start?

a. *Life With Luigi*

b. *Charlie Chan*

c. *The Goldbergs*

d. *I Remember Mama*

GAME 23 Q2 ANSWER b
"Chewie" was the nickname of Han Solo's Wookie friend Chewbacca in the *Star Wars* movies. To date, he has not been asked to appear in any Walt Disney cartoon features.

3. In which of the following films is Stallone clean shaven throughout the entire movie?

a. *Nighthawks* (1979)

b. *First Blood* (1983)

c. *Get Carter* (2001)

d. *Over the Top* (1987)

GAME 43 Q2 ANSWER c
Although Meredith "appeared" in five of the films, he "acted" in only four. In *Rocky IV*, Meredith is seen in a montage sequence in which Rocky is remembering his past. The scenes are from existing footage from earlier films in the series.

3. Before embarking on his solo career, Vince Gill was the lead singer of:

a. Supertramp

b. Little Feat

c. Pure Prairie League

d. Bachman-Turner Overdrive

GAME 63 Q2 ANSWER a
Also featured on the cover is Christopher Lee, the great Count Dracula of "countless" vampire films.

10. Which song was *not* a hit for Billy Idol?

a. "White Wedding"

b. "Goody Two Shoes"

c. "Hot in the City"

d. "Eyes Without a Face"

George Peppard, a.k.a. Colonel John "Hannibal" Smith, led the team of renegade Vietnam vets-for-hire. Mr. T. played mechanic "B.A.," Dirk Benedict was master imposter "Face," and Dwight Schultz played pilot Murdoch. In later seasons, *The A Team* members worked as government agents under Robert Vaughn's General Stockwell.

---

10. Which film gave us the line, "You're gonna need a bigger boat"?

a. *Moby Dick* (1956)

b. *Jaws* (1975)

c. *The African Queen* (1951)

d. *Orca: The Killer Whale* (1977)

Oliver Stone's screenplay for Brian De Palma's *Scarface* used the word 206 times, Martin Scorsese's *Goodfellas* used it 246 times, and Quentin Tarantino's *Pulp Fiction* topped the scales at 257. Sometimes you gotta say, "What the f–," like in *Risky Business*.

---

10. In which James Bond film does 007's car turn into an underwater submarine?

a. *The Spy Who Loved Me* (1977)

b. *Live and Let Die* (1973)

c. *Moonraker* (1979)

d. *You Only Live Twice* (1967)

A fine Lamborghini found its way into *The Cannonball Run* (1981); Mark Hamill was in search of a stolen Corvette in *Corvette Summer* (1978); and Michael J. Fox zoomed *Back to the Future* (1985) in a DeLorean "time-machine."

---

10. Political/foreign affairs correspondent P.J. O'Rourke co-wrote the screenplay for which "easy" movie?

a. *Easy Rider* (1969)

b. *Five Easy Pieces* (1970)

c. *Easy Money* (1983)

d. *The Big Easy* (1987)

In addition to writing his own story, the multi-talented "Velvet Fog" also wrote about drummer Buddy Rich (*Traps the Drum Wonder: The Life of Buddy Rich*) and singer Judy Garland (*The Other Side of the Rainbow: With Judy Garland on the Dawn Patrol*). When Bing Crosby was on my show, Mel Torme was the singer he praised the most.

4. *American Graffiti* (1973) was written and directed by what noted filmmaker?

a. Steven Spielberg

b. George Lucas

c. Martin Scorsese

d. Barry Levinson

GAME 3 Q3 ANSWER a

This 1978 film, based on The Beatles' 1967 album, featured Barry, Maurice, and Robin Gibb (The Bee Gees) as the title band, and Peter Frampton as "the one and only Billy Shears." At that time, the Gibbs' brother Andy was a successful solo recording artist. The movie also featured George Burns and Steve Martin as characters from Beatles' songs.

---

4. In *Cool World* (1992), who does cartoon creation "Holli Would" seduce in her attempt to become human?

a. Brad Pitt

b. Gabriel Byrne

c. Frank Sinatra, Jr.

d. Alec Baldwin

GAME 23 Q3 ANSWER a

Reed played Pasquale, owner of Pasquale's Spaghetti Palace, on both the radio and television shows. Incidentally, Luigi was played by J. Carrol Naish, who also played the title character on the *Charlie Chan* television show.

---

4. What was the name of the 1984 comedy that paired Stallone with Dolly Parton?

a. *Singin' West*

b. *Rhinestone*

c. *The Flexin' Cowboy*

d. *Go for the Rodeo*

GAME 43 Q3 ANSWER d

In *Nighthawks,* Stallone has a full beard. In *Get Carter,* he sports a full goatee. As John Rambo in *First Blood,* he has a moustache in the Vietnam flashback scenes. Stallone's clean-shaven role in *Over the Top* is as a widower who competes with his wealthy father-in-law for the custody of his son.

---

4. Which group does *not* include a performer's name in its name?

a. ELP

b. BTO

c. CCR

d. CSN

GAME 63 Q3 ANSWER c

Gill joined PPL in 1979, after the group had already logged most of its hits. Previously, he performed with a band called Mountain Smoke, which coincidentally, opened for Pure Prairie League earlier in the 1970s.

9. Which member of NBC's *The A Team* was a slightly deranged pilot?

a. "Hannibal" Smith
b. "B.A." Barracus
c. "Face" Peck
d. "Howlin' Mad" Murdoch

GAME 18 Q8 ANSWER b
Although its season debut in 1979 had low ratings, this sitcom, which took place in an exclusive all-girls boarding school, ran until 1988. Three original roles (including Ringwald's) were cut at the start of the second season. Actors who appeared regularly on the show included George Clooney, Juliette Lewis, and Seth Green.

9. Which film uses the "F"-word the most times?

a. *Scarface* (1983)
b. *Pulp Fiction* (1994)
c. *Goodfellas* (1990)
d. *Risky Business* (1983)

GAME 38 Q8 ANSWER d
The oft-parodied line comes from this overacted King Vidor film (it's entirely possible that Davis was commenting on the film's quality). *Beyond the Forest* was released just a year before Davis redeemed her film career with *All About Eve*.

9. What kind of car did Burt Reynolds drive in *Smokey and the Bandit* (1977)?

a. Lamborghini
b. Corvette
c. Trans Am
d. DeLorean

GAME 58 Q8 ANSWER a
Jaunty Jalopies recounts a 1920s-era Monte Carlo Rally; *The Great Race* recounts the 1908 New York-to-Paris auto race; and *The Gumball Rally* and *Cannonball Run* were both inspired by automotive journalist Brock Yates's real and very illegal "Cannonball Baker Sea-to-Shining-Sea Memorial Trophy Dash" of the early 1970s.

9. *It Wasn't All Velvet* is the autobiography of:

a. Elizabeth Taylor
b. Mel Torme
c. John Kraft
d. David Lynch

GAME 78 Q8 ANSWER c
Chris O'Donnell starred in the film version of Grisham's *The Chamber* (1996); Matthew McConaughey was in *A Time to Kill* (1996); and Matt Damon was cast in *The Rainmaker* (1997).

5. On which TV show could you hear someone being told to "Kiss my grits"?

a. *Good Times*

b. *Alice*

c. *Sanford and Son*

d. *Happy Days*

GAME 3 Q4 ANSWER b

Although it may seem like TV's *Happy Days* was a take-off on *American Graffiti*, the opposite is true. Lucas's second film was inspired by Garry Marshall's 1971 pilot for the sitcom. The movie was released in 1973, and the TV show premiered in 1974.

---

5. One of TV's traditional holiday favorites, *A Charlie Brown Christmas* first aired in what year?

a. 1965

b. 1967

c. 1964

d. 1968

GAME 23 Q4 ANSWER b

In Ralph Bakshi's answer to *Who Framed Roger Rabbit* (1988), Kim Basinger is cartoon vixen Holli. Byrne is cartoonist Jack Deebs, and the perfect foil for Holli's plan to become human. Pitt is a human detective who lives in the cartoon world. Frank Sinatra, Jr. appears as himself, and sings a duet with Holli on the soundtrack.

---

5. Which film did Stallone write, direct, produce, star in, and even sing the title song?

a. *Staying Alive* (1983)

b. *Rambo: First Blood, Part II* (1985)

c. *Driven* (2001)

d. *Paradise Alley* (1978)

GAME 43 Q4 ANSWER b

Sly as a country singer? You betcha! Though it's considered something of a camp classic these days, this film was a flop when it opened. It did, however, prove that Stallone had a good sense of humor about moviemaking. My favorite scene is when he is on a farm, singing "Devil With the Blue Dress On," and even the chickens run screaming.

---

5. Which band once was Linda Ronstadt's backup band?

a. The Band

b. The Eagles

c. Styx

d. REO Speedwagon

GAME 63 Q4 ANSWER c

The Golliwogs changed its name in 1967 to Creedence Clearwater Revival, borrowing a friend's name and some words culled from a beer commercial. The others are Emerson, Lake & Palmer; Bachman-Turner Overdrive; and Crosby, Stills & Nash.

8. Which Brat Packer played on NBC's *The Facts of Life* during its first season?

a. Ally Sheedy

b. Molly Ringwald

c. Demi Moore

d. Sarah Jessica Parker

GAME 18 Q7 ANSWER c
Michael J. Fox shot to stardom playing Alex, the ultra-conservative son of liberal parents. *Family Ties,* which ran from 1982 to 1989, was reputedly Reagan's favorite TV show.

---

8. Bette Davis complains, "What a dump!" in which film?

a. *All About Eve* (1950)

b. *The Little Foxes* (1941)

c. *Satan Met a Lady* (1936)

d. *Beyond the Forest* (1949)

GAME 38 Q7 ANSWER b
These were the words of actor Lewis Stone, as the observant Dr. Otternschlag, when referring to Berlin's most expansive hotel. *Grand Hotel* starred Garbo at the height of her game. She was only twenty-six years old when she played Grusinskaya, the aging and eccentric ballerina who only "vants to be alone."

---

8. Which movie's automobile race did *not* start in New York?

a. *Those Daring Young Men in Their Jaunty Jalopies* (1969)

b. *The Great Race* (1965)

c. *The Gumball Rally* (1976)

d. *Cannonball Run* (1981)

GAME 58 Q7 ANSWER b
Falk, best-known as TV's *Columbo,* teams up with Lemmon in this hilarious comedy. He plays Max Meen, loyal supporter of Lemmon's character Professor Fate. Their high jinks are similar to those of Laurel & Hardy, to whom the picture was dedicated.

---

8. Who has *not* played the lead in a film based on the writing of John Grisham?

a. Chris O'Donnell

b. Matthew McConaughey

c. Ben Affleck

d. Matt Damon

GAME 78 Q7 ANSWER d
Costner was first cast as Jack Ryan in *The Hunt for Red October* (1990). Instead, Alec Baldwin took the role, but he turned down the role in the next film, *Patriot Games* (1992). Harrison Ford stepped into the role for that film and the next, *Clear and Present Danger* (1994). Ben Affleck then played Jack Ryan in *The Sum of All Fears* (2002).

6. *Roots,* one of the most remarkable achievements in television history, was based on which author's bestseller?

a. John Jakes

b. Alex Haley

c. Sidney Sheldon

d. Jacqueline Susann

GAME 3 Q5 ANSWER b
The diner's outspoken waitress Flo (Polly Holliday) coined this sassy expression. *Alice* was based on the Martin Scorsese film *Alice Doesn't Live Here Anymore* (1975). Coincidentally, when Holliday spun off *Alice* to star in her own sitcom, she was replaced by Diane Ladd, who played Flo in the original movie.

---

6. Which television show holds the title for longest-running prime time animated series?

a. *The Flintstones*

b. *The Jetsons*

c. *The Simpsons*

d. *King of the Hill*

GAME 23 Q5 ANSWER a
Charles Schulz' first *Peanuts* special aired on December 9, 1965 on CBS. Although Schulz died in 2000, his beloved characters and TV specials will continue to entertain viewers.

---

6. Who was Stallone's co-star in *Tango & Cash?*

a. James Woods

b. Wesley Snipes

c. Kurt Russell

d. John Lithgow

GAME 43 Q5 ANSWER d
Released in 1978 to so-so reviews, this tale of an up-and-coming wrestler and the brother who trains and believes in him had its roots in Stallone's own past, growing up in New York's Hell's Kitchen. Sly should probably not sing so much, though—that would be better left to his brother Frank, I think.

---

6. After Ace Frehley left KISS in 1982, how many lead guitarists were in the group before Frehley rejoined in 1996?

a. One

b. Two

c. Three

d. Four

GAME 63 Q5 ANSWER b
The Eagles were first assembled by producer John Boylan as the backup band for Linda Ronstadt's second album, *Silk Purses* (1970). This was two years before The Eagles' self-titled debut.

7. On NBC's *Family Ties*, who was Alex P. Keaton's idol?

a. Ronald Reagan
b. J.P. Morgan
c. Richard Nixon
d. Muhammad Ali

GAME 18 Q6 ANSWER c
Building on the success of "We Are the World," rock recording artists' largest charity event took place simultaneously in stadiums in the United States and the UK. Top artists performed some of their most popular songs to raise money for famine relief in Ethiopia.

---

7. "People come, people go. Nothing ever happens . . ." where?

a. *Casablanca* (1942)
b. *Grand Hotel* (1932)
c. *Key Largo* (1948)
d. *Chinatown* (1974)

GAME 38 Q6 ANSWER c
Clerow "Flip" Wilson's best-known routines involved the sassy Geraldine, who always talked about her boyfriend Killer. One of twenty-four children, Flip got his nickname while in the Air Force, because his comedy routines "flipped" out his company.

---

7. Who played Jack Lemmon's henchman in Blake Edwards' *The Great Race* (1965)?

a. Tony Curtis
b. Peter Falk
c. Dick Shawn
d. Jack Klugman

GAME 58 Q6 ANSWER c
Speed drove the powerful Mach 5 as he raced Racer X to the delight and concern of girlfriend Trixie, kid brother Spritle, and pet monkey Chim-Chim.

---

7. Who has *not* played the lead in a film based on the novels of Tom Clancy?

a. Harrison Ford
b. Alec Baldwin
c. Ben Affleck
d. Kevin Costner

GAME 78 Q6 ANSWER b
Before writing *The Exorcist*, Blatty was known for writing the screenplays to the Blake Edwards films *What Did You Do In The War, Daddy?* and *Peter Gunn*. He also helped turn *A Shot in the Dark* from a stage adaptation into an Inspector Clouseau film. Blatty later wrote and directed *The Ninth Configuration* (1980) and 1990's *The Exorcist III*.

From Silents to "Talkies"

Most people have seen and enjoyed Gene Kelly's delightful 1955 musical comedy *Singin' in the Rain*, which spoofed Hollywood's transition from silent movies to sound films. Although many of the great silent film stars did fall by the wayside when "talkies" came in—as Kelly's film so brilliantly shows—that period was not quite as bad as it's been portrayed both in the press and in the cinema.

For example, there has long been a widespread myth that silent actor John Gilbert lost his film career because of an extremely squeaky voice. In fact, Gilbert's voice was not squeaky at all, and the performer went on to make many, many early sound films, including the wonderful *Queen Christina*. Pound for pound, larynx for larynx, John Gilbert had an all-around good voice. I wouldn't say he had a voice like Ronald Colman or the magnificent Orson Welles, but he could deliver his lines as well as the next player. In fact, Gilbert made sound films until 1934, his last film being *The Captain Hates the Sea*. I think the real reason his career went south was that he simply went out of vogue. It's common enough in the entertainment biz for this to happen, and it has certainly happened more than once. (Just ask Buster Keaton or John Travolta.)

When talkies were first made, Hollywood tried to round up as many Broadway actors and actresses with good speaking voices as possible. One of my favorites, a man I think of with great affection, was Conrad Nagel. He had been a successful Broadway star and had starred in some silent films as well. Strangely, he was also dating my wife, Lois, around the time she convinced me to add her to my growing wealth of beloved collectibles.

Conrad Nagel once told me one of the great stories about early sound films. Sometime around 1929 or 1930—

at the beginning of sound pictures—Conrad was acting in seven movies simultaneously. The actor moved from room to room, from soundstage to soundstage, with his lines written on off-camera blackboards. He had no idea of the films' various plots. Wherever he was, he simply read the words off the boards, and every film came out just great. In each performance, he seemed to know exactly what he was saying. This, to me, shows the true brilliance of a gifted actor. In addition to his film career, Conrad won a number of diction awards and was an emcee on various early radio shows like *The Silver Theatre*. His voice was one of his strongest gifts.

The move from silent movies to sound films didn't affect only actors, by the way. Directors also faced a host of challenges when the big change came. For example, D.W. Griffith—director of silent classics such as *Orphans of the Storm* and *Birth of a Nation*—found that the brilliant storytelling techniques which had served him so well in silent films were no help to him once sound came in. His last film in 1931 was called *The Struggle,* and the title was an apt description of Griffith's attempt to make a sound film that both literally and figuratively spoke to the filmgoer. Griffith's career as a filmmaker was over, and by his death in 1948, his legacy as the founding father of silent film had been all but forgotten.

Yes, the transition from silent to sound claimed some casualties, but on the other hand, it proved to be a boon to a number of big-city stage performers, including James Cagney, Joan Blondell, and Humphrey Bogart. Bogart—previously an actor on Broadway—didn't even catch on as a star until 1936, when he appeared in *The Petrified Forest.* It was a very tumultuous time, and I'm not so sure that films got any better with sound. In many cases, it seems they just got louder.

GAME 3

7. Who was the Rhodes scholar who wrote "Me and Bobby McGee"?

a. Janis Joplin

b. Kris Kristofferson

c. Roger Miller

d. Johnny Cash

GAME 3 Q6 ANSWER b
The twelve-hour ABC adaptation of the book aired on eight consecutive nights in January 1977. All eight telecasts ranked among the top twenty highest-rated single programs of all time. Two years later, the network aired the twelve-hour sequel, *Roots: The Next Generation*, over seven nights.

GAME 23

7. Which *This Is Spinal Tap* (1984) band member provides the voices for over twenty characters on *The Simpsons*?

a. Michael McKean

b. Harry Shearer

c. Christopher Guest

d. Ed Begley, Jr.

GAME 23 Q6 ANSWER c
Still going strong, *The Simpsons* first aired in January 1990. *The Flintstones* had a six-year run, beginning in 1960. *The Jetsons* aired on prime time only during its first 1962/63 season. *King of the Hill*, which is currently still on the air, debuted in 1997.

GAME 43

7. Who played the partner to Stallone's half-deaf, overweight police officer in *Cop Land*?

a. Janeane Garofalo

b. Sandra Bullock

c. Lili Taylor

d. Christina Ricci

GAME 43 Q6 ANSWER c
Stallone and Russell both showed their naked butts in this 1989 cop flick. Other highlights include Jack Palance as the film's nasty villain, and an up-and-coming Teri Hatcher as Stallone's beautiful sister (before she became known as TV's sexiest Lois Lane ever in *The Adventures of Lois & Clark*).

GAME 63

7. Which of the following guitarists joined supergroup Yes in the early '80s?

a. Trevor Rabin

b. Steve Howe

c. Steve Hackett

d. Peter Banks

GAME 63 Q6 ANSWER c
The three guitarists were Vinnie Vincent, Mark St. John, and Bruce Kulick. When Frehley first departed in 1982, Vinnie Vincent was brought in to record the solos on *Creatures of the Night*. Strangely, the album's first cover featured Ace on the cover and not Vinnie. Vincent was kept for only one more album before getting the *kiss*-off . . .

6. In what year was the "Live Aid" concert event held?

a. 1982

b. 1984

c. 1985

d. 1986

GAME 18 Q5 ANSWER a
Although Matt Groening's short films about Bart's family appeared occasionally on *The Tracey Ullman Show*, Homer and the family didn't debut on their own until 1990.

6. Which TV character was known for saying "What you see is what you get"?

a. Alice Kramden

b. Ginger Grant

c. Geraldine Jones

d. Florence Johnston

GAME 38 Q5 ANSWER b
William Powell received an Oscar nomination for his 1934 portrayal of Nick Charles in the first of six films based on Dashiell Hammett's characters. Dash modeled the boozy detective couple, Nick and Nora, on his own relationship with writer Lillian Hellman.

6. What was the name of the car in *Speed Racer*?

a. K.I.T.T.

b. General Lee

c. Mach 5

d. Mother

GAME 58 Q5 ANSWER d
All four films won various Oscars, but of them, only *Airport* was up for Best Picture. Nominated for ten awards, it lost Best Film to *Patton* and Best Screenplay to *M*A*S*H*, but Helen Hayes beat co-star Maureen Stapleton to take the Best Supporting Actress Award. Of other disaster films, *The Towering Inferno* (1974) also received a Best Picture nomination.

6. Who wrote the novel and screenplay for *The Exorcist*?

a. Robert Bloch

b. William Peter Blatty

c. Frederick Knott

d. Ira Levin

GAME 78 Q5 ANSWER b
Based on Richard Matheson's novel *I Am Legend*, *The Omega Man* stars Charlton Heston as a man under attack by a race of zombies spawned by germ warfare.

8. What folk rock singer sang "Operator (That's Not the Way It Feels)"?

a. Arlo Guthrie
b. Jim Croce
c. James Taylor
d. Jackson Browne

GAME 3 Q7 ANSWER b
Texas native Kristofferson went to Oxford University in 1958. He left in 1960 to become a U.S. Army helicopter pilot, and then moved to Nashville after turning down a teaching position at West Point. "Me and Bobby McGee" was a country hit for Roger Miller two years before Joplin's posthumous hit in 1971.

---

8. Which of the following actors appeared in a movie with cartoon characters Tom and Jerry?

a. Betty Grable
b. Frank Sinatra
c. Esther Williams
d. Jerry Lewis

GAME 23 Q7 ANSWER b
Mr. Burns, Smithers, Ned Flanders, and Principal Skinner are among the characters voiced by the former *Saturday Night Live* writer and cast member. Shearer, a former child actor, appeared in *Abbott and Costello Go to Mars* (1953) and *The Robe* (1953). He also played Frankie, (the "Eddie Haskell") part, in the 1957 *Leave It to Beaver* pilot.

---

8. In the comedy *Oscar,* who plays Stallone's dying father in the first scene of the film?

a. Don Ameche
b. Kirk Douglas
c. Burt Lancaster
d. Eli Wallach

GAME 43 Q7 ANSWER a
Cop Land was considered a return to form for Stallone, who gained nearly forty pounds to convey his character's heavy sense of inner collapse and isolation. *Cop Land* also pitted Stallone against acting heavyweights Robert DeNiro, Harvey Keitel, and Ray Liotta.

---

8. What '90s rock group paired "madman" guitarist Ted Nugent with band members from Night Ranger and Styx?

a. Poison
b. The Black Crowes
c. Damn Yankees
d. Skid Row

GAME 63 Q7 ANSWER a
Peter Banks was the group's first guitarist in the late '60s, followed by Steve Howe, who joined the group in 1971 and stayed there until 1980. Steve Hackett played guitar in fellow progressive rock band Genesis throughout the early '70s, and later joined Steve Howe in the '80s group GTR (they had a hit with their song "When the Heart Meets the Mind").

GAME 18

5. Which show was *not* part of FOX-TV's 1987/88 inaugural season?

a. *The Simpsons*

b. *Married . . . With Children*

c. *The Tracey Ullman Show*

d. *Second Chance*

GAME 18 Q4 ANSWER b
This film of an obsessive romance between two teenagers also marked the film debuts of Jami Gertz, James Spader, and Tom Cruise.

GAME 38

5. "A dry martini you always shake to waltz time" came from which film?

a. *Days of Wine and Roses* (1962)

b. *The Thin Man* (1934)

c. *Dr. No* (1962)

d. *Cocktail* (1988)

GAME 38 Q4 ANSWER a
This 1943 romantic comedy starred Jean Arthur and Joel McCrea, and featured Charles Coburn as Arthur's older gentleman roommate. The film received six Academy Award nominations, but the only Oscar went to Best Supporting Actor Coburn as the aging Cupid, who also got to deliver the line.

GAME 58

5. Which 1970s disaster flick was nominated for a Best Picture Oscar?

a. *Earthquake* (1974)

b. *The Hindenburg* (1975)

c. *The Poseidon Adventure* (1972)

d. *Airport* (1970)

GAME 58 Q4 ANSWER c
William Boyd's black-clothed Hoppy could usually be seen astride his white horse, Topper. Dale Evans rode Buttermilk. Zorro sat atop Phantom (and sometimes Tornado). Rex was Sergeant Preston of the Yukon's faithful mount.

GAME 78

5. Which of these thrillers involves a world destroyed by biological warfare?

a. *The Ipcress File* (1965)

b. *The Omega Man* (1971)

c. *The Odessa File* (1974)

d. *The Terminal Man* (1974)

GAME 78 Q4 ANSWER a
Erich Segal was a professor of the classics at Yale and at Oxford. His rewrite of *Yellow Submarine* (1968) was the first script Segal participated in writing that made it to the screen. *Love Story* (novel *and* screenplay) came in 1970. The film has been criticized increasingly for being too sappy. I love sentimental stories, so I'm a big fan of *Love Story*—on principle.

9. Which sexy blonde was married to *Six Million Dollar Man* Lee Majors during the '70s?

a. Suzanne Somers

b. Cheryl Ladd

c. Farrah Fawcett

d. Bo Derek

GAME 3 Q8 ANSWER b
Croce's 1972 classic song reached #17 on the charts before his "Bad, Bad Leroy Brown" went to #1 in 1973. He died that same year in a plane crash.

9. Who was *not* one of *Casper the Friendly Ghost's* ghostly cartoon uncles?

a. Shrieker

b. Stinkie

c. Fatso

d. Stretch

GAME 23 Q8 ANSWER c
In *Dangerous When Wet* (1953), Williams shared an underwater sequence with the famous cat and mouse. The film co-starred Fernando Lamas, whom she married before retiring from show business. Williams began making public appearances again after Lamas's death.

9. Where does director Sylvester Stallone's cameo appearance take place in *Staying Alive*?

a. In a bar

b. At a boxing match

c. On a busy city street

d. At a dance audition

GAME 43 Q8 ANSWER b
Directed by John *"Animal House"* Landis, this 1991 film has Kirk Douglas really hamming it up in his hilarious deathbed scene. He comically slaps his son hard across the face every time he wants to make a point.

9. Phil Collins went from just drummer to drummer *and* lead vocalist of Genesis in 1975. Who sang before?

a. Simon LeBon

b. Robert Palmer

c. Jon Anderson

d. Peter Gabriel

GAME 63 Q8 ANSWER c
Nugent got together with Night Ranger bassist and lead vocalist Jack Blades, and Styx lead guitarist and singer Tommy Shaw for two albums. Completing the group was young power drummer Michael Cartellone.

GAME 18

4. Who co-starred opposite Martin Hewitt in Franco Zeffirelli's teen romance *Endless Love* (1981)?

a. Demi Moore

b. Brooke Shields

c. Jodie Foster

d. Ally Sheedy

GAME 18 Q3 ANSWER b

Performers including Boy George, Paul McCartney, Phil Collins, and Sting; and members of Duran Duran, U2, and Kool and the Gang were among those in the single twenty-four-hour recording session for the song penned by Bob Geldof and Midge Ure. The recording sold over 2 million copies in its first ten days.

GAME 38

4. What movie gave us the line, "Damn the torpedoes! Full steam ahead!"?

a. *The More, the Merrier* (1943)

b. *Grand Hotel* (1932)

c. *Operation Petticoat* (1959)

d. *All About Eve* (1950)

GAME 38 Q3 ANSWER c

This is the immortal last line spoken by Charles Foster Kane's business manager, Mr. Bernstein, played by the great Mercury Theatre actor Everett Sloane.

GAME 58

4. What was the name of Hopalong Cassidy's horse?

a. Buttermilk

b. Phantom

c. Topper

d. Rex

GAME 58 Q3 ANSWER d

In *Citizen Kane* (1941), Kane receives one as a Christmas gift from Mr. Thatcher ("You're too old to be calling me Mr. Thatcher, Charles." "You're too old to be called anything else."). "Rosebud" was named by Mercury Theatre writer Howard Teichmann, who wrote *The Solid Gold Cadillac* (with George S. Kaufman, 1956) and *Lonelyhearts* (1959).

GAME 78

4. The author of what novel co-wrote the screenplay for *Yellow Submarine*?

a. *Love Story*

b. *The Andromeda Strain*

c. *The Magic Christian*

d. *Fear and Loathing in Las Vegas*

GAME 78 Q3 ANSWER c

The script was co-written by Bradbury and director John Huston. Bradbury's writing found its way to TV in the late '70s with the mini-series *The Martian Chronicles,* starring Rock Hudson and Roddy McDowell.

GAME 3

10. Which '70s hit became the theme song for a popular TV series in the '80s and '90s?

a. "Lonely Boy"

b. "Brandy"

c. "Laughter in the Rain"

d. "Thank You for Being a Friend"

GAME 3 Q9 ANSWER c
At the time, Fawcett and Majors were TV's sexiest real-life couple with both *Charlie's Angels* and *The Six Million Dollar Man* scoring big ratings on ABC. Fawcett even appeared in four episodes of her husband's show, which ran from 1972 to 1978. The two were married from 1973 to 1982.

---

10. Which of the *South Park* kids is "big boned"?

a. Stan Marsh

b. Eric Cartman

c. Kenny McCormick

d. Kyle Broflovski

GAME 23 Q9 ANSWER a
Unlike the round-headed Casper, the ghostly trio (Uncles Stinkie, Fatso, and Stretch) were of the pointy-head variety. Casper's friends included Wendy the Good Little Witch and Nightmare the Galloping Ghost. On the other side of nice, there was Casper's nemesis, Spooky the Tough Little Ghost.

---

10. In 1978, Stallone starred in a movie about labor unions. What was the name of the film?

a. *Strike!*

b. *Union*

c. *Bosses & Workers*

d. *F.I.S.T.*

GAME 43 Q9 ANSWER c
In this sequel to *Saturday Night Fever*, Stallone can be seen wearing an expensive fur coat and tough-guy shades in his cameo with John Travolta. Many critics disapproved of Stallone's handling of the Tony Manero story, feeling that he had taken a gritty coming-of-age story and turned it into a kind of *Rocky* for the leotard set.

---

10. Which popular heavy metal act did bassist Rudy Sarzo join after leaving Quiet Riot in 1986?

a. Dio

b. Def Leppard

c. Whitesnake

d. Ozzy Osbourne

GAME 63 Q9 ANSWER d
Gabriel had been the group's theatrical lead vocalist since 1969. When Gabriel left, Collins took over vocals. The result was a string of radio-friendly songs, record sales in the millions, and a Top 10 hit in 1983 ("That's All"). Seems our boy Collins knew the rhythm of a cash register as well as a drum kit.

3. Which song was recorded by Band Aid, the pop-music charity group for Ethiopia?

a. "We Are the World"

b. "Do They Know It's Christmas?"

c. "Sun City"

d. "God Bless the U.S.A."

GAME 18 Q2 ANSWER c

Andrew Ridgeley and George Michael formed Wham! in 1982. The duo split in 1986, giving a sold-out farewell concert at London's Wembley Stadium that was attended by 72,000 fans. Post Wham!, George Michael maintained a hold on pop music through the 1990s with hits like "Faith," "I Want Your Sex," and "Father Figure."

---

3. "Old age, it's the only disease . . . that you don't look forward to being cured of." Name the film:

a. *The African Queen* (1951)

b. *Cocoon* (1985)

c. *Citizen Kane* (1941)

d. *Little Big Man* (1970)

GAME 38 Q2 ANSWER b

This film won six of its thirteen nominated Academy Awards, including Best Director (Robert Zemeckis), Best Actor (Tom Hanks), and Best Picture. Through the eyes of simple-minded, kind-hearted Forrest Gump, the film chronicles historic moments from the late 1950s through the 1970s.

---

3. What was the name of Charles Foster "Citizen" Kane's *other* sled?

a. Red Ryder

b. Lightning

c. Santa Fe

d. Crusader

GAME 58 Q2 ANSWER c

Perlman appeared on *Taxi* from 1979 to 1982 as Zena, Louie's "nice girl." Danson and Wendt each appeared on the show only once—Danson as Elaine's hairdresser Vincenzo, and Wendt as an exterminator. Incidentally, Perlman and DeVito were married on the *Taxi* set during a lunch break in 1982.

---

3. Author Ray Bradbury co-wrote the award-winning screenplay for which film?

a. *Planet of the Apes* (1968)

b. *Ben-Hur* (1959)

c. *Moby Dick* (1956)

d. *Bridge on the River Kwai* (1957)

GAME 78 Q2 ANSWER a

In 1979, Sean Connery and Donald Sutherland starred in *The Great Train Robbery*, based on Crichton's 1975 novel. Crichton had already directed his original screenplay *Westworld* (1973), and his adaptation of Robin Cook's novel *Coma* (1978).

11. Maureen McGovern sang the theme song to which disaster film?

a. *Jaws* (1975)

b. *The Poseidon Adventure* (1972)

c. *Avalanche* (1978)

d. *Airport* (1970)

GAME 3 Q10 ANSWER d
Andrew Gold's tune barely reached the Top 20 when it was first released in 1978. Its popularity increased in 1985, when it was adopted as the theme song for *The Golden Girls*. Gold's other contribution to television is the theme for Paul Reiser's *Mad About You*, which ran from 1992 to 1999.

11. Judy Garland provided the voice to a cat in which animated film?

a. *The Aristocats*

b. *Gay Purr-ee*

c. *Alice in Wonderland*

d. *That Darn Cat!*

GAME 23 Q10 ANSWER b
Actually, Eric is overweight, thanks to a mother who is constantly feeding him "comfort foods" like chocolate chicken pot pies. This Comedy Central animated series, starring a group of foul-mouthed kids, began as a five-minute video Christmas card that was produced for a Fox studio executive.

11. In the prison flick *Lock Up* (1989), who plays Stallone's sadistic warden?

a. Brian Dennehy

b. Donald Sutherland

c. Rutger Hauer

d. Jack Palance

GAME 43 Q10 ANSWER d
After the immense success of *Rocky* in 1976, Stallone realized that he could act in class-A productions. For *F.I.S.T.*, he cut his hair short and really got into the character of Johnny Kovak, inspired by real-life Jimmy Hoffa. The film features great performances from Peter Boyle, Melinda Dillon, and Rod Steiger as a crusading United States senator.

11. After leaving Ritchie Blackmore's group Rainbow in 1984, for which guitar hero did Joe Lynn Turner sing?

a. Neal Schon

b. Jeff Beck

c. Jimmy Page

d. Yngwie Malmsteen

GAME 63 Q10 ANSWER c
Sarzo joined Whitesnake in 1987. But in 1997, the bass guitarist returned to Quiet Riot.

GAME 18

2. In 1984, Wham!'s first single hit the top of the charts. What was it?

a. "Careless Whisper"

b. "Freedom"

c. "Wake Me Up Before You Go Go"

d. "Everything She Wants"

GAME 18 Q1 ANSWER a

Kevin Bacon's leading role of a city boy in a rural town where rock music and dancing are banned was first offered to rocker Jon Bon Jovi, who turned it down to concentrate on his music career.

GAME 38

2. The line "Life is like a box of chocolates" is from:

a. *Chocolat* (2000)

b. *Forrest Gump* (1994)

c. *Willy Wonka and the Chocolate Factory* (1971)

d. *Love Is a Many Splendored Thing* (1955)

GAME 38 Q1 ANSWER a

The 4'8" actor Gary Coleman played little Arnold Jackson, who, with older brother Willis (Todd Bridges), was adopted by their late mother's employer. She was a housekeeper for Park Avenue millionaire Phillip Drummond (Conrad Bain).

GAME 58

2. Which *Cheers* regular appeared as a recurring character on *Taxi*?

a. Ted Danson

b. Shelley Long

c. Rhea Perlman

d. George Wendt

GAME 58 Q1 ANSWER d

The bright orange 1969 Dodge Charger had a Confederate flag painted on its roof. Dozens of '69 Chargers were used during the show's 1979 to 1985 run. With all the wear and tear from those jumps and chases, one "General Lee" rarely made it through the production of a single episode.

GAME 78

2. Which author has directed a film from his own screenplay adaptation of his novel?

a. Michael Crichton

b. Robin Cook

c. John Grisham

d. Stephen King

GAME 78 Q1 ANSWER a

In May of 2002, the Remainders celebrated their tenth anniversary, performing at a concert in New York City. Each author has had the distinction of seeing his or her work made into film and/or TV properties over the years. I remember the days when most rock stars couldn't even *read*, let alone write.

12. Actor/composer Paul Williams penned which hit song by the Carpenters?

a. "For All We Know"

b. "We've Only Just Begun"

c. "Close to You"

d. "Top of the World"

GAME 3 Q11 ANSWER b
The year was 1972, and the song was "The Morning After." McGovern also sang "We May Never Love Like This Again," the theme to *The Towering Inferno* (1974). Both songs won Academy Awards for Best Song.

12. Which sci-fi series has *not* yet had a Saturday-morning TV cartoon program?

a. *Star Trek*

b. *Planet of the Apes*

c. *Battlestar Galactica*

d. *Star Wars*

GAME 23 Q11 ANSWER b
The lead cats in this 1962 film were voiced by Garland and Robert Goulet. The movie featured music by Yip Harburg and Harold Arlen, composers for *The Wizard of Oz.*

12. In how many films does Michael Caine appear with Sylvester Stallone?

a. None

b. One

c. Two

d. Three

GAME 43 Q11 ANSWER b
Brian Dennehy played the sadistic police chief in *First Blood.* Rutger Hauer played the sadistic terrorist in *Nighthawks.* Jack Palance played the sadistic corporate drug smuggler in *Tango & Cash.* By pitting himself against all these sadistic villains, I'm beginning to wonder: is Stallone a masochist?

12. Which Rolling Stones album was the last for bassist Bill Wyman?

a. *Steel Wheels*

b. *Bridges to Babylon*

c. *Voodoo Lounge*

d. *Dirty Work*

GAME 63 Q11 ANSWER d
Yngwie (pronounced *ing-vay*) has recorded albums with both Turner and Graham Bonnet, also a former singer from Rainbow. Blackmore now dedicates himself completely to Renaissance music with his new group Blackmore's Night. Members of his live group have included singer/songwriter Marci Geller and percussionist Alex Alexander.

GAME 18

1. In which 1984 film do Lori Singer, Sarah Jessica Parker, and Chris Penn strut their stuff across a stage?

a. *Footloose*

b. *Flashdance*

c. *Dirty Dancing*

d. *Fame*

The answer to this question is on:

page 240, top frame, right side.

GAME 38

1. "Whatchoo talkin' 'bout, Willis?" was a catch phrase from which sitcom?

a. *Diff'rent Strokes*

b. *Good Times*

c. *Webster*

d. *What's Happening!!*

The answer to this question is on:

page 240, second frame, right side.

GAME 58

1. What was the name of Bo and Luke's car on *The Dukes of Hazzard*?

a. K.I.T.T.

b. Stonewall

c. Daisy

d. General Lee

The answer to this question is on:

page 240, third frame, right side.

GAME 78

1. Authors Stephen King, Amy Tan, and Dave Barry form which rock group?

a. The Rock Bottom Remainders

b. Thirty Odd Foot of Grunts

c. Franz Liszt Backlist

d. The Traveling Wilburys

The answer to this question is on:

page 240, bottom frame, right side.

GAME 4

Memory Lane
Grab Bag

*Turn to page 44
for the first question.*

The song started life as a commercial jingle for a bank before becoming a #2 hit in 1970. Williams also wrote "Rainy Days and Mondays," which was recorded by the Carpenters in 1971, and also rose to #2.

GAME 24

Memory Lane
Grab Bag

*Turn to page 44
for the first question.*

From 1973 to 1975, the *Star Trek* animated series won acclaim on NBC and an Emmy in 1975 for Outstanding Entertainment Children's Series. *Return to the Planet of the Apes* lasted only one season on NBC from 1975 to 1976, and *The Ewoks,* produced by George Lucas, aired on ABC from 1985 to 1987.

GAME 44

Memory Lane
Grab Bag

*Turn to page 44
for the first question.*

Caine and Stallone first appeared together in John Huston's 1981 war film *Victory.* In it they played WWII soldiers who escaped their German prison camp by winning a soccer match against the Nazi team. They met again on film when Caine made a small cameo in Stallone's 2001 remake of Caine's own 1971 film *Get Carter.*

GAME 64

Memory Lane
Grab Bag

*Turn to page 44
for the first question.*

Amidst public bickering about band loyalty between Stones lead vocalist Mick Jagger and guitarist Keith Richards, the normally quiet Wyman split from the group in 1992 to concentrate on roots music—the music he loves best.

GAME 18

The '80s

Brat Packs, Band Aids, and the Boss

Turn to page 239 for the first question.

GAME 17 Q12 ANSWER c

With a total of twenty-six, Disney still holds the record as the person who has been awarded the most Oscars in history. In 1953, he won in four categories—Documentary Feature (*The Living Desert*), Documentary Short Subject (*The Alaskan Eskimo*), Cartoon Short Subject (*Toot, Whistle, Plunk and Boom*), and Two-Reel Short Subject (*Bear Country*).

GAME 38

Say What?

Identify the Quote

Turn to page 239 for the first question.

GAME 37 Q12 ANSWER b

After starring in such TV shows as *Surfside 6* and films like *A Summer Place* in the early '60s, Troy Donahue (whose real name was Merle Johnson) took a career nosedive from which he really never recovered. Fellow '50s heartthrob Tab Hunter's career took off again in the '80s when he appeared in *Grease 2* and John Waters' camp classic *Polyester*.

GAME 58

Way to Go!

Basic Transportation

Turn to page 239 for the first question.

GAME 57 Q12 ANSWER b

Both actresses sing in this nostalgic film—Mia Farrow sings "I Don't Want to Walk Without You" at a USO dance, and Diane Keaton sings "You'd Be So Nice to Come Home To" at a New Year's Eve party.

GAME 78

Writer's Block

Tales From the Script

Turn to page 239 for the first question.

GAME 77 Q12 ANSWER b

Composed by Elmer Bernstein, whose work on the film won an Academy Award nomination for Best Score, the theme of *The Magnificent Seven* not only played an important role in the film's success, but also became a familiar part of American culture through its use in Marlboro ads.

GAME 4

1. Which *devil*-ishly good film won an Oscar for Best Original Score?

a. *Rosemary's Baby* (1968)

b. *The Exorcist* (1973)

c. *Poltergeist* (1982)

d. *The Omen* (1976)

The answer to this question is on:

page 45, top frame, right side.

GAME 24

1. Which acclaimed actor died a mere ten days after shooting a death scene in his last film?

a. James Dean

b. Edward G. Robinson

c. Montgomery Clift

d. Humphrey Bogart

The answer to this question is on:

page 45, second frame, right side.

GAME 44

1. Who directed Forest Whitaker as jazz legend Charlie Parker in *Bird* (1988)?

a. Clint Eastwood

b. Alan Parker

c. Spike Lee

d. Robert Altman

The answer to this question is on:

page 45, third frame, right side.

GAME 64

1. Which of the following artists did *not* have an album go to #1 posthumously?

a. John Lennon

b. Elvis Presley

c. Roy Orbison

d. Nat King Cole

The answer to this question is on:

page 45, bottom frame, right side.

44

12. Walt Disney received an Oscar for which film?

a. *Cinderella* (1950)

b. *Bambi* (1942)

c. *The Living Desert* (1953)

d. *Mary Poppins* (1964)

GAME 17 Q11 ANSWER b
Erika Eleniak, later *Playboy's* July 1989 Playmate of the Month, was the "pretty girl" whom Elliott kisses after saving the frogs from dissection in science class. Spielberg directed this scene to look like the one with John Wayne and Maureen O'Hara in *The Quiet Man,* which E.T. is watching on TV while Elliot is at school.

12. Which late '50s heartthrob played Merle Johnson, Connie Corleone's boyfriend in 1974's *The Godfather Part II*?

a. Tab Hunter

b. Troy Donahue

c. Rock Hudson

d. Geoffrey Hunter

GAME 37 Q11 ANSWER b
In *The Hurricane,* Denzel portrayed boxer Rubin "Hurricane" Carter. In *Remember the Titans,* he played high school football coach Herman Boone. And in *Cry Freedom,* Denzel played South African black activist Steven Biko.

12. In which Woody Allen film do both Diane Keaton and Mia Farrow appear?

a. *The Purple Rose of Cairo*

b. *Radio Days*

c. *Manhattan*

d. *A Midsummer Night's Sex Comedy*

GAME 57 Q11 ANSWER d
Allen has said often that *Stardust Memories* remains one of his most heartfelt and personal films—the film that came closest to what he envisioned when he first wrote the screenplay. Well, I know why it's one of my favorites—it's the first film to feature a beautiful blonde named Sharon Stone.

12. The signature music for Marlboro cigarettes was originally written for which of the following Westerns?

a. *High Noon* (1952)

b. *The Magnificent Seven* (1960)

c. *Shane* (1953)

d. *How the West Was Won* (1962)

GAME 77 Q11 ANSWER b
The 1967 film *El Dorado* was loosely based on the 1959 film *Rio Bravo.* Both were directed by Howard Hawks and both star Wayne as a federal marshall trying to help his friend, a drunken sheriff. Dean Martin plays the sheriff in *Rio Bravo,* and Robert Mitchum has the role in *El Dorado.*

2. Which of the following movies was *not* directed by Rob Reiner?

a. *Ghosts of Mississippi* (1996)

b. *A Few Good Men* (1992)

c. *Sleepless in Seattle* (1993)

d. *When Harry Met Sally* (1989)

GAME 4 Q1 ANSWER d
Actually, acclaimed film composer Jerry Goldsmith wrote the music for both *The Omen* (an Oscar winner for him in 1976) and *Poltergeist* (1982), which was produced by Steven Spielberg and directed by Tobe "Texas Chainsaw Massacre" Hooper.

2. Which of the following was *not* a Norman Lear-produced TV show?

a. *All in the Family*

b. *The Jeffersons*

c. *Maude*

d. *Chico & the Man*

GAME 24 Q1 ANSWER b
For his last scene in the 1973 film *Soylent Green*, Robinson's character was required to watch the natural beauties of the world flash before him on a screen as he prepared to die. Robinson, a very dignified and private man, had kept his illness from the cast and crew.

2. Which Oliver Stone film does *not* feature a cameo by an '80s pop star?

a. *Platoon* (1986)

b. *The Doors* (1991)

c. *Born on the Fourth of July* (1989)

d. *Talk Radio* (1988)

GAME 44 Q1 ANSWER a
Eastwood has long been a jazz aficionado. He can be seen playing piano in the action film *In the Line of Fire* (1993). Spike Lee also directed a film about jazz called *Mo' Better Blues* (1991), as did Robert Altman with his film *Kansas City* (1996). Alan Parker directed a film about a working-class Irish white soul band called *The Commitments* (1991).

2. Who was known as "The Highness of Hi-De-Ho"?

a. Fats Waller

b. Cab Calloway

c. Louis Armstrong

d. Count Basie

GAME 64 Q1 ANSWER d
It was daughter Natalie Cole's *Unforgettable . . . With Love* that went to #1 in 1991. Digital technology enabled her to sing "Unforgettable" with her dad, who had the original hit. Lennon's *Double Fantasy* hit #1 after his 1980 assassination; Orbison's *Mystery Girl* reached #1 after his death in 1988; and in 2002, the top spot went to *Elvis 30 #1 Hits*.

11. Elliott (Henry Thomas) kisses which future *Baywatch* babe in *E.T. The Extra-Terrestrial* (1982)?

a. Pamela Anderson

b. Erika Eleniak

c. Nicole Eggert

d. Donna D'Errico

GAME 17 Q10 ANSWER d
Instead of saying "How!," the American Indians on *Howdy Doody* had their own greetings. Princess Summerfall Winterspring would greet people with, "Kowagoopa," Chief Thunderthud used "Kowabunga" as both greeting and exclamation. The word's change in spelling occurred over time without explanation.

11. In which film did Denzel Washington play a role that was *not* based on a real person?

a. *The Hurricane* (1999)

b. *Mississippi Masala* (1991)

c. *Remember the Titans* (2000)

d. *Cry Freedom* (1987)

GAME 37 Q10 ANSWER c
Clint Eastwood is close to the President in both *In the Line of Fire* and *Absolute Power*, but neither president is portrayed by Nicholson. Bill Pullman played the heroic President in *Independence Day*.

11. Which of his films has Woody Allen often declared to be his personal favorite?

a. *Interiors* (1978)

b. *Zelig* (1983)

c. *Crimes and Misdemeanors* (1989)

d. *Stardust Memories* (1980)

GAME 57 Q10 ANSWER c
Although both Diane Keaton and Mia Farrow starred in several of Allen's films and were personally involved with him, neither was ever married to him. To date, Allen has been married three times—to Harlene Rosen, Louise Lasser, and Soon-Yi Previn.

11. Which two John Wayne Westerns share the same basic plot?

a. *Fort Apache* and *She Wore a Yellow Ribbon*

b. *El Dorado* and *Rio Bravo*

c. *Rio Grande* and *Rio Lobo*

d. *Rio Bravo* and *Rio Grande*

GAME 77 Q10 ANSWER d
Brian Dennehy is just one of the many actors who helped make *Silverado* a popular Western that appealed to *all* types of audiences. It is the story of four unlikely comrades—played by Kevin Kline, Scott Glenn, Kevin Costner, and Danny Glover—who team up to fight the injustices in a small town.

GAME 4

3. Which of the following films contains the famous line, "Don't let's ask for the moon; we have the stars."

a. *Now, Voyager* (1942)

b. *Dark Victory* (1939)

c. *The Three Faces of Eve* (1957)

d. *The Spiral Staircase* (1946)

GAME 4 Q2 ANSWER c

Famous in the '70s as Mike "Meathead" Stivic on *All in the Family*, Reiner's appearance in Nora Ephron's *Sleepless in Seattle* marked his return to acting. Since then, he has appeared in Woody Allen's *Bullets Over Broadway* (1994), Ron Howard's *EdTV* (1999), and Albert Brooks' *The Muse* (1999), in which he portrays himself.

GAME 24

3. Who played Archie Bunker's business partner in the spinoff series *Archie Bunker's Place*?

a. Barnard Hughes

b. Don Ameche

c. Martin Balsam

d. Anne Meara

GAME 24 Q2 ANSWER d

Lear's *All in the Family* spawned a number of popular CBS sitcoms, including *The Jeffersons* and *Maude*. NBC's *Chico & the Man* starred screen veteran Jack Albertson and comedian Freddie Prinze.

GAME 44

3. Which of the following movies did *not* feature Dudley Moore in the starring role?

a. *Lovesick* (1983)

b. *Modern Romance* (1981)

c. *Six Weeks* (1982)

d. *Micki & Maude* (1984)

GAME 44 Q2 ANSWER d

One of the army grunts in *Platoon* was Corey Glover, the charismatic lead singer for the rock group Living Colour. In *The Doors*, punk rocker Billy Idol played one of Jim Morrison's drinking buddies, while Edie Brickell, lead singer of the New Bohemians, sang Bob Dylan's "A Hard Rain's a-Gonna Fall" in *Born on the Fourth of July*.

GAME 64

3. The only instrumental to reach #1 on *Billboard* was:

a. "A Fifth of Beethoven"

b. "Wipe Out"

c. "Theme from *A Summer Place*"

d. "Love's Theme"

GAME 64 Q2 ANSWER b

Cabell Calloway III was an original. The bandleader/singer/actor's biggest hit is undoubtedly "Minnie the Moocher." A new generation was introduced to Calloway in the 1980 film *The Blues Brothers*, in which he sang his famous song as opening act to Jake and Elwood Blues.

10. Where did the term "cowabunga" originate?

a. *The Simpsons*

b. *Teenage Mutant Ninja Turtles*

c. *It's the Great Pumpkin, Charlie Brown*

d. *The Howdy Doody Show*

GAME 17 Q9 ANSWER b

Courage of Lassie features Elizabeth Taylor, who made one of her first films in 1943 with *Lassie Come Home*. Although played by the star of other *Lassie* pictures, the dog's name in this movie was Bill.

10. Jack Nicholson plays the President of the United States in which film?

a. *In the Line of Fire* (1993)

b. *Absolute Power* (1997)

c. *Mars Attacks* (1996)

d. *Independence Day* (1996)

GAME 37 Q9 ANSWER a

Both the film and the TV show were created by writer Aaron Sorkin. In the movie, which was directed by Rob Reiner, Martin Sheen played A.J. MacInerny, Chief of Staff to Michael Douglas's President Shepherd.

10. Of the following four actresses, who was married to Woody Allen?

a. Mia Farrow

b. Diane Keaton

c. Louise Lasser

d. Dianne Wiest

GAME 57 Q9 ANSWER c

This film stars Sean Penn as a self-absorbed Dixieland jazz guitarist named Emmet Ray, whose playing style is evocative of the great Gypsy guitarist Reinhardt. Interestingly, this story was the genesis of Allen's first proposed film script in 1969 called *The Jazz Baby*. The idea was rejected, and Allen made *Take the Money and Run* instead.

10. Which actor plays the corrupt sheriff in the 1985 movie *Silverado*?

a. James Coburn

b. Scott Glenn

c. Richard Boone

d. Brian Dennehy

GAME 77 Q9 ANSWER b

Robert Redford stars as a rugged mountain man in this film directed by Sydney Pollack. The two have worked together on a number of movies, including *This Property Is Condemned* (1966), *The Way We Were* (1973), *Three Days of the Condor* (1975), *The Electric Horseman* (1979), *Out of Africa* (1985), and *Havana* (1990).

4. Which Roger Corman film featured William Shatner as a Bible-thumping racist minister?

a. *The Wild Angels* (1966)

b. *The Raven* (1963)

c. *The Intruder* (1961)

d. *Bloody Mama* (1970)

GAME 4 Q3 ANSWER a

Delivered by Bette Davis, the star of this 1942 classic, the line is directed at Paul Henreid, who plays the married man with whom she falls in love. Although she cannot marry the man she adores, Davis's character is helping to raise his daughter—a fact that binds the characters together and gives her life purpose and meaning.

4. Which actor from TV's *Alice* also appeared in the movie *Alice Doesn't Live Here Anymore*?

a. Philip McKeon

b. Vic Tayback

c. Polly Holliday

d. Beth Howland

GAME 24 Q3 ANSWER c

Martin Balsam shared cents and sensibility with Archie as his business partner, Murray Klein, at Archie Bunker's Place—a restaurant/tavern that was originally Kelsey's Bar during the *All in the Family* days. Archie had talked Edith into letting him mortgage the house to buy it. The show ran from 1979 to 1981.

4. Which of the following groups did *not* use its name as the title of its first album?

a. KISS

b. The Beatles

c. Black Sabbath

d. Led Zeppelin

GAME 44 Q3 ANSWER b

Lovesick starred Moore as a psychiatrist. *Six Weeks* featured Dudley Moore with Mary Tyler Moore (no relation), as they try to comfort a terminally sick young girl. *Micki & Maude* paired Moore with writer/director Blake Edwards, who gave Moore his star-making role in *10. Modern Romance* is an Albert Brooks comedy.

4. On *Laverne & Shirley*, what was Laverne's favorite drink?

a. Scotch and soda

b. Milk and Pepsi

c. Coffee, black with sugar

d. Shotz beer

GAME 64 Q3 ANSWER c

The 1959 film *A Summer Place* brought us the original teen romance of Troy Donahue and Sandra Dee. Nearly twenty years later, this film's theme song by Percy Faith provided background music as Thomas Hulce tries to score with a pretty young girl in *National Lampoon's Animal House* (1978).

9. Which *Lassie* film didn't feature a dog named "Lassie"?

a. *Lassie Come Home* (1943)

b. *Courage of Lassie* (1946)

c. *Challenge to Lassie* (1949)

d. *The Magic of Lassie* (1978)

GAME 17 Q8 ANSWER a
After playing Ted for two seasons, Hinnant originated the role of Schroeder in the off-Broadway musical *You're a Good Man, Charlie Brown*. But not everything Hinnant did was family fare. He also supplied the voice for the title character in the 1972 X-rated cartoon feature *Fritz the Cat*.

---

9. Which presidential movie featured *The West Wing's* Martin Sheen as a presidential advisor?

a. *The American President* (1995)

b. *Dave* (1993)

c. *Air Force One* (1997)

d. *Primary Colors* (1998)

GAME 37 Q8 ANSWER b
The producers of PT 109 and President Kennedy himself wanted Warren Beatty to play the role. The Kennedy family, however, didn't approve of Beatty's reputation as a womanizer and requested that the part go to someone else.

---

9. On which pioneering jazz musician did Woody Allen base his 1999 film *Sweet and Lowdown*?

a. Dizzy Gillespie

b. Woody Herman

c. Django Reinhardt

d. Artie Shaw

GAME 57 Q8 ANSWER b
Originally named after *anhedonia* (a psychoanalytic term for the inability to enjoy *anything*), the film's title was changed as a subtle play on Diane Keaton's real name—Diane Hall. *Annie Hall* started as a murder mystery. Allen and co-writer Marshall Brickman revisited the idea in 1993's *Manhattan Murder Mystery*.

---

9. Which is *not* a Clint Eastwood Western?

a. *High Plains Drifter* (1973)

b. *Jeremiah Johnson* (1972)

c. *Pale Rider* (1985)

d. *Hang 'Em High* (1968)

GAME 77 Q8 ANSWER c
The seven rough-and-tough hombres who stand up to cutthroat Eli Wallach in this 1960 Western include Yul Brynner, Steve McQueen, Horst Buchholz, Charles Bronson, Robert Vaughn, Brad Dexter, and James Coburn. Although Brynner was the only real "name" when the film was made, nearly all of the others quickly rose in the acting ranks afterwards.

5. In which Robert DeNiro film does his first wife, Diahnne Abbott, sing?

a. *Mean Streets* (1973)

b. *New York, New York* (1977)

c. *Taxi Driver* (1976)

d. *The King of Comedy* (1982)

GAME 4 Q4 ANSWER c
King of the "B" movies, Roger Corman actually had quite a controversial film in *The Intruder* (also reissued under the titles *I Hate Your Guts!*, *The Stranger*, and *Shame*). Those who know Shatner principally as Captain Kirk or T.J. Hooker might be shocked to see him playing such a despicable character.

5. One of the following was *not* a TV show. Which one?

a. *The Jimmy Stewart Show*

b. *The Tony Randall Show*

c. *The Art Carney Show*

d. *The Dean Martin Show*

GAME 24 Q4 ANSWER b
Tayback played Mel, the diner's grouchy owner and cook. In the series, which ran from 1976 to 1985, Linda Lavin played Alice. Polly Holliday was Flo, the gum-chewing brassy waitress who made "Kiss my grits!" a national catch phrase. Beth Howland was the timid Vera, and Philip McKeon played Tommy, Alice's son.

5. Which rock group stuck by its drummer after he lost an arm in a car accident?

a. Lynyrd Skynyrd

b. Smashing Pumpkins

c. Mötley Crüe

d. Def Leppard

GAME 44 Q4 ANSWER b
In the UK, the first album by The Beatles in 1963 was called *Please Please Me*. In 1964, their first album released in the United States was called *Meet the Beatles* (called *With the Beatles* in the UK). Both Led Zeppelin and Black Sabbath released their eponymously titled debut albums in 1969, while KISS released its first album in 1973.

5. On *Three's Company*, what was the name of Jack's restaurant?

a. Regal Beagle

b. Robin's Nest

c. Jack's Bistro

d. Monk's

GAME 64 Q4 ANSWER b
Laverne also loved Scooter Pies. Starring Cindy Williams and Penny Marshall as bottlecappers at Milwaukee's Shotz Brewery, *Laverne & Shirley* (1976 to 1983) was one of Garry Marshall's successful spinoffs from *Happy Days*.

8. Which cast member of *The Electric Company* played Cathy's boyfriend Ted on *The Patty Duke Show*?

a. Skip Hinnant

b. Jimmy Boyd

c. Ken Roberts

d. Gene Wilder

Bob Clampett's *Time for Beany* and *The Beany and Cecil Show* featured Beany, the little boy with the propeller hat; his uncle, Captain Huffenpuff; and Cecil, the seasick sea monster. Cecil's voice was that of comedian/ad man extraordinaire Stan Freberg.

---

8. Who portrayed John F. Kennedy in *PT 109*?

a. James Franciscus

b. Cliff Robertson

c. Henry Fonda

d. Robert Culp

Sinatra was 5'11". Show business people are a height-conscious lot, but who am I to challenge Burt Reynolds' claim to be 6' tall, and Tom Cruise's claim to be 5'7"? As "height-challenged" showman Billy Rose once told me, "I'm taller than anybody I know when I stand on my wallet."

---

8. What was the original working title of *Annie Hall*?

a. *What's It All About, Alvie?*

b. *Anhedonia*

c. *Dynamite Ham*

d. *The Universe Is Expanding*

Woody Allen is a great champion of early twentieth-century popular music. He used "I'll Be Seeing You" in both his 1989 film *Crimes and Misdemeanors* and his short film *Oedipus Wrecks*, in the three-part *New York Stories*. "He Loves and She Loves" and "Embraceable You" by George Gershwin were featured prominently in Allen's *Manhattan* (1979).

---

8. Which of the following actors is *not* among *The Magnificent Seven's* team of heroes?

a. Yul Brynner

b. Brad Dexter

c. James Garner

d. Robert Vaughn

Katy Jurado received glowing reviews for her tough-as-nails portrayal of Helen Ramirez, the marshal's former lover. Many expected her to win the Best Supporting Actress Oscar. However, producer Stanley Kramer accidentally listed the entire cast as leading players, so the Oscar went to Gloria Grahame instead for *The Bad and the Beautiful*.

6. Which performer received an Oscar nomination for playing someone who was *also* nominated for an acting Oscar?

a. Steven Boyd

b. Robert Downey, Jr.

c. Faye Dunaway

d. Martin Landau

6. On *Welcome Back, Kotter,* what was the name of Gabe Kotter's wife?

a. Annie

b. Laurie

c. Julie

d. Barbara

6. Who did Louis "Satchmo" Armstrong go fishin' with in the hit song "Gone Fishin'"?

a. Bing Crosby

b. Perry Como

c. Dean Martin

d. Nat King Cole

6. What was the name of the restaurant located above *Cheers*?

a. Gary's Olde Towne Tavern

b. Melville's

c. Frank's Place

d. Phil's Place

GAME 4 Q5 ANSWER b
Abbott appeared in three films with her husband, all of which were directed by Martin Scorsese. In *Taxi Driver,* she was the ticket counter girl in a seamy porno theater; in *New York, New York,* she appeared briefly as a Billie Holiday-esque nightclub singer; and in *The King of Comedy,* she played a pretty bartender named Rita.

GAME 24 Q5 ANSWER c
Jimmy Stewart's short-lived show aired on NBC during the 1971/72 season. Tony Randall's show on CBS debuted in 1976 and lasted for one season. Dean Martin's weekly variety show on NBC premiered in 1965 and ran for nine seasons.

GAME 44 Q5 ANSWER d
Although Def Leppard was able to stick by its stickman Rick Savage, and continue rocking the world, tragedy again struck the band when guitarist and co-founder Steve Clark died in 1991.

GAME 64 Q5 ANSWER c
The Regal Beagle was the favored hangout throughout most of the show's run from 1977 to 1984. Then when Jack opened his Bistro in November 1982, it became a second hangout. This restaurant was also featured in the spinoff *Three's a Crowd.*

7. What was the name of the seasick sea serpent?

a. Sigmund

b. Cecil

c. Beany

d. Ollie

Gordon was originated in 1969 by Matt Robinson, one of the show's producers and father of actress Holly Robinson Peete. Robinson later wrote for ABC's *Sanford and Son* and *Eight is Enough*. Gordon's character was also played by Hal Miller from 1971 to 1973, and by Roscoe Orman since 1973.

---

7. Which actor is *not* over six feet tall?

a. Burt Lancaster

b. George C. Scott

c. Frank Sinatra

d. Clint Eastwood

John Barrymore first played the role in 1920; Fredric March won an Oscar for his portrayal in 1931; and Boris Karloff played the part in *Abbott and Costello Meet Dr. Jekyll and Mr. Hyde* (1953). Others who've played the role include Spencer Tracy, Anthony Perkins in *Edge of Sanity* (1989), and John Malkovich in *Mary Reilly* (1996).

---

7. What song recurs throughout Woody Allen's comedy "musical" *Everyone Says I Love You* (1996)?

a. "I'm Through With Love"

b. "I'll Be Seeing You"

c. "He Loves and She Loves"

d. "Embraceable You"

Allen has shot many of his New York films in black and white. Among them is *Broadway Danny Rose*, one of two 1984 films in which I appeared. (The other is *Ghostbusters*, in which I appear in glorious color).

---

7. Who plays Gary Cooper's former lover in the 1952 movie *High Noon*?

a. Ava Gardner

b. Barbara Stanwyck

c. Dolores Del Rio

d. Katy Jurado

Mario Van Peebles starred in and directed this film, which features father Melvin Van Peebles (a pioneering director of blaxploitation cinema of the '70s) along with "Shaft" superstar Isaac Hayes, and Pam *Foxy Brown* Grier. An earlier Western also named *Posse* (1975) was directed by and starred Kirk Douglas.

TV Talk Shows . . .
Yesterday and Today

The talk shows of the sixties, seventies, and early eighties were really quite tame in comparison with the talk shows of today. Talk shows hosted by commentators like Mike Douglas, Merv Griffin, and Phil Donahue were replaced in past years by guys like Geraldo Rivera, the late Morton Downey, Jr., and Jerry Springer. The earlier shows were a little more moderate in terms of what people said and how they said it. There wasn't as much confrontation as there is now. I have always favored conversation over confrontation. I think we're seeing the results of all this confrontation now on TV—the airwaves are not as restrictive but the pop culture has become so sarcastic, so rough and angry. You know, there used to be a time when people actually watched TV to be entertained and for enjoyment. What happened?

Don't get me wrong—many of our best late-night talk show hosts act as mirrors of our culture, and they would be false and hollow talking heads if they didn't attempt to be truthful with their humor. And I do think that both David Letterman and Jay Leno were wonderfully sincere when they went back on the air to soothe the viewing public with laughter and remembrance just after the terrible terrorist attacks on Manhattan's Twin Towers and The Pentagon in Washington, DC on September 11, 2001. My only complaint is that, on the average, many of the talk show hosts have gotten so cruel and mean-spirited with everything. I often blush when they start knocking the president or have discussions about the most recent sex scandals as if they're giving out holiday pie recipes. Nobody is better than anybody else, and I think it's kind of arrogant the way some talk show hosts act as if they are above it all. Truthfully, I feel embarrassed for most folks when they get into trouble like that. I respect privacy and I really think we'd all be a lot better off leaving certain things alone. It's time to give our culture a facelift, if you ask me. It's not about censorship, it's about common sense.

I'm particularly fond of Conan O'Brien—and not just because I was the first guest on his first show in 1993. Conan has a real sense of television history—he had me on the show because, as the new kid on the block, he wanted some on-air advice and a blessing from an old mentor like me. He's a great young guy with a quick wit and a clever way of putting a show together. We often go browsing together through the Times Square flea markets in New York City, looking for hard-to-find items. Conan plays guitar and is always in search of vintage guitars. He just loves them.

Some television hosts just can't seem to live without their show. When *The Ed Sullivan Show* went off the air, Ed seemed to go to pieces. He loved that show, and it was his entire life. I respected the program—in fact, it was the only TV show that I watched every week, bar none. Ed Sullivan was not a particularly funny man, but Ed knew this and recognized it early in his career. He always told me that his job in life was to be a pointer—on the show, he would point at the stars on his program and share what he saw. He dominated the field for many years. Then all the big shows were pulled off the air. Even though many of these shows had huge ratings, the networks took them off the air in one fell swoop. Apparently, the networks were after a different demographic audience in the ratings war—it was the sixties, and they wanted the kids as viewers. I didn't give them the chance. The last segment of *The Joe Franklin Show* aired on August 6, 1993 after 21,425 shows. Johnny Carson and I are both aware of the best secret in show business—knowing when to end the act.

7. In *The Shining* (1980), what movie are Shelley Duvall and son Danny Lloyd watching on TV?

a. *Bambi*

b. *Smokey and the Bandit*

c. *Summer of '42*

d. *Breakfast at Tiffany's*

GAME 4 Q6 ANSWER b
Robert Downey, Jr. was nominated for his portrayal of Charlie Chaplin in the 1992 film *Chaplin*. Chaplin received a nomination for Best Actor in a Leading Role for his performance in the 1940 film *The Great Dictator*, which he also wrote and directed, and for which he composed the music.

---

7. On *Happy Days*, who was Richie Cunningham's long-time steady girl?

a. Lori Beth

b. Peggy Sue

c. Mary Lou

d. Sandra Dee

GAME 24 Q6 ANSWER c
As Mr. Kotter's wife, actress Marcia Strassman won the hearts of viewers as well as her TV husband's students, the "Sweathogs." During the show's fourth and final 1978/79 season, Strassman became the school's vice principal to fill the void left by star Gabe Kaplan's absence from the show.

---

7. Which hard rocker played a significant role in helping Van Halen get a record deal?

a. Gene Simmons

b. Ozzy Osbourne

c. Jimmy Page

d. Pete Townshend

GAME 44 Q6 ANSWER a
The song inspired a comedy starring Danny Glover and Joe Pesci called (you guessed it) *Gone Fishin'* (1997). Unfortunately, the movie wasn't as popular with folks as the song was.

---

7. On *Seinfeld*, where did Jerry, Elaine, George, and Kramer regularly go to nosh?

a. Tom's

b. Monk's

c. Zabar's

d. Babu's

GAME 64 Q6 ANSWER b
Melville's was nothing more than the restaurant above Cheers until the show's ninth season. That's when the restaurant's egotistical new owner, John Allen Hill (Keene Curtis), was introduced to the series. Hill immediately "locked horns" with Sam, and was the focus of a number of comical episodes.

6. The four original adult characters on *Sesame Street* were Bob, Susan, Mr. Hooper, and:

a. Melvin

b. Gordon

c. Jim

d. Ernie

GAME 17 Q5 ANSWER b
Beany received four nominations and won three times—in 1950, 1951, and 1953. It lost in 1956 to *Lassie*. *Kukla* was nominated nine times, and won twice—in 1954 and 1971. *Ding Dong School* was nominated four times with no wins. *Howdy Doody* was nominated twice with no wins.

6. Who never played the lead role in *Dr. Jekyll and Mr. Hyde*?

a. John Barrymore

b. Lon Chaney

c. Fredric March

d. Boris Karloff

GAME 37 Q5 ANSWER c
Redford did many of his own stunts in this movie. During the filming of one fight sequence with former professional wrestler Hank Garrett, Redford's nose was broken by an errant right hand. Redford didn't mention it until they finished shooting the scene (two hours later!).

6. Which Woody Allen film was shot in black and white?

a. *Hannah and Her Sisters* (1986)

b. *A Midsummer Night's Sex Comedy* (1982)

c. *Annie Hall* (1977)

d. *Celebrity* (1998)

GAME 57 Q5 ANSWER b
In *Bananas* and *Broadway Danny Rose*, Cosell appears as himself. In *Sleeper*, Woody Allen's character, Miles Monroe, on being shown archival footage of Cosell from "Wide World of Sports," confirms that watching the show is a mild form of torture . . .

6. Which Western is about African-American frontier life in the Old West?

a. *Posse* (1993)

b. *Bad Girls* (1994)

c. *Dead Man* (1996)

d. *Quigley Down Under* (1990)

GAME 77 Q5 ANSWER b
In this movie, John Wayne searches for his niece (played by Natalie Wood) who was captured by Indians after they massacred her family. Wayne, believing his niece has been contaminated through her contact with the Indians, plans to kill her. In the end, however, he welcomes her home.

8. What film starring Dustin Hoffman was banned in the UK upon its release?

a. *Kramer vs. Kramer* (1979)

b. *Marathon Man* (1976)

c. *Lenny* (1974)

d. *Straw Dogs* (1972)

Directed by Richard Mulligan, *Summer of '42* is a bittersweet story about a lonely married woman and the young teenage boy with whom she has an affair. Nothing is accidental in Kubrick films, and it's been said that he chose this movie to set up an Oedipal struggle between Jack Nicholson and his son with Shelley Duvall in the middle.

---

8. Who played Rocky Dennis, the disfigured teenager with a tender heart, in *Mask* (1985)?

a. Andrew McCarthy

b. Michael J. Fox

c. Eric Stoltz

d. Anthony Michael Hall

The names Peggy Sue and Mary Lou are found in rock-and-roll songs by Buddy Holly ("Peggy Sue") and Ricky Nelson ("Hello, Mary Lou"). Sandra Dee was a popular "teen" actress in the 1960s and the model for Olivia Newton-John's character in *Grease* (1978).

---

8. Which R&B singer won a Grammy only after his fatal plane crash in December 1967?

a. Otis Redding

b. Sam Cooke

c. Marvin Gaye

d. Wilson Pickett

Gene Simmons produced Van Halen's demo, which led the group to be signed by record producer Ted Templeman at Warner Brothers. In 1978, Van Halen toured the United States as the opening act for Black Sabbath. By tour's end, Van Halen was a headliner in its own right.

---

8. All of these singers have served time in a jail cell. Which one was *not* jailed for a drug-related offense?

a. Paul McCartney

b. David Crosby

c. Merle Haggard

d. Ike Turner

The diner was called Monk's on the show, but the real-life place was actually Tom's Restaurant, located on Manhattan's upper West Side. This is the same "Tom's Diner" of which Suzanne Vega wrote in her 1987 hit song.

5. Which children's program won the most Emmys?

a. *Kukla, Fran, and Ollie*
b. *Time for Beany*
c. *Ding Dong School*
d. *Howdy Doody*

Like *Sesame Street, The Electric Company* was produced by the Children's Television Workshop. Irene Cara was a member of the show's "Short Circus." Bill Cosby appeared from 1971 to 1972. Morgan Freeman and Rita Moreno rode out the series. Others who lent their voices to characters included Mel Brooks, Joan Rivers, and Gene Wilder.

5. In which film is Robert Redford a CIA agent who is running for his life?

a. *The Great Waldo Pepper* (1975)
b. *Brubaker* (1980)
c. *Three Days of the Condor* (1975)
d. *The Chase* (1966)

Bruce Lee had many "last films," as he died before their release dates. *Game of Death,* about a kung fu star who fakes his own death, was filmed in 1972, but released six years later. Jackie Chan appeared with Lee in a number of other martial arts films, including *The Chinese Connection* (1973)

5. Howard Cosell was in all of these Woody Allen films except:

a. *Bananas* (1971)
b. *Take the Money and Run* (1969)
c. *Sleeper* (1973)
d. *Broadway Danny Rose* (1984)

Play It Again, Sam was directed by Herbert Ross. Martin Ritt directed Allen and Zero Mostel in *The Front.* The star-studded James Bond spoof *Casino Royale* was directed by John Huston and four other directors—none of whom was Allen.

5. Which Western explores racism?

a. *She Wore a Yellow Ribbon* (1949)
b. *The Searchers* (1956)
c. *Butch Cassidy and the Sundance Kid* (1969)
d. *The Man Who Shot Liberty Valance* (1962)

Ford directed John Wayne in all four. Wayne played Cavalry Captain then Commander Kirby York in *Fort Apache* and *Rio Grande.* In between, Wayne played a retiring Cavalry officer in *She Wore a Yellow Ribbon* (1949). In 1956's *The Searchers,* the Duke played a Civil War veteran, an anti-hero that you might find in a spaghetti Western.

9. What was the name of the movie that paired John Travolta and Olivia Newton-John for the second time?

a. *Grease 2* (1982)

b. *Two of a Kind* (1983)

c. *The Experts* (1989)

d. *Xanadu* (1980)

GAME 4 Q8 ANSWER d
This film by maverick director Sam Peckinpah was released around the same time as Stanley Kubrick's *A Clockwork Orange*. Both films were banned in the UK in 1972 for their disturbing depictions of social violence. *Straw Dogs* was considered Peckinpah's most violent film since his vicious 1969 Western *The Wild Bunch*.

9. Who was supposed to play Michael Corleone's daughter Mary in *The Godfather Part III* (1990)?

a. Madonna

b. Winona Ryder

c. Lea Thompson

d. Bridget Fonda

GAME 24 Q8 ANSWER c
After giving what many considered a great screen performance opposite Cher in this film, Stoltz was suprisingly *not* nominated for an Oscar. That same year, he was hired and then fired from the Steven Spielberg-produced film *Back to the Future* (the role went to Michael J. Fox). Stoltz went on to play Helen Hunt's ex-boyfriend on TV's *Mad About You*.

9. Jack Lemmon and Walter Matthau first appeared together in what film?

a. *The Odd Couple*

b. *The Fortune Cookie*

c. *The Front Page*

d. *Grumpy Old Men*

GAME 44 Q8 ANSWER a
1967 was Redding's year. Along with Jimi Hendrix, he had electrified the audience at the Monterey Pop Festival. His sudden death was tragic, but Redding received a number of posthumous awards, including Grammys for Best Rhythm & Blues Vocal Performance and Best Rhythm & Blues Song for "(Sittin' On) The Dock of the Bay" in 1968.

9. Who is the sniper that San Francisco cop Harry Callahan is after in *Dirty Harry*?

a. Scorpio

b. Taurus

c. Virgo

d. Capricorn

GAME 64 Q8 ANSWER c
Haggard was arrested for breaking and entering a restaurant in 1957 at the age of twenty. Sentenced to five years at San Quentin, Haggard didn't allow incarceration to get in his way—he brewed beer in his cell and headed an inmate gambling ring.

4. All of these actors were regulars on *The Electric Company* except:

a. Bill Cosby

b. Jennifer Beals

c. Irene Cara

d. Morgan Freeman

GAME 17 Q3 ANSWER c

Rita Moreno was a regular on PBS's *The Electric Company*. On *Sesame Street*, Raul Julia played Rafael, Alan Arkin was Larry, and Ruth Buzzi appeared as Ruthie. Other well-known actors who have appeared as characters on the show include Charlotte Rae as Molly the Mail Lady and Savion Glover as Savion.

---

4. In Bruce Lee's *Game of Death* (1978), Lee fights with all of these actors *except:*

a. Chuck Norris

b. Jackie Chan

c. Kareem Abdul-Jabbar

d. Sammo Hung

GAME 37 Q3 ANSWER c

The Maltese Falcon (1941) was the directorial debut of John Huston and the first talkie for "Fat Man" Sydney Greenstreet. Both received Oscar nominations but no awards. Bogart didn't receive his first nomination until the following year for *Casablanca* (1942).

---

4. Which of the following films did Woody Allen direct?

a. *The Front* (1976)

b. *Play It Again, Sam* (1972)

c. *Casino Royale* (1967)

d. *Mighty Aphrodite* (1995)

GAME 57 Q3 ANSWER d

Allen also wrote the screenplay for this 1965 film, which starred Peter O'Toole and Peter Sellers. Burt Bacharach and Hal David penned the movie's title song, which was a monster hit for Welsh singer Tom Jones.

---

4. Which film was *not* part of John Ford's "Cavalry trilogy"?

a. *Fort Apache* (1948)

b. *She Wore a Yellow Ribbon* (1949)

c. *Rio Grande* (1950)

d. *The Searchers* (1956)

GAME 77 Q3 ANSWER b

Estevez, Sutherland, and Sheen were joined by Lou Diamond Phillips, Dermot Mulroney, and Casey Siemaszko as the six "young guns" of this 1988 movie, whose tagline was: "Six Reasons Why the West Was Wild."

10. Which is *not a Planet of the Apes* sequel?

a. *Conquest of the Planet of the Apes*

b. *Battle for the . . .*

c. *Escape from the . . .*

d. *Revenge of the . . .*

Two of a Kind brought together the stars after the success of 1978's *Grease*. This film was not nearly as popular, although it has become a bit of a campy cult film. Highlights include Gene Hackman as the voice of God and Oliver Reed as the Devil, who sings "Rain" by The Beatles from scene to scene.

---

10. Legendary movie producer David O. Selznick married which of the following actresses:

a. Marion Davies

b. Norma Shearer

c. Jennifer Jones

d. Marlene Dietrich

Due to a case of severe exhaustion, Ryder had to bow out of Coppola's film—she later worked with the director on *Bram Stoker's Dracula* in 1992. Sofia Coppola, Francis Ford's daughter, suffered much harsh criticism for her performance in the role, but later won critical acclaim as director of *The Virgin Suicides* (2000).

---

10. What was Michael Landon's first film?

a. *This Gun for Hire* (1942)

b. *They Were Expendable* (1945)

c. *I Was a Teenage Werewolf* (1957)

d. *The Little Shop of Horrors* (1960)

After *The Fortune Cookie* (1966), Lemmon and Matthau appeared together in *The Odd Couple, The Front Page, Buddy Buddy, JFK, Grumpy Old Men, Grumpier Old Men, Out to Sea,* and *Odd Couple 2*. Billy Wilder wrote and directed *The Fortune Cookie, The Front Page,* and *Buddy Buddy*.

---

10. In what 1967 movie does Audrey Hepburn play a blind woman who must defend herself against small-time hoods?

a. *Two for the Road*

b. *Afraid of the Dark*

c. *Wait Until Dark*

d. *Charade*

Actor Andrew Robinson, who played the part of Scorpio, received death threats because of his role in this 1971 movie. Starring Clint Eastwood, *Dirty Harry* is loosely based on San Francisco's Zodiac Killer, who was active at the time.

3. All of these actors played characters on *Sesame Street* except:

a. Raul Julia

b. Alan Arkin

c. Rita Moreno

d. Ruth Buzzi

GAME 17 Q2 ANSWER b
Paramount's answer to the popular Andy Hardy series, Henry Aldrich and his family made a leap from radio to the silver screen in 1939. The series included eleven films, which were made over a five-year period. In 1949, *The Aldrich Family* leapt to television, where it found a home on NBC until 1953.

---

3. What is Bogart's name in *The Maltese Falcon*?

a. Rick Blaine

b. Philip Marlowe

c. Sam Spade

d. Duke Mantee

GAME 37 Q2 ANSWER c
Both Brando and DeNiro played Don Vito Corleone. Brando was cast in the original *Godfather;* DeNiro played Corleone as a young immigrant in the sequel. *The Score* was a heist film, co-starring the two giants and Edward Norton.

---

3. Woody Allen first acted in which movie?

a. *Annie Hall*

b. *Play It Again, Sam*

c. *Take the Money and Run*

d. *What's New, Pussycat?*

GAME 57 Q2 ANSWER c
Although he is credited with co-directing *What's Up, Tiger Lily?* in 1966, it wasn't until 1969's *Take the Money and Run* that Allen sat alone at the helm. In the last scene of the film, he is interviewed on-camera with a director's viewfinder around his neck.

---

3. Who was *not* among the *Young Guns*?

a. Emilio Estevez

b. Robert Downey, Jr.

c. Kiefer Sutherland

d. Charlie Sheen

GAME 77 Q2 ANSWER d
On *The Roy Rogers Show*, Rogers had a horse named Trigger and Pat Brady had a jeep called Nellybelle. Red Conners was sidekick to Hopalong Cassidy, and Pat Buttram was Gene Autry's pal.

11. Which actress did Alfred Hitchcock originally want to play the female lead in *Vertigo* (1958)?

a. Vera Miles
b. Grace Kelly
c. Janet Leigh
d. Doris Day

GAME 4 Q10 ANSWER d
This popular film series yielded four sequels: *Beneath the Planet of the Apes* (1970), *Escape from the Planet of the Apes* (1971), *Conquest of the Planet of the Apes* (1972), and *Battle for the Planet of the Apes* (1973). The franchise also yielded a mid-70s live-action TV series, a Saturday morning cartoon series, and a remake of the original film in 2001.

11. With whom did Orson Welles share a Best Original Screenplay Oscar for *Citizen Kane* (1941)?

a. Herman J. Mankiewicz
b. John Houseman
c. Gregg Toland
d. Bernard Herrmann

GAME 24 Q10 ANSWER c
Born Phylis Isley, this pretty young actress won over Selznick, who gave her the name Jennifer Jones and introduced her to the public in 1942. Selznick divorced his wife (Louis B. Mayer's daughter) and married Jones in 1949. He had hoped that 1946's *Duel in the Sun* would provide Jones with an Oscar-winning role. He was wrong.

11. Kate Smith's hit song "God Bless America" was written by:

a. George Gershwin
b. Irving Berlin
c. Cole Porter
d. Louis Armstrong

GAME 44 Q10 ANSWER c
This B-movie cost only $82,000 to make and grossed over $2 million. Its huge success gave birth to other cheaply produced teen pictures of the day, like *I Was a Teenage Frankenstein* in 1957 and *I Married a Monster from Outer Space* in 1958.

11. In *Chocolat*, the favorite treat of Roux, played by Johnny Depp, is:

a. Dark chocolate truffles
b. "Nipples of Venus"
c. Hot chocolate
d. Chocolate gateau

GAME 64 Q10 ANSWER c
For her performance, Hepburn was an Oscar nominee for Best Actress. In 1998, *My Cousin Vinny* star Marisa Tomei played Audrey Hepburn's character in a Broadway run of *Wait Until Dark*, while *Pulp Fiction* director Quentin Tarantino appeared in the role originally played by Alan Arkin.

2. What was the first movie to feature the line "Hen-REEE!!! Henry Aldrich!"?

a. *Henry Aldrich for President*
b. *What a Life*
c. *Life with Henry*
d. *The Aldrich Family*

GAME 17 Q1 ANSWER b
Schwartz began his writing career in radio with *The Bob Hope Show* in 1939. During his long television career, he wrote, rewrote, and/or produced over 700 shows, including *The Red Skelton Show* and *My Favorite Martian* (both for CBS) before creating, writing and producing *Gilligan's Island* in 1963.

---

2. In which movie do both Marlon Brando and Robert DeNiro appear?

a. *The Godfather* (1972)
b. *The Godfather Part II* (1974)
c. *The Score* (2001)
d. *Once Upon a Time in America* (1984)

GAME 37 Q1 ANSWER a
Nicholson lost Best Supporting Actor for this 1969 film to Gig Young (*They Shoot Horses, Don't They?*) To date, Nicholson has won three Oscars—Best Actor for *One Flew Over the Cuckoo's Nest* (1975), Best Supporting Actor for *Terms of Endearment* (1983), and Best Actor for *As Good As It Gets* (1997).

---

2. The first movie Woody Allen directed on his own was:

a. *Casino Royale*
b. *Play It Again, Sam*
c. *Take the Money and Run*
d. *Sleeper*

GAME 57 Q1 ANSWER b
To date, Allen has been nominated for twenty Academy Awards and has received three. For *Annie Hall* (1977), he won Oscars for Best Director and Best Screenplay, which he shared with co-writer Marshall Brickman. He also received a Best Screenplay Oscar for *Hannah and Her Sisters* (1986).

---

2. Who was Roy Rogers' jeep-driving sidekick?

a. Red Connors
b. Gene Autry
c. Pat Buttram
d. Pat Brady

GAME 77 Q1 ANSWER c
Weaver's deputy with a limp left the show in 1964, and Ken Curtis came on as new deputy Festus Haggen. Burt Reynolds played the half-breed blacksmith Quint Asper from 1962 to 1965, and Buck Taylor was gunsmith Newly O'Brien from 1967 until the show's end in 1975.

12. Which rock group's 1972 album is comprised of only one song that runs for over forty minutes?

a. Yes

b. King Crimson

c. Jethro Tull

d. Led Zeppelin

Hitchcock was very fond of Vera Miles. She had starred alongside Henry Fonda in *The Wrong Man* (1956), and Hitchcock thought she would be ideal for *Vertigo.* When she announced that she was pregnant and could not star in the film, Hitch was furious. Kim Novak got the role.

---

12. Which of the following movie actors is *not* yet a Pulitzer Prize-winning or nominated playwright?

a. Jason Miller

b. Sam Sheperd

c. Eric Bogosian

d. Steve Martin

Mankiewicz, who was a close friend of William Randolph Hearst and Marion Davies, co-wrote the film's first-rate screenplay, which was loosely based on Hearst's life. John Houseman co-produced the movie, Gregg Toland was the cinematographer, and Bernard Herrmann composed the music.

---

12. Which song is on the soundtrack of *Singin' in the Rain*?

a. "Make 'Em Laugh"

b. "Be a Clown"

c. "Laughter in the Rain"

d. "Tears of a Clown"

It was twenty years after Irving Berlin wrote "God Bless America" that Kate Smith was able to convince him that the song was worthwhile. Berlin donated all the money he made on that song to the Boy Scouts, the Girl Scouts, and the war effort.

---

12. *"Food Fight!"* In which film will you hear this line?

a. *Revenge of the Nerds*

b. *National Lampoon's Animal House*

c. *Dead Man on Campus*

d. *Ferris Bueller's Day Off*

This 1992 film—a charming tale that centers on the owner of a French chocolate shop—received five Oscar nominations, including Best Picture, Best Actress in a Leading Role (Juliette Binoche), and Best Actress in a Supporting Role (Judi Dench).

1. Sherwood Schwartz created the show and co-wrote the theme song for *Gilligan's Island* and what other show?

a. *Nanny and the Professor*

b. *The Brady Bunch*

c. *The Partridge Family*

d. *The Flintstones*

The answer to this question is on:

page 226, top frame, right side.

---

1. In which film was Jack Nicholson first nominated for an Oscar?

a. *Easy Rider*

b. *One Flew Over the Cuckoo's Nest*

c. *Terms of Endearment*

d. *Chinatown*

The answer to this question is on:

page 226, second frame, right side.

---

1. How many Oscars has Woody Allen won?

a. None

b. Three

c. Six

d. Nine

The answer to this question is on:

page 226, third frame, right side.

---

1. Who played Deputy Chester B. Goode on *Gunsmoke*?

a. Burt Reynolds

b. Ken Curtis

c. Dennis Weaver

d. Buck Taylor

The answer to this question is on:

page 226, bottom frame, right side.

225

GAME 5

And the Winner Is . . .

Nominees and Award Winners

Turn to page 58 for the first question.

Thick as a Brick is an album of only one song of the same title. Written by frontman and flautist Ian Anderson, the song, as originally released in record format, runs across both sides of the record and still remains interesting. Since I still have a record player at home, I have no trouble listening to it as originally intended—I'm good that way.

GAME 25

A Plague on Both Your Houses

Famous Deaths and Death Scenes

Turn to page 58 for the first question.

The late Jason Miller won the Pulitzer in 1973 for *That Championship Season*, while Sam Shepard won in 1978 for *Buried Child*. Eric Bogosian was a 1988 Pulitzer finalist for his one-man play *Talk Radio* (later made into a film by Oliver Stone). Steve Martin wrote the play *Picasso at the Lapin Agile*, but has yet to be nominated for a Pulitzer.

GAME 45

Let 'em All Talk

Talk Show Trivia

Turn to page 58 for the first question.

Donald O'Connor's bravura performance of this song is one of the film's highlights. The soundtrack is composed of songs that Herb Nacio Brown and producer Arthur Freed wrote for early MGM musicals. "Make 'Em Laugh," however, was written specifically for *Singin' in the Rain*.

GAME 65

British Invasion

Chart Toppers From Across the Sea

Turn to page 58 for the first question.

Originally, this 1978 comedy classic surrounding the high jinks of a disreputable college fraternity was to be filmed at the University of Missouri; however, permission was rescinded when the President of the University read the script. Filming eventually took place at the University of Oregon.

GAME 17

Rated G

Wholesome Family Fare

Turn to page 225 for the first question.

GAME 16 Q12 ANSWER c

Lee J. Cobb, Dustin Hoffman, and Brian Dennehy have all played Willy Loman in made-for-TV adaptations of the Arthur Miller play. Kevin Kline's portrayal of this character appears in Garry Marshall's comedy romp *Soapdish* (1991). In it, Kline plays an out-of-work soap star who is stuck playing *Death of a Salesman* in a Florida supper club theater.

GAME 37

Follow My Lead

Those Magnificent Leading Men

Turn to page 225 for the first question.

GAME 36 Q12 ANSWER b

When Chevy Chase left *Saturday Night Live* after just one season, his film debut as a leading man paired him with Goldie Hawn in 1978's critically acclaimed *Foul Play*. In 1980, they worked together again in Neil Simon's *Seems Like Old Times*. Hawn was also the first guest on Chase's short-lived late-night talk show in 1993.

GAME 57

Going "Bananas"

Play It Again, Woody Allen

Turn to page 225 for the first question.

GAME 56 Q12 ANSWER b

This 1967 winner is from the family musical *Doctor Dolittle*, starring Rex Harrison. The animated film *Pocahontas* (1995) had the award-winning "Colors of the Wind." "You'll Be in My Heart" is from *Tarzan* (1999), and "Can You Feel the Love Tonight?" is from *The Lion King* (1994).

GAME 77

Ride 'em Cowboy

Western Entertainment

Turn to page 225 for the first question.

GAME 76 Q12 ANSWER a

Cruise was one of the Greasers in Coppola's 1983 film of S.E. Hinton's *The Outsiders*. Cruise was nominated for Best Actor in 1989 for his work in Oliver Stone's *Born on the Fourth of July*, then appeared in 1992 with second wife Nicole Kidman in Ron Howard's *Far and Away*. Cruise and Spielberg first worked together in 2002 on *Minority Report*.

GAME 5

1. Julia Roberts won an Oscar for her performance in:

a. *Steel Magnolias* (1989)

b. *Pretty Woman* (1990)

c. *Sleeping With the Enemy* (1991)

d. *Erin Brockovich* (2000)

The answer to this question is on:

page 59, top frame, right side.

GAME 25

1. What are Captain Kirk's last words before dying in *Star Trek VII: Generations*?

a. "It was fun . . . Oh, my."

b. "Khan!"

c. ". . . I'll die alone."

d. "Klingon bastards, you've killed my son."

The answer to this question is on:

page 59, second frame, right side.

GAME 45

1. On which Norman Lear "Fernwood" show did Martin Mull play Garth Gimble?

a. *Mary Hartman, Mary Hartman*

b. *Forever Fernwood*

c. *Fernwood 2-Night*

d. *America 2-Night*

The answer to this question is on:

page 59, third frame, right side.

GAME 65

1. Which song was *not* a hit for Gerry and the Pacemakers?

a. "Ferry 'Cross the Mersey"

b. "You'll Never Walk Alone"

c. "Till There Was You"

d. "Don't Let the Sun Catch You Crying"

The answer to this question is on:

page 59, bottom frame, right side.

12. Who has *not* played Willy Loman in a film version of *Death of a Salesman*?

a. Dustin Hoffman

b. Kevin Kline

c. Hume Cronyn

d. Lee J. Cobb

GAME 16 Q11 ANSWER a

Herrmann was nominated for the scores for Brian De Palma's *Obsession* and Martin Scorsese's *Taxi Driver*, both released in 1976. (He died the same night he finished recording the score for *Taxi Driver*.) Herrmann won the award posthumously for *Obsession*, a remake of Hitchcock's *Vertigo* (1958).

12. How many movies have Chevy Chase and Goldie Hawn starred in together?

a. One

b. Two

c. Three

d. Four

GAME 36 Q11 ANSWER d

Hanks must love to swim, because nearly every one of his films has him going for a dip. He even ends up in the water in *Apollo 13* (1995), the story of the country's ill-fated 1970 moon mission.

12. Which Oscar-winning song is *not* from an animated motion picture?

a. "Colors of the Wind"

b. "Talk to the Animals"

c. "You'll Be in My Heart"

d. "Can You Feel the Love Tonight?"

GAME 56 Q11 ANSWER d

Although it didn't win the Oscar, Marvin Hamlisch's song for the 1977 Bond film *The Spy Who Loved Me*, was a huge hit. Award winner "Take My Breath Away" is from *Top Gun* (1986), "The Time of My Life" is from *Dirty Dancing* (1987), and "Let the River Run" is from *Working Girl* (1988).

12. Which film director did Tom Cruise work with first?

a. Francis Ford Coppola

b. Steven Spielberg

c. Ron Howard

d. Oliver Stone

GAME 76 Q11 ANSWER c

McCartney and fellow Beatles shared the Best Original Score Oscar for *Let It Be*. He and wife Linda earned a Best Song nomination for "Live and Let Die," but lost to Marvin Hamlisch's "The Way We Were." McCartney's "Vanilla Sky" was also nominated, but lost to Randy Newman's "If I Didn't Have You" from *Monster's Inc.*

2. Which Gene Hackman film won the most Academy Awards?

a. *The French Connection* (1971)

b. *The Poseidon Adventure* (1972)

c. *Bonnie and Clyde* (1967)

d. *Unforgiven* (1992)

GAME 5 Q1 ANSWER d
Roberts also received a Best Actress nomination for her role as the prostitute with a heart of gold in the grown-up fairy tale *Pretty Woman* (1990) and a Best Supporting Actress nomination the year before as Shelby, Sally Field's daughter in *Steel Magnolias* (1989). Both roles earned her Golden Globe awards.

---

2. Which movie was Natalie Wood filming when she died?

a. *Bob & Carol & Ted & Alice*

b. *Sex and the Single Girl*

c. *Brainstorm*

d. *Rebel Without a Cause*

GAME 25 Q1 ANSWER a
After helping Captain Picard (Patrick Stewart) defeat the villainous Malcolm McDowell, Kirk is fatally injured. Many consider Kirk's last lines to be Shatner's best acting, while others preferred him shouting Khan's name in *Star Trek II*, bemoaning his son's death in *Star Trek III*, or predicting his own end in *Star Trek V*.

---

2. Which *Tonight Show* host was a featured panelist on *What's My Line?* in the 1950s?

a. Jack Paar

b. Ernie Kovacs

c. Steve Allen

d. Johnny Carson

GAME 45 Q1 ANSWER a
All four shows took place in the fictional town of Fernwood, Ohio. In *Mary Hartman, Mary Hartman*, Mull's character Garth Gimble was killed. Mull appeared as Garth's twin brother Barth on *Fernwood 2-Night* and *America 2-Night*. When Louise Lasser left the role of Mary Hartman after 325 episodes, the show was renamed *Forever Fernwood*.

---

2. Which British band is *not* mentioned in the lyrics of "All the Young Dudes"?

a. T. Rex

b. The Rolling Stones

c. The Beatles

d. The Kinks

GAME 65 Q1 ANSWER c
In 1964, Gerry and the Pacemakers had hits with "Ferry 'Cross the Mersey" and "Don't Let the Sun Catch You Crying." In 1985, lead singer Gerry Marsden hit #1 with a new recording of "You'll Never Walk Alone," becoming the first British artist to top the charts twice with two renditions of the same song.

11. Which composer has competed against himself in the Oscars and won?

a. Bernard Herrmann
b. Jerry Goldsmith
c. John Williams
d. Danny Elfman

GAME 16 Q10 ANSWER b
The people who appear as themselves in this film are Dick Cavett, Marshall McLuhan, and Truman Capote, who does a brief walk-by as what Alvy calls "the winner of the Truman Capote Look-Alike Award." Ruth Gordon and Jeff Goldblum also appear in little cameos as nondescript characters.

11. Which film does *not* have Tom Hanks swimming at any point?

a. *Splash* (1984)
b. *Forrest Gump* (1994)
c. *Cast Away* (2000)
d. *Big* (1988)

GAME 36 Q10 ANSWER c
Jeff Goldblum's character (known simply as "Motorcycle Man") appears throughout the film but never speaks. As an interesting counterpoint, Hal Phillip Walker, the presidential candidate of the film, is always heard but never seen.

11. Which song is *not* an Oscar winner?

a. "Take My Breath Away"
b. "The Time of My Life"
c. "Let the River Run"
d. "Nobody Does It Better"

GAME 56 Q10 ANSWER a
Loretta Lynn reached this status in 1965 at age thirty. Twenty-five years later, Sissy Spacek won the Best Actress Oscar portraying Lynn in *Coal Miner's Daughter.*

11. Paul McCartney won an Oscar for his music in which film?

a. *Vanilla Sky* (2001)
b. *I Am Sam* (2001)
c. *Let It Be* (1970)
d. *Live and Let Die* (1973)

GAME 76 Q10 ANSWER b
Roy, the other card-playing regular, was Oscar's accountant. But only Officer Murray Greschler, played by Al Molinaro on TV and Herb Edelman in the movie, became a recurring minor character on the sitcom.

3. A 1975 remake of "Misty" earned a Grammy Award for which novelty act?

a. Ray Stevens

b. Weird Al Yankovic

c. Victor Borge

d. The Chipmunks

GAME 5 Q2 ANSWER a

The French Connection won five Oscars, including Hackman's first as Best Actor. He also won a Best Supporting Actor Oscar for *Unforgiven*. Hackman was also nominated for Best Supporting Actor in *Bonnie and Clyde* and *I Never Sang for My Father* (1970), and for Best Actor in *Mississippi Burning* (1988).

3. In which of the following films does Jimmy Stewart die onscreen?

a. *The Glenn Miller Story* (1954)

b. *Bandolero!* (1968)

c. *Rope* (1948)

d. *Vertigo* (1958)

GAME 25 Q2 ANSWER c

Wood spent Thanksgiving 1981 on her yacht with husband Robert Wagner and *Brainstorm* co-star Christopher Walken. The next morning, she was found floating nearly a mile away, dressed in a nightgown and down jacket. The mystery surrounding her death was never solved.

3. Which TV talk show did The J. Geils Band agree to appear on in 1983?

a. *Late Night With David Letterman*

b. *The Joe Franklin Show*

c. *The Tonight Show*

d. *The Mike Douglas Show*

GAME 45 Q2 ANSWER c

Allen coined the question, "Is it bigger than a breadbox?" while a panelist. By the 1960s, panelists included Bennett Cerf, Arlene Francis, Dorothy Kilgallen, and a guest celebrity. Incidentally, John Daly not only hosted the show for its entire seventeen-year network run, but also anchored the ABC evening news.

3. What was the first song Tom Jones took to the top of the charts?

a. "What's New Pussycat?"

b. "Delilah"

c. "It's Not Unusual"

d. "She's a Lady"

GAME 65 Q2 ANSWER d

When David Bowie wrote "All the Young Dudes" for Mott the Hoople in 1972, "Bang a Gong (Get It On)" was a big hit for T. Rex. The lyrics of Bowie's song also make sly references to The Beatles' "Revolution" and The Rolling Stones' "Mother's Little Helper." The Kinks are not mentioned at all.

GAME 16

10. How many people show up as themselves in *Annie Hall* (1977)?

a. Two
b. Three
c. Four
d. Five

GAME 16 Q9 ANSWER a

Released with an "X" rating, *Midnight Cowboy* received an "R" rating after winning an Oscar and scoring with the public. *Henry & June* was the first film to receive the "NC-17" rating, followed by *Henry: Portrait of a Serial Killer*. *Last Tango in Paris* only recently was changed from "X" to "NC-17," more for the crudity of Brando's language than for nudity.

GAME 36

10. Which actor does not speak a single word in *Nashville*, Robert Altman's 1975 masterpiece?

a. Hal Phillip Walker
b. Scott Glenn
c. Jeff Goldblum
d. Keenan Wynn

GAME 36 Q9 ANSWER d

Buffalo Springfield was home to both Stephen Stills and Neil Young. The Hollies had Graham Nash, and The Byrds had rebellious guitarist/singer David Crosby. The Yardbirds was a breeding ground for guitar heroes, though. During the 1960s, the group had Eric Clapton, Jimmy Page, and Jeff Beck in the group at different times.

GAME 56

10. Who was country music's first female millionaire?

a. Loretta Lynn
b. Patsy Kline
c. Shania Twain
d. Tammy Wynette

GAME 56 Q9 ANSWER a

National Public Radio put on this expanded radio-drama version of George Lucas's epic tale. Mark Hamill was joined on the air by Anthony Daniels, who played C-3PO in the film. In the movie, David Prowse walked around as Darth Vader while James Earl Jones provided the voice—Brock Peters did the voice for NPR.

GAME 76

10. Who was *not* one of the poker-playing pals on *The Odd Couple*?

a. Murray
b. Mickey
c. Speed
d. Vinnie

GAME 76 Q9 ANSWER a

Leave It to Beaver was the first prime time program to *show* a toilet (just the tank, not the seat), but it was the Bunkers who finally proved that one worked.

4. *Citizen Kane* won the Academy Award for:

a. Best Picture

b. Best Original Screenplay

c. Best Cinematography

d. Best Film Editing

GAME 5 Q3 ANSWER a

Stevens, both a class-act songwriter and wacky humorist, has won two Grammys to date. His first was in the category of Best Male Vocalist for his 1970 song, "Everything Is Beautiful." For "Misty," his 1975 remake of the Gardner and Burke classic, Ray received his second Grammy for Best Arrangement Accompanying Vocalist(s).

---

4. Which former child star did *not* die of a drug overdose?

a. River Phoenix

b. Carl "Alfalfa" Switzer

c. Dana Plato

d. Anissa Jones

GAME 25 Q3 ANSWER b

Starring with Dean Martin as the outlaw Bishop Brothers, Stewart is killed during a gunfight with Mexican bandits. As Glenn Miller, Stewart dies in *The Glenn Miller Story,* but it happens offscreen. Hitchcock has Stewart discover a corpse in a trunk in *Rope,* then makes him take the blame for no less than three deaths in *Vertigo.*

---

4. Which talk show host got his nose broken by an unruly guest?

a. Howard Stern

b. Geraldo Rivera

c. Morton Downey, Jr.

d. Jerry Springer

GAME 45 Q3 ANSWER b

That's right, my friends, back in 1983, during the height of the band's popularity, my show was the only one The J. Geils Band agreed to do. At that time, they had two hit singles-"Freeze Frame" and "Centerfold." Martin Paint was my show's sponsor, so the band decided to have paint poured all over them at the end of the show.

---

4. Which British group had big hits with "She's Not There" and "Time of the Season"?

a. The Zombies

b. The Yardbirds

c. The Moody Blues

d. Herman's Hermits

GAME 65 Q3 ANSWER c

The Welsh singer, born Thomas Jones Woodward, changed his stage name from Tommy Scott to Tom Jones after the release of the successful 1963 film of the same name. His first hit made it to #1 in Britain and was a Top 10 hit in the United States.

9. To date, what has been the only X-rated film to win the Best Picture Oscar?

a. *Midnight Cowboy* (1969)

b. *Last Tango in Paris* (1972)

c. *Henry & June* (1990)

d. *Henry: Portrait of a Serial Killer* (1990)

GAME 16 Q8 ANSWER a
Neighbors, which was released in 1981, paired Belushi with frequent partner Dan Ackroyd. Earlier that same year, Belushi won the hearts of moviegoers with his sensitive performance opposite Blair Brown in the romantic comedy *Continental Divide.*

---

9. Which '60s rock group did *not* contain a member of the rock group CSNY (Crosby, Stills, Nash and Young)?

a. Buffalo Springfield

b. The Hollies

c. The Byrds

d. The Yardbirds

GAME 36 Q8 ANSWER a
In 1967, Carole King and then-husband Gerry Goffin wrote "Pleasant Valley Sunday" for The Monkees. King also wrote James Taylor's hit "You've Got a Friend," and was awarded one of four Grammys in 1971 for her hit song "It's Too Late" from *Tapestry,* her Grammy-winning album.

---

9. Which *Star Wars* cast member was the only one to appear in a radio version of the film in 1981?

a. Mark Hamill

b. Carrie Fisher

c. David Prowse

d. Sir Alec Guinness

GAME 56 Q8 ANSWER b
Dean, who was killed in a car accident a few days after completing *Giant,* received a Best Actor nomination for it in 1956. He lost, however, to Yul Brynner, who took home the award for his performance in *The King and I.*

---

9. The first prime time television program that had a toilet flushing was:

a. *All in the Family*

b. *Leave It to Beaver*

c. *Seinfeld*

d. *Get Smart*

GAME 76 Q8 ANSWER c
Kasdan's first industry assignment was co-writing the script for *The Empire Strikes Back* (1980) with George Lucas. He began directing his own work with *Body Heat* (1981) and *The Big Chill* (1983), and then continued to dazzle audiences and critics alike with such films as *Silverado* (1985), *The Accidental Tourist* (1988), and *Grand Canyon* (1991).

5. Who received an Oscar nomination as the beekeeper in the 1997 film *Ulee's Gold*?

a. Peter Fonda

b. Dennis Hopper

c. Jack Nicholson

d. Geoffrey Rush

GAME 5 Q4 ANSWER b
This 1941 film classic was nominated for nine Academy Awards, including Best Picture, Actor, Director, and Score. It left with only one—Best Screenplay.

5. Which Rat Pack member died at the youngest age?

a. Dean Martin

b. Sammy Davis, Jr.

c. Frank Sinatra

d. Peter Lawford

GAME 25 Q4 ANSWER b
The freckle-faced, off-key crooner of the "Our Gang/Little Rascals" comedy series was shot to death in 1959 at age thirty-one. Conflicting stories surround how and why the incident occurred.

5. Which well-known game show panelist had her own TV talk show?

a. Peggy Cass

b. Dorothy Kilgallen

c. Arlene Francis

d. Jaye P. Morgan

GAME 45 Q4 ANSWER b
A member of the Ku Klux Klan smashed Rivera's nose with a chair during a segment of *Geraldo.* A former lawyer and newscaster, Geraldo, no stranger to fighting, once boxed Frank Stallone (Sylvester's brother) on Howard Stern's show. Geraldo won.

5. Which Rolling Stone played saxophone on a Beatles' song?

a. Mick Jagger

b. Keith Richards

c. Brian Jones

d. Bill Wyman

GAME 65 Q4 ANSWER a
One of the hipper British groups in the mid-1960s, The Zombies recorded songs that were used in film soundtracks by George Lucas in *More American Graffiti* (1978), and by Penny Marshall in *Awakenings* (1991).

8. What was John Belushi's last film before he died in 1982?

a. *Neighbors*

b. *Continental Divide*

c. *The Blues Brothers*

d. *1941*

GAME 16 Q7 ANSWER d
Don't Look Now was the directorial debut of acclaimed cinematographer Nicholas Roeg. Based on a short story by Daphne du Maurier, this tale of a grieving young couple that receives messages from their recently deceased daughter featured the great acting of Donald Sutherland and Julie Christie.

---

8. Which female recording artist wrote a hit song for The Monkees?

a. Carole King

b. Carly Simon

c. Linda Ronstadt

d. Joni Mitchell

GAME 36 Q7 ANSWER c
Although Ryder was the film's executive producer, Angelina Jolie stole the show with a bravura performance that earned her the Best Supporting Actress Oscar in 2000.

---

8. Who was the first performer to be nominated posthumously for an acting Oscar?

a. Sal Mineo

b. James Dean

c. Peter Finch

d. Bobby Darren

GAME 56 Q7 ANSWER a
With four Oscars for her performances in *Morning Glory* (1933), *Guess Who's Coming to Dinner* (1967), *The Lion in Winter* (1968), and *On Golden Pond* (1981), Katharine Hepburn leads the pack.

---

8. Who wrote the screenplay for *Raiders of the Lost Ark* (1981)?

a. Robert Altman

b. Steven Spielberg

c. Lawrence Kasdan

d. David Mamet

GAME 76 Q7 ANSWER c
Singer Sheryl Crow was convinced to take the part in this movie by cast members Owen Wilson and Dwight Yoakam. Crow's successful singing career began with a McDonald's commercial. She then backed up artists, including Don Henley, George Harrison, Rod Stewart, and Sting. Crow also sang backup for Michael Jackson's *Bad* tour in 1987.

GAME 5

6. Which actor was *not* Oscar nominated for the same role in two different movies?

a. John Wayne

b. Paul Newman

c. Bing Crosby

d. Al Pacino

Peter Fonda first shot to film stardom in 1969's *Easy Rider* and then faded into obscurity. His only noticeable movie part after that was as a biker in *The Cannonball Run* (1981). In *Ulee's Gold,* Fonda based some of his performance on his father, who was an amateur beekeeper.

GAME 25

6. All of these actors died during the production of their last movie *except:*

a. Bruce Lee

b. Clark Gable

c. Vic Morrow

d. Bela Lugosi

Lawford was the sole Brit of the famous Rat Pack and did much to embody the group's laid-back "cool." His first Hollywood film was at age fifteen in *Lord Jeff* (1938). He was at the height of celebrity when he married John F. Kennedy's sister Patricia in 1954. Lawford died on Christmas Eve 1984 at age sixty-one.

GAME 45

6. Which controversial comic broke into tears on *The Arsenio Hall Show* in 1990?

a. George Carlin

b. Andrew "Dice" Clay

c. Roseanne

d. Richard Pryor

Although Dorothy Kilgallen did host a radio show with her husband, it was the lovely and charming Arlene Francis who hosted NBC's *Home* and *The Arlene Francis Show* in the 1950s. Following her short run on TV, Francis moved the show to radio, where it aired for nearly twenty-five years.

GAME 65

6. Who has *not* been a lead vocalist for the British heavy metal band Black Sabbath?

a. Ozzy Osbourne

b. Ronnie James Dio

c. Ian Gillan

d. Bruce Dickinson

Jones played sax on The Beatles' joke song "You Know My Name (Look Up the Number)" which was recorded in 1967 but not released until late 1969. He also played sitar on the Stones' song "Paint It Black," and vibes on "Under My Thumb."

7. Which film was *not* directed by Roman Polanski?

a. *Repulsion* (1965)

b. *Rosemary's Baby* (1968)

c. *Chinatown* (1974)

d. *Don't Look Now* (1973)

GAME 16 Q6 ANSWER a
Robert Altman's *Nashville* marked Lily Tomlin's acting debut in motion pictures. Altman regular Robert Duqui also starred in both films.

---

7. Which Petula Clark hit is featured in *Girl, Interrupted* (1999), starring Winona Ryder?

a. "Don't Sleep in the Subway"

b. "Sign of the Times"

c. "Downtown"

d. "My Love"

GAME 36 Q6 ANSWER a
Raspy-voiced Joplin's posthumous #1 hit was written by actor/songwriter Kris Kristofferon. A few months after recording the song in 1970 for Pearl, her final album, Joplin died of an overdose. "Me and Bobby McGee" was released as a single in March of 1971, and quickly reached #1, where it remained for two weeks.

---

7. Who holds the most Oscars for acting?

a. Katherine Hepburn

b. Ingrid Bergman

c. Jack Nicholson

d. Sir Laurence Olivier

GAME 56 Q6 ANSWER a
Starring Anne Bancroft and Shirley MacLaine, this movie received eleven nominations. To date, the only other movie to share this same fate is *The Color Purple* (1985).

---

7. Which singer is cast as a junkie who is murdered in the first few minutes of *The Minus Man* (1999)?

a. Linda Ronstadt

b. Whitney Houston

c. Sheryl Crow

d. Mariah Carey

GAME 76 Q6 ANSWER d
The End was directed by its star, Burt Reynolds. Reiner does, however, appear in this film as Reynolds' doctor (who collapses of a heart attack while exercising). Among Reiner's directing credits are the Steve Martin films *The Jerk*, *Dead Men Don't Wear Plaid*, *The Man with Two Brains*, and *All of Me*.

Marilyn & Me

I met Marilyn Monroe on a radio show called *Luncheon at Sardi's*. Marilyn was on one side of me, and on the other side was a performer named Molly Picon who was an old-time Jewish actress—she played Frank Sinatra's mother in a movie called *Come Blow Your Horn* in 1963. Marilyn and I became quite close as friends but we were never intimate. She loved men, though—and they loved her right back. It's no accident that she married such remarkable men as baseball legend Joe DiMaggio and playwright Arthur Miller. Marilyn was one of the most alluring women in the world. You can imagine how hard it was for me to resist her.

Anyway, Marilyn and I began work on her autobiography and we got on quite well together. I can truthfully say that she liked me. She was taken away from the book project before we had a chance to finish, though. Someone pointed out to her that she was under contract to another publisher. By then, Marilyn and I had finished about three-quarters of the book. The remainder of the book was written by a woman named Laurie Palmer, who specialized in press releases and the like.

I saw Marilyn only a few times after our initial collaboration. She was always pleasant, gorgeous, and very lady-like. She was a very bright woman, not an airhead, as so much of the celebrity gossip mill would have you believe. She knew exactly what she was doing all the time. She negotiated her own movie contracts. A real smart cookie. I've met other beautiful, interesting blonde actresses since Marilyn—Jayne Mansfield, for example, had a genius IQ and played the violin just wonderfully. Marilyn was special, though. Knowing her was a privilege and a thrill—I still see her in my dreams from time to time, and she's as beautiful as she ever was.

Burns & Allen—
A Memory Lane Romance

One of my favorite comedy duos ever was George Burns and Gracie Allen. These two performers worked together wonderfully. It was more than that, though—they remain one of Hollywood's great romances. Burns and Allen met in the days of vaudeville. Today, many more people recognize George Burns than Gracie Allen. This is only because of his later fame in films during the 1970s. Gracie was a wonderful woman, very smart, quick-witted, and tenacious. When they first started out, Burns was the dope and Allen was the straight man (uh, *woman*). They soon reversed it, however, since Gracie was able to get so many more laughs in the dope slot.

Legend has it that Burns once had a small fling during his marriage to Gracie. However, he immediately felt so guilty about it that he went out and bought her a gorgeous silver centerpiece that she had wanted—that and a $10,000 diamond ring. As far as he knew, she wasn't aware of his fling. Of course, one day about twenty-five years later, he picked up the phone in the house and overheard Gracie saying, "Yeah, well, I wish George would have another fling so I could get another centerpiece."

Sometime in the late 1950s, Gracie developed heart disease. According to the story I heard, when Gracie's health was at its worst, George went out and bought her an expensive mink coat. He presented it to her in a beautifully wrapped gift box in mid-March with a tag on it saying "Don't open until Christmas." George and Gracie both knew that she would not be there by then, but they allowed themselves to believe that they would still be together. A very loving couple. The world could use more of them.

GAME 5

7. James Cagney won his only Oscar for his role in what movie?

a. *Angels With Dirty Faces* (1938)

b. *Ragtime* (1981)

c. *Yankee Doodle Dandy* (1942)

d. *Love Me or Leave Me* (1955)

GAME 5 Q6 ANSWER a

Crosby was nominated as Father O'Malley in *Going My Way* and *The Bells of St. Mary's;* Newman, for playing Fast Eddie Felson in *The Hustler* and *The Color of Money;* and Pacino, for his role as Michael Corleone in the first two *Godfather* films. Wayne was nominated for the role of Rooster Cogburn in *True Grit* but not in *Rooster Cogburn.*

GAME 25

7. Which cigar-smoking celebrity died in a car accident?

a. Groucho Marx

b. Ernie Kovacs

c. George Burns

d. Edward G. Robinson

GAME 25 Q6 ANSWER b

Lee died mysteriously while filming his final movie, *Game of Death* (1978). Vic Morrow died in a helicopter crash on the set of *Twilight Zone: The Movie* (1983). Lugosi's last scenes were in Ed Wood's famous flop *Plan 9 from Outer Space* (1956). Gable had just finished filming *The Misfits* (1962) when he suffered a heart attack and died a few days later.

GAME 45

7. Which talk show host had to break up a fight between Andy Kaufman and pro wrestler Jerry "The King" Lawler?

a. David Letterman

b. Johnny Carson

c. Tom Snyder

d. Joe Franklin (a.k.a. "me")

GAME 45 Q6 ANSWER b

On the eve of his first film, *The Adventures of Ford Fairlane* (1990), the "Diceman" reacted to his much-publicized banning from MTV for life and a tumultuous guest appearance on *Saturday Night Live* with a teary-eyed defense of his act. *Ford Fairlane* flopped, but it did produce hit single "Cradle of Love" for Billy Idol.

GAME 65

7. Which British rocker appeared in The Who's film *Quadrophenia* (1979)?

a. Elvis Costello

b. Sting

c. Mick Jagger

d. John Lydon (a.k.a. Johnny Rotten)

GAME 65 Q6 ANSWER d

Dickinson has been the lead vocalist of fellow British metal band Iron Maiden since 1983. He is responsible for giving the band's lyrics a significant face-lift, quoting from the Bible and drawing influence from English poet Samuel Taylor Coleridge's classic poem "The Rime of the Ancient Mariner."

6. Which actor appeared in both Robert Altman's *Nashville* (1975) and *Short Cuts* (1993)?

a. Lily Tomlin

b. Ned Beatty

c. Karen Black

d. Shelley Duvall

GAME 16 Q5 ANSWER b
Family Business starred Matthew Broderick, who had been offered the part of Alex P. Keaton on NBC-TV's *Family Ties*. Broderick passed the film up in favor of Broadway, and Fox took on the role that would make him famous.

---

6. What was Janis Joplin's only #1 hit?

a. "Me and Bobby McGee"

b. "Piece of My Heart"

c. "Mercedes Benz"

d. "Try (Just a Little Bit Harder)"

GAME 36 Q5 ANSWER b
Although Patricia Arquette played the lead female role opposite Christian Slater in 1993's *True Romance* (written by Tarantino), it was in fact her sister, Rosanna Arquette, who plays the body-pierced shrew of a wife to drug-dealer Eric Stoltz.

---

6. Which of the following films received the most Oscar nominations without a single win?

a. *The Turning Point* (1977)

b. *Giant* (1956)

c. *Lord of the Rings* (2001)

d. *Tootsie* (1982)

GAME 56 Q5 ANSWER b
In this 1987 film adaptation of John Updike's novel, a trio of beautiful witches unknowingly conjures up the devil (Jack Nicholson) when attempting to find the "ultimate" man. Nicholson acted with Pfeiffer once again in Mike Nichols' 1994 film *Wolf*.

---

6. Which film was *not* directed by Carl Reiner?

a. *Enter Laughing* (1967)

b. *Where's Poppa?* (1970)

c. *Oh, God!* (1977)

d. *The End* (1978)

GAME 76 Q5 ANSWER d
"You come in here with a head full of mush and you leave thinking like a lawyer." So said Harvard Law School's Professor Kingsfield (played by John Houseman) in this 1973 film. Co-stars included Timothy Bottoms as a struggling law student, and Lindsay Wagner as Houseman's daughter and Bottoms' girlfriend.

8. The Oscar for Best Actor in 1955 went to:

a. James Dean in *East of Eden*

b. Frank Sinatra in *The Man With the Golden Arm*

c. Spencer Tracy in *Bad Day at Black Rock*

d. Ernest Borgnine in *Marty*

GAME 5 Q7 ANSWER c

Yankee Doodle Dandy gave Cagney a chance to return to his tap-dancing vaudevillian roots, and to help boost morale during World War II.

---

8. Which of the following actors died of a heart attack during the filming of a scene?

a. Errol Flynn

b. Buster Keaton

c. Gloria Grahame

d. Tyrone Power

GAME 25 Q7 ANSWER b

Kovacs was killed in 1962 when his Chevrolet Corvair skidded in the rain into a utility pole. (The car was highlighted in Ralph Nader's 1965 book, *Unsafe at Any Speed*.) Kovacs's cigar was a trademark prop, and he did a series of creative commercials for Dutch Masters. Kovacs's gravestone carries the epitaph, "Nothing in moderation."

---

8. Who sang to Johnny Carson on his next-to-last show on May 22, 1992?

a. Liza Minnelli

b. Barbra Streisand

c. Carol Burnett

d. Bette Midler

GAME 45 Q7 ANSWER a

A favorite guest of Letterman's, Andy Kaufman appeared with Lawler in 1982, a few months after their wrestling match had "apparently" put Kaufman into a neck brace. During an argument on the show, Lawler wound up slapping Kaufman right out of his chair. Everyone thought it was a real fight—me included. The fight was, in fact, staged.

---

8. Which British guitar hero had Rod Stewart as lead vocalist in the late 1960s?

a. Jeff Beck

b. Ritchie Blackmore

c. Eric Clapton

d. Jimmy Page

GAME 65 Q7 ANSWER b

Sting, whose real name is Gordon Sumner, plays a charismatic Mod gang leader named Ace in *Quadrophenia*. Although this film, produced by Who frontman Roger Daltrey, was moderately successful upon its release, Sting has starred mostly in stinkers. *Brimstone and Treacle* (1982), *Dune* (1984), and *The Bride* (1985) were all box-office duds.

5. Michael J. Fox starred in all of the following films *except:*

a. *Bright Lights, Big City* (1998)

b. *Family Business* (1989)

c. *Casualties of War* (1989)

d. *Light of Day* (1987)

GAME 16 Q4 ANSWER b

In spite of some box office disappointments, Brian De Palma has proven himself a gifted Hollywood director with films like *Carrie* (1976), *Dressed to Kill* (1980), *The Untouchables* (1987), and *Mission: Impossible* (1996). Just like his "Master of Suspense" predecessor Alfred Hitchcock, De Palma has never been nominated for an Academy Award.

---

5. Which of the following actors does *not* have a small role in Quentin Tarantino's *Pulp Fiction* (1994)?

a. Eric Stoltz

b. Patricia Arquette

c. Christopher Walken

d. Steve Buscemi

GAME 36 Q4 ANSWER c

Volunteers was a second attempt to successfully pair Tom Hanks with John Candy after their box office hit *Splash* (1984). Although *Volunteers* didn't do well at the box office, Hanks met Rita Wilson during the filming, and found romantic success with her—they were married shortly after the movie's release.

---

5. Along with Cher and Michelle Pfeiffer, who was the third witch in *The Witches of Eastwick*?

a. Angelica Houston

b. Susan Sarandon

c. Jane Fonda

d. Faye Dunaway

GAME 56 Q4 ANSWER c

Although no female has yet won this award, Wertmuller received a nomination for her direction of *Seven Beauties* (1976). To date, the only other female to receive a directing nomination is Jane Campion for *The Piano* (1993).

---

5. Who did *not* appear in the movie *The Paper Chase*?

a. Lindsay Wagner

b. Timothy Bottoms

c. John Houseman

d. Jane Kaczmarek

GAME 76 Q4 ANSWER b

Greystoke received three nominations, for Best Screenplay, Makeup, and Supporting Actor (Ralph Richardson). Leading lady Andie McDowell had trouble with her accent, so her voice was dubbed by Glenn Close. Co-screenwriter Robert Towne was so unhappy with the finished film, he gave his writing credit to P.H. Vazak, his pet sheepdog. The dog lost.

9. Which performer has been nominated for the most Oscars?

a. Jack Nicholson
b. Katharine Hepburn
c. Spencer Tracy
d. Laurence Olivier

Marty also won Oscars for Best Picture and Best Director, and for Paddy Cheyevsky's adaptation of his own play. Its line: "Whaddya wanna do tonight?" became the catch phrase of the day. In 1954, Borgnine also appeared in *Bad Day at Black Rock*, in which he says, "You mess with me and I'll kick a lung out of you." This did *not* become a catch phrase.

---

9. Where was Doors frontman Jim Morrison living when he died at age twenty-seven in 1971?

a. Los Angeles, California
b. Paris, France
c. Ghana, Africa
d. Seville, Spain

While on location for *Solomom & Sheba* in Madrid, Spain, Power died while filming a strenuous duel with actor George Sanders. He was forty-four years old. His scenes were later reshot with Yul Brynner in the role, but Power can still be seen in some of the film's long shots.

---

9. Whose talk show set wound up in Kramer's apartment in a *Seinfeld* episode?

a. Dick Cavett
b. Dinah Shore
c. Merv Griffin
d. Mike Douglas

As Carson listened quietly with tears in his eyes, the Divine Miss M poignantly performed "You Made Me Love You" (fondly parodied as "You Made Me Watch You"), "Here's That Rainy Day," and "One for My Baby."

---

9. How many drummers have appeared on studio albums by The Who, to date?

a. One
b. Two
c. Three
d. Four

Fresh from his tour of duty with The Yardbirds (which, incidentally, also employed the lead guitar services of both Eric Clapton and Jimmy Page), Jeff Beck put together his own group with Rod Stewart on lead vocals. The first album, *Truth*, is still regarded as one of the seminal rock-blues records of the 1960s.

4. Who directed the box office bomb *Bonfire of the Vanities* (1990)?

a. Ron Howard
b. Brian De Palma
c. Sydney Pollack
d. Michael Cimino

GAME 16 Q3 ANSWER b
Fresh from his Best Actor Oscar win for *The Goodbye Girl* (1977), Dreyfuss was not available for the George Lucas-produced sequel. Candy Clark and Paul LeMat returned as Debbie and John Milner, respectively, and so did Harrison Ford as the drag racer-turned-cop Bob Falfa.

---

4. On which film did Tom Hanks meet his future wife Rita Wilson?

a. *Bachelor Party* (1984)
b. *Punchline* (1988)
c. *Volunteers* (1985)
d. *Every Time We Say Goodbye* (1986)

GAME 36 Q3 ANSWER c
Actually, the other three actors have played musicians in films as well. Bridges played a moody jazz pianist in *The Fabulous Baker Boys* (1989), rock musician Marshall Crenshaw played Buddy Holly in the Richie Valens biopic *La Bamba* (1987), and Ed Begley, Jr. played drummer John "Stumpy" Pepys in Rob Reiner's *This Is Spinal Tap* (1984).

---

4. Which of the following women was an Oscar nominee for Best Director?

a. Nora Ephron
b. Barbra Streisand
c. Lina Wertmuller
d. Penny Marshall

GAME 56 Q3 ANSWER a
The award for Best Actor went to Peter Finch (posthumously); Best Actress, to Faye Dunaway; and Best Supporting Actress, to Beatrice Straight. To date, the only other movie to win three out of four acting awards is *A Streetcar Named Desire* (1951).

---

4. Which Tarzan film got the most Oscar nominations?

a. *Tarzan the Ape Man*
b. *Greystoke: The Legend of Tarzan, Lord of the Apes*
c. *Tarzan's Greatest Adventure*
d. *Disney's Tarzan*

GAME 76 Q3 ANSWER b
John Bridges directed this film about the Los Angeles fitness scene. *Perfect* also featured Marilu Henner and Laraine Newman, and boasted cameos from Carly Simon and Rolling Stone founder Jann Wenner. Travolta starred with Olivia Newton-John in *Two of a Kind*, Cynthia Rhodes in *Staying Alive*, and Debra Winger in *Urban Cowboy*.

10. Which of these Oscar-nominated comic actors did *not* win an Academy Award for his acting?

a. Dan Aykroyd

b. Woody Allen

c. Art Carney

d. Robin Williams

Hepburn has twelve nominations to her credit, all for Best Leading Actress. Her first win was for her second film, *Morning Glory* (1933). Her next was thirty-four years later for *Guess Who's Coming to Dinner*. She also won Oscars for *The Lion in Winter* (1968) and *On Golden Pond* (1982). No one else has won four Oscars for acting.

---

10. Which screenplay was Orson Welles rewriting on the night he died in 1985?

a. *The Dreamers*

b. *The Other Side of the Wind*

c. *The Big Brass Ring*

d. *The Magic Show*

Trying to live the life of the hardworking poet in Paris, France, Morrison was found dead in the bathtub by his long-time girlfriend, Pamela Courson. Interestingly, Morrison refers to each of these locations in his songs: Los Angeles ("L.A. Woman"); Africa ("Wild Child"); and Spain ("Spanish Caravan"). Paris, France is never mentioned in any Doors songs.

---

10. To date, who has been a national network TV late-night talk show host the longest?

a. Steve Allen

b. Jack Paar

c. David Letterman

d. Johnny Carson

In a 1998 episode, Kramer (Michael Richards) finds the set in a dumpster and puts it in his apartment. He then treats anyone who comes in as a guest on the brought-back-to-life talk show. Merv Griffin is one of TV's most successful game show producers, responsible for such shows as *Wheel of Fortune* and *Jeopardy*.

---

10. Which Rolling Stones album cover was designed by Andy Warhol?

a. *Sticky Fingers*

b. *Exile on Main Street*

c. *Some Girls*

d. *Tattoo You*

There have been only two drummers for The Who in the recording of studio albums: original drummer Keith Moon, who died at age thirty-two of an overdose; and Kenny Jones, who was the original drummer for The Small Faces.

3. Which actor from *American Graffiti* (1973) did *not* appear in the sequel, *More American Graffiti* (1978)?

a. Candy Clark

b. Richard Dreyfuss

c. Harrison Ford

d. Paul LeMat

GAME 16 Q2 ANSWER d

The year before, John Hurt starred in Ridley Scott's classic sci-fi horror film, *Alien* (1979). As the sensitive but hopelessly disfigured John Merrick, Hurt delivers the movie's most famous line, "I am not an animal!"

3. Who played rock-and-roll pioneer Buddy Holly in *The Buddy Holly Story* (1978)?

a. Jeff Bridges

b. Ed Begley Jr.

c. Gary Busey

d. Marshall Crenshaw

GAME 36 Q2 ANSWER b

Robbie Robertson, lead guitarist of The Band, has provided music in other Scorsese films like *The King of Comedy* (1982) and *The Color of Money* (1986). Led Zeppelin and Lynyrd Skynyrd have released live concert motion pictures—Led Zeppelin with *The Song Remains the Same* (1976), and Lynyrd Skynyrd with *Freebird . . . The Movie* (1996).

3. Which of the following films won three out of four Oscars for acting?

a. *Network* (1976)

b. *The Godfather* (1972)

c. *Dances with Wolves* (1990)

d. *Titanic* (1997)

GAME 56 Q2 ANSWER c

For her performances in *The Great Ziegfeld* (1936) and *The Good Earth* (1937), Luise Rainer was awarded the Best Actress Oscar. Back in the early 1970s, Luise's appearance on my show was one of the shining moments of my career.

3. Which John Travolta film starred Jamie Lee Curtis?

a. *Two of a Kind* (1983)

b. *Perfect* (1985)

c. *Staying Alive* (1983)

d. *Urban Cowboy* (1980)

GAME 76 Q2 ANSWER b

After releasing seven albums from 1972 to 1980, founding members Donald Fagen and Walter Becker ended their partnership as Steely Dan. A new Steely Dan album did not appear until 2000, when *Two Against Nature* won a Best Album Grammy along with three more for Best Pop Performance, Best Pop Vocal, and Best Engineered Album.

11. Which performer has won more Grammys?

a. Diana Ross
b. Barry Manilow
c. Donna Summer
d. Neil Diamond

GAME 5 Q10 ANSWER b
Although Allen was nominated for Best Actor in *Annie Hall* (1977), he lost to Richard Dreyfuss for his role in *The Goodbye Girl*. Best Supporting Actor awards were won by Art Carney for *Harry and Tonto* (1974), Dan Aykroyd for *Driving Miss Daisy* (1989), and Robin Williams for *Good Will Hunting* (1997).

11. How many crime bosses does Michael Corleone have killed during the baptism sequence at the end of *The Godfather*?

a. Three
b. Four
c. Five
d. Six

GAME 25 Q10 ANSWER d
Welles had tremendous difficulty in getting any of his film ideas produced in Hollywood after *Citizen Kane* (1941). *The Magic Show* had been planned as a kind of documentary on one of Welles' favorite subjects—magic. Orson once told me he would rather perform five minutes of magic tricks than act in any of Shakespeare's plays.

11. Which talk show host wrestled with women in an immense bowl of tossed salad?

a. Jay Leno
b. Steve Allen
c. Jack Paar
d. Conan O'Brien

GAME 45 Q10 ANSWER d
Although I remain the host who's been on TV the longest, at forty-three years, Carson took over NBC-TV's nationally broadcast *The Tonight Show* from Jack Paar, and ran with it for nearly thirty years, from October 1962 to May 1992. He retired after 4,531 episodes.

11. With which group did Eric Clapton record "Sunshine of Your Love"?

a. The Yardbirds
b. Cream
c. Derek & the Dominoes
d. Blind Faith

GAME 65 Q10 ANSWER a
That famous image of the tight pants with a real zipper on the album's front cover was pure Warhol, and echoed what he did with *The Velvet Underground & Nico* album, which featured a peelable banana.

2. Which British actor portrayed John Merrick in David Lynch's film *The Elephant Man* (1980)?

a. David Warner
b. Derek Jacobi
c. Alan Bates
d. John Hurt

GAME 16 Q1 ANSWER c
Though he was trained by German film-makers to shoot movies inside large film studios, Hitchcock often made many of his films on location. When shooting *The Wrong Man* with Henry Fonda, Hitch filmed all around the borough of Queens, because that's where the real story had taken place.

2. Which band was featured in Martin Scorsese's film *The Last Waltz* (1978)?

a. The Allman Brothers
b. The Band
c. Led Zeppelin
d. Lynyrd Skynyrd

GAME 36 Q1 ANSWER c
For at least thirty years, Hollywood directors have held the right to use this pseudonym if the final film is considered bad. This concept was satirized in the film *An Alan P. Smithee Film: Burn, Hollywood, Burn* (1998). The film's screenplay was written by Joe Eszterhas, controversial screenwriter of films like *Basic Instinct* (1992) and *Showgirls* (1996).

2. Who was the first person to win a best acting Oscar two years in a row?

a. Spencer Tracy
b. Tom Hanks
c. Luise Rainer
d. Katherine Hepburn

GAME 56 Q1 ANSWER b
For her performance in *Children of a Lesser God* (1986), Matlin won at age twenty-one. Though Tatum O'Neal and Anna Paquin were much younger than Matlin when they won Oscars for *Paper Moon* and *The Piano*, respectively, they won for *supporting* roles and not *lead* parts.

2. To date, how many Best Album Grammys has Steely Dan won?

a. None
b. One
c. Two
d. Three

GAME 76 Q1 ANSWER c
Glenn Ford was the good guy in this film, while ex-Marine Lee Marvin left his mark quite literally as a rotten thug. Richard Widmark gained instant notoriety in his first film *Kiss of Death* (1947) by pushing an old lady down a flight of stairs. Robert Mitchum frightened moviegoers everywhere as a psychotic preacher in *Night of the Hunter* (1955).

12. Who is the only performer to win an Oscar, an Emmy, a Grammy, and a Tony?

a. Barbra Streisand
b. Rita Moreno
c. Bernadette Peters
d. Carol Burnett

Donna Summer won five Grammys for "Last Dance" (1978), "Hot Stuff" (1979), "He's a Rebel" (1983), "Forgive Me" (1984), and "Carry On" (1997). Barry Manilow and Neil Diamond won one Grammy each—Manilow for "Copacabana" (1978) and Diamond for the score of *Jonathan Livingston Seagull* (1973). Diana Ross has not yet won a Grammy.

---

12. Which of the following musicians died in a helicopter crash?

a. John Bonham
b. Stevie Ray Vaughan
c. Jim Croce
d. Randy Rhoads

To establish full dominion over the organized crime syndicate, Michael has Barzini, Tattaglia, Stracci, Cuneo, and Jewish mobster Moe Greene *whacked,* as they say. He then orders the deaths of Tessio (Abe Vigoda) and brother-in-law Carlo (Gianni Russo), both of whom betrayed the family. In all, twenty-three people get killed in this movie.

---

12. Who hosted the public television talk show *Firing Line*?

a. Art Linkletter
b. Gore Vidal
c. William F. Buckley
d. Dick Cavett

Steve Allen, *The Tonight Show*'s original host in the mid-50s, was one of the funniest and nicest men I've ever known. He could also be very silly, like when he wrestled in salad or jumped into nine feet of Jell-O. I would say that Andy Kaufman's decision to wrestle women in the '70s and '80s was partly influenced by Allen's antics.

---

12. Which of the following hit songs was *not* sung by British singer Petula Clark?

a. "My Love"
b. "Don't Sleep in the Subway"
c. "Alfie"
d. "I Couldn't Live Without Your Love"

Paired with expert bass player and vocalist Jack Bruce and drummer Ginger Baker, Clapton had other big hits with Cream—"Strange Brew," "White Room," and "Badge" (co-written with Beatle George Harrison). After the group disbanded, Clapton went on to record one of his biggest hits, "Layla," with Derek & the Dominoes.

1. Which Hitchcock movie was partially filmed in Queens, New York?

a. *Topaz* (1969)

b. *Torn Curtain* (1966)

c. *The Wrong Man* (1956)

d. *I Confess* (1952)

The answer to this question is on:

page 212, top frame, right side.

1. An "Alan P. Smithee Film" is:

a. A film with no stars

b. A film with no screenplay

c. A film so bad that the director uses a pseudonym

d. A pornographic film

The answer to this question is on:

page 212, second frame, right side.

1. Who is the youngest female to win an Oscar for Best Actress in a Leading Role?

a. Anna Paquin

b. Marlee Matlin

c. Tatum O'Neal

d. Kirsten Dunst

The answer to this question is on:

page 212, third frame, right side.

1. Which actor throws a pot of scalding hot coffee into Gloria Grahame's face in *The Big Heat* (1953)?

a. Robert Mitchum

b. Richard Widmark

c. Lee Marvin

d. Glenn Ford

The answer to this question is on:

page 212, bottom frame, right side.

GAME 6

The Fab Four

How Well Do You Know The Beatles?

Turn to page 72 for the first question.

Moreno won a Best Supporting Actress Oscar for *West Side Story* (1962); two Emmys, one in 1977 for *The Muppet Show* and another in 1978 for *The Rockford Files;* a Grammy for her performance on 1972's *The Electric Company Album;* and a Tony in 1975 for her role as Googie Gomez in *The Ritz.*

GAME 26

Affairs to Remember

Notorious Couplings

Turn to page 72 for the first question.

Led Zeppelin drummer Bonham died in his sleep in 1980. Jim Croce died in a 1974 plane crash, while Ozzy Osbourne's guitarist Randy Rhoads died in 1982 aboard a plane that collided with a tour bus. Vaughan's helicopter crashed in Alpine Valley, Wisconsin, just after a concert with Eric Clapton in 1990.

GAME 46

Welcome to the '60s

A Decade of Peace, Love, and a Dozen Trivia Questions

Turn to page 72 for the first question.

During the show's run from 1965 to 1999, Buckley interviewed such diverse guests as Groucho Marx, "Beat" writer Jack Kerouac, and feminist Germaine Greer in an effort to inspire thought-provoking debate on a variety of issues. With my show, I've always preferred communication over confrontation—that's just my style.

GAME 66

A Rose by Any Other Name

Shakespeare Rears His Head

Turn to page 72 for the first question.

Written by Burt Bacharach and Hal David for the 1966 Michael Caine film of the same name, "Alfie" was a huge #1 hit for Cilla Black. The hit recording was produced by the brilliant Beatles record producer George Martin.

GAME 16

Memory Lane Grab Bag

Turn to page 211 for the first question.

GAME 15 Q12 ANSWER c
Robbie Rist played the blonde, bespectacled Cousin Oliver for the show's final six episodes. Robbie also appeared as Glendon, David Hartman's kid-next-door, in *Lucas Tanner;* and as David Baxter, the adopted son of Ted and Georgette, on *The Mary Tyler Moore Show*. Robbie is now a voiceover artist (he was one of the *Teenage Mutant Ninja Turtles*).

GAME 36

Memory Lane Grab Bag

Turn to page 211 for the first question.

GAME 35 Q12 ANSWER c
When novelist William Goldman wrote the screenplay for this film, it was first called *The Sundance Kid and Butch Cassidy*. The title was changed after Newman was cast as Butch Cassidy. The film's producer Darryl F. Zanuck wanted Newman to play Sundance, but director George Roy Hill wanted relative newcomer Robert Redford in the part.

GAME 56

Memory Lane Grab Bag

Turn to page 211 for the first question.

GAME 55 Q12 ANSWER b
Though he had only a few proper piano lessons as a youngster, Chico hobbled together enough of a playing technique to be able to tickle the ivories in his own unique and inimitable way. In many of the Marx Brothers films, you can see Chico shooting at notes on the keyboard as if his finger were a gun.

GAME 76

Memory Lane Grab Bag

Turn to page 211 for the first question.

GAME 75 Q12 ANSWER d
The Thin Red Line is set in the Pacific during World War II. Woody Harrelson, John Travolta, and George Clooney all agreed to cameos as military men just for the chance to work with legendary director Malick. Tommy Lee Jones played a psychologically scarred Vietnam vet in Oliver Stone's *Heaven and Earth* (1993).

GAME 6

1. John Lennon had only one solo #1 hit. What was it?

a. "Imagine"

b. "Whatever Gets You Through the Night"

c. "Instant Karma"

d. "Watching the Wheels"

The answer to this question is on:

page 73, top frame, right side.

GAME 26

1. Which Taylor was once married to Barbara Stanwyck?

a. Robert Taylor

b. Rod Taylor

c. Rip Taylor

d. Dub Taylor

The answer to this question is on:

page 73, second frame, right side.

GAME 46

1. Mr. Bob Dylan is the man behind which of these gentlemen?

a. Mr. Bojangles

b. Mr. Tambourine Man

c. Mean Mr. Mustard

d. Mr. Big Stuff

The answer to this question is on:

page 73, third frame, right side.

GAME 66

1. Which Humphrey Bogart movie ends with his character quoting from *The Tempest*?

a. *The African Queen* (1951)

b. *Angels With Dirty Faces* (1938)

c. *The Maltese Falcon* (1941)

d. *Key Largo* (1948)

The answer to this question is on:

page 73, bottom frame, right side.

72

12. Who was the cousin who lived with *The Brady Bunch* during the show's last season?

a. Ricky

b. Andrew

c. Oliver

d. Robbie

GAME 15 Q11 ANSWER d
Billy Gray played Bud, whose character's real name was Jim, Jr. He was joined by sisters Betty (Elinor Donahue), and Kathy (Lauren Chapin). *Father Knows Best* began as a radio show in 1948, starring Robert Young. Young followed the show to television when it first aired in 1954.

---

12. Who was supposed to play The Sundance Kid in *Butch Cassidy and the Sundance Kid* (1969)?

a. Warren Beatty

b. Clint Eastwood

c. Paul Newman

d. James Brolin

GAME 35 Q11 ANSWER c
Charles Grodin eventually played the part to deadpan perfection. DeNiro and Williams had been good friends ever since Williams was America's favorite alien on *Mork & Mindy.* Though they didn't work together on *Midnight Run,* DeNiro and Williams both did act a few years later in *Awakenings,* directed by "Laverne" herself, Penny Marshall.

---

12. Everybody knows that Harpo Marx played the harp. What musical instrument did Chico Marx play?

a. Drums

b. Piano

c. Trumpet

d. Tuba

GAME 55 Q11 ANSWER c
Released in 1950, this was the last Marx Brothers movie. The film was really a starring vehicle for Harpo, and Groucho had no real desire to appear in it. Then he saw Marilyn and suddenly became interested in the film. I can't blame him—Marilyn was one of the most beautiful women ever to walk the earth. Wonderful lady, simply stunning.

---

12. Which actor does *not* make a cameo appearance in Terrence Malick's *The Thin Red Line* (1998)?

a. Woody Harrelson

b. John Travolta

c. George Clooney

d. Tommy Lee Jones

GAME 75 Q11 ANSWER b
Due to the film's harsh anti-French sentiment, *Paths of Glory* was banned in France. Stanley Kramer gave us *On the Beach* in 1959, while British director Ronale Neame made *Tunes of Glory* in 1960. John Frankenheimer's first feature film was *The Manchurian Candidate* (1962).

2. When did the Silver Beetles become The Beatles?

a. 1958

b. 1960

c. 1961

d. 1964

The single, released in 1974, featured Elton John on piano and organ. After Lennon's death in 1980, Elton John's tribute song to him, "Empty Garden (Hey Hey, Johnny)," was on *Billboard's* Top 40 for seventeen weeks and peaked at #13.

---

2. Which of the following men was never married to Ava Gardner?

a. Frank Sinatra

b. Howard Hughes

c. Mickey Rooney

d. Artie Shaw

Stanwyck and matinee idol Robert Taylor were married from 1939 to 1951. They starred together in *His Brother's Wife* (1936) and *This Is My Affair* (1937).

---

2. Whose opening act was booed from the stage during The Monkees' 1967 U.S. tour?

a. Janis Joplin

b. Jimi Hendrix

c. Procol Harum

d. Stone Poneys

Bob Dylan met Roger McGuinn, lead guitarist of The Byrds, in January 1965. Dylan liked The Byrds and offered them his song "Mr. Tambourine Man" for their first album. This song was The Byrds' first hit, reaching #6 that June, and kicking off the folk rock era.

---

2. Which sci-fi film is based on a Shakespearean play?

a. *The Day the Earth Stood Still* (1951)

b. *Forbidden Planet* (1956)

c. *Metropolis* (1927)

d. *When Worlds Collide* (1951)

In Act IV of *The Tempest,* Prospero offers, "We are such stuff as dreams are made on, and our little life is rounded with a sleep." At the end of *The Maltese Falcon*, Sgt. Polhaus lifts the bird statue and asks, "What is it?" Sam Spade's response: "The, uh, stuff dreams are made of."

11. The son's name on *Father Knows Best* was:

a. Jeff

b. Danny

c. Barry

d. Bud

GAME 15 Q10 ANSWER b
Terry, played by Sherry Jackson, was one of the original Williams children. She and brother Rusty (Rusty Hamer), were later joined by stepsister Linda (Angela Cartwright).

11. Who was first approached to star opposite Robert DeNiro in *Midnight Run* (1988)?

a. Richard Dreyfuss

b. Danny DeVito

c. Robin Williams

d. Ted Danson

GAME 35 Q10 ANSWER b
The five actors considered for the part of Ness were Van Heflin, Van Johnson, Fred MacMurray, Jack Lord, and Cliff Robertson. *The Untouchables* ran on TV from 1959 to 1963, and was later made into a blockbuster motion picture by director Brian De Palma in 1987.

11. Marilyn Monroe had a small part in which Marx Brothers movie?

a. *A Night in Casablanca* (1946)

b. *The Big Store* (1941)

c. *Love Happy* (1949)

d. *A Girl in Every Port* (1952)

GAME 55 Q10 ANSWER a
After almost shooting himself, Allen's character goes for a walk and ends up in a revival house that's showing *Duck Soup*. In a poignant moment that stands as perhaps one of Allen's most optimistic film statements, the character decides that the fun of the Marx Brothers is what makes life worth living. I couldn't agree more.

11. Who directed the classic World War I film *Paths of Glory* (1958)?

a. Stanley Kramer

b. Stanley Kubrick

c. John Frankenheimer

d. Ronald Neame

GAME 75 Q10 ANSWER c
When Andrews' character returns from World War II combat, he soon discovers that he and his war bride (Virginia Mayo) have little in common. In the final scene, he declares his love for Peggy (Teresa Wright)—a sweet yet straightforward girl who shares his love of home and family.

GAME 6

3. Which Beatle is barefoot on the cover of _Abbey Road_?

a. John Lennon

b. Paul McCartney

c. George Harrison

d. Ringo Starr

The group was first known as The Quarrymen all those years ago in 1957. They then became Johnny & the Moondogs, and then The Silver Beetles. They became The Beatles in 1960. John's inspired spelling of "Beat"les was more of a reference to the rhythm of rock-and-roll than to the hipness of beatniks.

GAME 26

3. Which singer was married to Ernest Borgnine for just over one month?

a. Julie Andrews

b. Ethel Merman

c. Mary Martin

d. Bernadette Peters

After a brief marriage to Mickey Rooney, Gardner was pursued by billionaire Howard Hughes, but she turned down his many proposals. Shortly after her second marriage to bandleader Artie Shaw ended, she began her scandalous affair with "family man" Frank Sinatra. They married immediately after Sinatra's legal separation, but divorced in 1957.

GAME 46

3. Anne Bancroft won an Oscar for her role in:

a. _The Graduate_ (1967)

b. _The Turning Point_ (1977)

c. _The Miracle Worker_ (1962)

d. _The Pumpkin Eater_ (1964)

Hendrix was already popular in the UK ("Hey, Joe" reached #6 on the charts there), but he hadn't yet made his breakout performance at the Monterey Pop Festival. Monkees' fans didn't know what to make of Hendrix and the incredibly loud volume at which he played. Tired of the booing, Hendrix quit the tour after two weeks.

GAME 66

3. Disney's _The Lion King_ (1994) is based on which Shakespearean tragedy?

a. _Romeo and Juliet_

b. _Hamlet_

c. _Macbeth_

d. _Titus Andronicus_

Besides being possibly one of the best sci-fi films of its time, _Forbidden Planet_ is based on _The Tempest_. Dr. Mobius (Walter Pidgeon) is Prospero, Altaira (Anne Francis) is his virginal Miranda, and Robby the Robot seems to be his Ariel (or maybe his Caliban).

10. Danny Williams' oldest child on *Make Room for Daddy* was:

a. Rusty
b. Terry
c. Patty
d. Linda

GAME 15 Q9 ANSWER d
Shelley Fabares played the role of teenager Mary Stone on this show, which premiered in 1958. In 1962, she recorded the hit song "Johnny Angel." Fabares went on to play Craig T. Nelson's love interest on *Coach*, a 1990s hit sitcom that aired on ABC.

10. Before Robert Stack won the role, how many actors were offered the part of Eliot Ness on TV's *The Untouchables*?

a. Four
b. Five
c. Six
d. Seven

GAME 35 Q9 ANSWER d
Screenwriter Buck Henry claims they wanted big-name California types in the leads: Robert Redford, Candace Bergen, Doris Day, and even Ronald Reagan. In the novel, Benjamin has blond hair and blue eyes, and is six feet tall.

10. Which 1933 Marx Brothers movie convinces Woody Allen's character to not kill himself in *Hannah and Her Sisters* (1986)?

a. *Duck Soup*
b. *Animal Crackers*
c. *A Night at the Opera*
d. *Monkey Business*

GAME 55 Q9 ANSWER d
In an episode that featured Lucille Ball dressed as Harpo, the pair reenacted a hilarious "mirror scene" pantomime. Although they had stopped making feature films in the 1940s, the Marx Brothers continued to appear on TV in the 1950s—most notably with Groucho as host of *You Bet Your Life*.

10. In *The Best Years of Our Lives*, with which actress does Dana Andrews find true love?

a. Virginia Mayo
b. Myrna Loy
c. Teresa Wright
d. Gene Tierney

GAME 75 Q9 ANSWER a
Directed by Norman Jewison, *In Country* showed audiences that Willis was more than a smirky sitcom heartthrob. In *Jacknife*, Robert DeNiro is cast as a troubled Vietnam veteran; James Caan stars in *Gardens of Stone;* and *The War* has Kevin Costner in the lead role.

4. Which George Harrison-penned Beatles tune was to become a hit single?

a. "While My Guitar Gently Weeps"

b. "Here Comes the Sun"

c. "Something"

d. "Taxman"

GAME 6 Q3 ANSWER b
His lack of shoes is considered one of the clues tied to the "Paul Is Dead" rumor, as is the license plate with the number 28 IF, a rumored reference to Paul's age *if* he were alive when the 1969 album was released. The album has sold more than 9 million copies.

---

4. Orson Welles was married to which pin-up girl?

a. Betty Grable

b. Rita Hayworth

c. Jayne Mansfield

d. Jane Russell

GAME 26 Q3 ANSWER b
Borgnine, who has been married five times, wed Merman in 1964. Their marriage, called one of "Hollywood's legendary fiascoes," by movie critic/reviewer Leonard Maltin, lasted only thirty-two days.

---

4. Which Lennon-McCartney tune was a hit for Peter and Gordon?

a. "Goodbye"

b. "Come and Get It"

c. "World Without Love"

d. "It's for You"

GAME 46 Q3 ANSWER c
Bancroft won a Tony for her portrayal of Annie Sullivan in 1959, and then an Oscar for playing the same role in the 1962 film. She also received Oscar nominations for her work in *The Pumpkin Eater, The Graduate, The Turning Point,* and *Agnes of God.*

---

4. Who did *not* appear in *Shakespeare in Love* (1998)?

a. Gwyneth Paltrow

b. Ralph Fiennes

c. Geoffrey Rush

d. Judi Dench

GAME 66 Q3 ANSWER b
Simba is visited by his father's ghost; is ambivalent about taking his place on the throne; and has to deal with his evil uncle, who is now married to Simba's mother. You do the math . . .

9. What was the name of Donna Reed's daughter on *The Donna Reed Show*?

a. Peggy

b. June

c. Barbara

d. Mary

The three beautiful sisters were constantly being sought after by various men throughout the series, which ran on CBS from 1963 to 1970. In 1965, crop-duster Steve Elliot won the heart of Betty Jo; they eventually wed and had a daughter, Kathy Jo.

---

9. Who did the writers want to play Benjamin Braddock in *The Graduate* (1967)?

a. Gene Wilder

b. Warren Beatty

c. Paul Simon

d. Robert Redford

River Phoenix was already cast to play the interviewer when he died of a drug overdose outside Johnny Depp's club, The Viper Room. Christian Slater took the part, and is said to have donated his entire paycheck from the movie to Phoenix's favorite charities.

---

9. Which Marx Brother made a guest appearance on *I Love Lucy* in 1955?

a. Zeppo

b. Groucho

c. Chico

d. Harpo

Whether or not you think this first of the Marx Brothers' MGM films is one of their funniest, you must see it for the state-room scene and the contract negotiation between Groucho and Chico ("You can't fool me. There ain't no sanity clause.")

---

9. What film featured Bruce Willis as an emotionally battered Vietnam vet?

a. *In Country* (1989)

b. *Jacknife* (1989)

c. *Gardens of Stone* (1987)

d. *The War* (1994)

Considered by the director as his Vietnam trilogy, Stone wrote and directed *Platoon* (won the Best Picture Oscar), *Born on the Fourth of July* (won the Best Director Oscar), and *Heaven and Earth*.

5. Which Beatle was the first to have a #1 hit single after the group broke up?

a. John Lennon

b. Paul McCartney

c. George Harrison

d. Ringo Starr

GAME 6 Q4 ANSWER c
Harrison's only #1 hit with The Beatles, "Something" (1969), was released as a double A-side single soon after the release of *Abbey Road*. Harrison's "Here Comes the Sun" later became a hit for Richie Havens, who recorded it in 1971.

---

5. Who has been married the most times?

a. Zsa Zsa Gabor

b. Mickey Rooney

c. Elizabeth Taylor

d. Lana Turner

GAME 26 Q4 ANSWER b
The Brooklyn-born Magarita Carmen Cansino got her first film contract at age sixteen. Welles was her second of five husbands. The two met while she was engaged to Victor Mature. The year after they divorced, Hayworth co-starred with her ex-husband in *The Lady From Shanghai* (1948), which was also written and directed by Welles.

---

5. Who played piano on the demo for The Shangri-Las' first hit "Remember [Walkin' in the Sand]" in 1964?

a. Billy Preston

b. Little Richard

c. Elton John

d. Billy Joel

GAME 46 Q4 ANSWER c
In addition to "World Without Love," Peter and Gordon also had hits with the Lennon-McCartney songs "Nobody I Know" and "I Don't Want to See You Again." "It's for You" saw chart action for both Cilla Black and Three Dog Night. Badfinger recorded "Come and Get It," and Mary Hopkin had a hit with "Goodbye."

---

5. Which Shakespeare-based film does *not* star Julia Stiles?

a. *O* (2001)

b. *10 Things I Hate About You* (1999)

c. *Hamlet* (2000)

d. *A Midsummer Night's Dream* (1999)

GAME 66 Q4 ANSWER b
Shakespeare was played by Ralph's (pronounced "Rafe's") brother, Joseph Fiennes. Their sister, Martha Fiennes, directed the 1999 film *Onegin*, starring brother Ralph and Liv Tyler.

8. Who was *not* a Bradley sister on TV's *Petticoat Junction*?

a. Billie Jo

b. Bobbie Jo

c. Betty Jo

d. Becky Jo

GAME 15 Q7 ANSWER c

The name of Cliff and Clair's oldest daughter, played by Sabrina LeBeauf, was Sondra. The other daughters were played by Lisa Bonet (Denise), Tempestt Bledsoe (Vanessa), and Keshia Knight Pulliam (Rudy, whose character's real name was Rudith Lillian).

8. Who was originally cast as Daniel Malloy, who has an *Interview With the Vampire*?

a. River Phoenix

b. Christian Slater

c. Johnny Depp

d. Brad Pitt

GAME 35 Q7 ANSWER c

Tina Louise played the role of the sexy movie star. And speaking of alternate casting, Carroll O'Connor read for the role of the Skipper, Dabney Coleman tested for the Professor, and Raquel Welch lost the part of Mary Ann. As for Gilligan, Jerry Van Dyke turned it down before Bob Denver was offered the title part.

8. Groucho Marx's character in *A Night at the Opera* (1935) is:

a. Hugo Z. Hackenbush

b. Jeffrey T. Spaulding

c. Rufus T. Firefly

d. Otis B. Driftwood

GAME 55 Q7 ANSWER c

This early 1930s show featured Groucho and Chico. A moneymaker for sponsor Esso Oil, it was dropped after twenty-six weeks. According to Groucho, "Company sales, as a result of our show, had risen precipitously. Profits doubled in that brief time, and Esso felt guilty taking the money. . . . Those were the days of *guilt*-edged securities."

8. To date, how many films specifically about the Vietnam War has Oliver Stone written and directed?

a. One

b. Two

c. Three

d. Four

GAME 75 Q7 ANSWER d

This line was written by John Milius and spoken by Robert Duvall's character, Colonel Kilgore, in Francis Ford Coppola's nightmarish Vietnam film. Although it went into production in 1975, *Apocalypse Now* was not released until after Hal Ashby's *Coming Home* and Michael Cimino's *The Deer Hunter* won Oscars in 1978.

6. Which of these songs was *not* sung by The Beatles when they first appeared on *The Ed Sullivan Show*?

a. "I Want to Hold Your Hand"

b. "I Saw Her Standing There"

c. "Love Me Do"

d. "She Loves You"

GAME 6 Q5 ANSWER c

Harrison's 1970 three-record set, *All Things Must Pass*, included the hit "My Sweet Lord." In 1976, a lawsuit established that the song's melody had been plagiarized from The Chiffons' 1963 #1 hit, "He's So Fine."

---

6. Who was married to Eddie Fisher when his affair with Elizabeth Taylor was made public?

a. Connie Stevens

b. Debbie Reynolds

c. Joan Collins

d. Jaye P. Morgan

GAME 26 Q5 ANSWER a

Now there might be some controversy here. Zsa Zsa, the author of *How to Catch a Man, How to Keep a Man, How to Get Rid of a Man*, was married nine times, but legally only eight, the same number as Mickey and Liz. Lana was married eight times, but like Zsa Zsa, one marriage was declared invalid.

---

6. Who played the guitar solo on The Beatles' hit "While My Guitar Gently Weeps"?

a. George Harrison

b. Eric Clapton

c. Carl Perkins

d. Bob Dylan

GAME 46 Q5 ANSWER d

The classically trained fourteen-year-old Long Islander was pressed to play the hastily written song, which had been composed by producer George "Shadow" Morton on his way to the basement recording studio. Because he wasn't a union member, Joel was never paid for the job.

---

6. Which film, based on one of Shakespeare's works, won Oscars for Best Direction and Best Picture?

a. *Hamlet* (1948)

b. *The Lion in Winter* (1968)

c. *West Side Story* (1961)

d. *Romeo and Juliet* (1968)

GAME 66 Q5 ANSWER d

In her short career, Julia Stiles has already managed to tackle modern retellings of *Othello, The Taming of the Shrew,* and *Hamlet.*

7. Who was *not* one of the Huxtable daughters on TV's *The Cosby Show*?

a. Denise

b. Vanessa

c. Sabrina

d. Rudy

GAME 15 Q6 ANSWER b
Chuck Cunningham, played by Gavan O'Herlihy and Randolph Roberts during the show's first season, was written out, and Fonzie was given the task of becoming Richie's mentor.

7. Which role on *Gilligan's Island* did Jayne Mansfield turn down?

a. Mary Ann

b. Lovey

c. Ginger

d. Jayne

GAME 35 Q6 ANSWER a
TV stardom did not come without a price for Selleck, who lost the opportunity to play Indiana Jones because the *Magnum, P.I.* producers would not release him. Instead, Harrison Ford was given the plum part and the rest, as they say, is movie history.

7. Which of the following radio shows was Groucho Marx's first?

a. *You Bet Your Life*

b. *The Flotsam Family*

c. *Flywheel, Shyster, and Flywheel*

d. *Tell It to Groucho*

GAME 55 Q6 ANSWER c
As loony Fredonian President Rufus T. Firefly, Groucho practically steals the show with his rapid-fire assault of wit and wisecracks. Throughout the film, he is aided and abetted in his hilarious acts of anarchy by brothers Chico and Harpo, who are cast as presidential spies Chicolini and Pinky. As usual, brother Zeppo plays the straight man.

7. "I love the smell of napalm in the morning." Which war film contains this classic line?

a. *Uncommon Valor* (1983)

b. *The Green Berets* (1968)

c. *The Deer Hunter* (1978)

d. *Apocalypse Now* (1979)

GAME 75 Q6 ANSWER c
Director Sam Fuller wrote *The Big Red One* based on his World War II experiences. *Hell in the Pacific* starred Lee Marvin with Toshiro Mifune, while *Force Ten from Navarone* had Harrison Ford in the leading role. *The Longest Day* starred just about everybody. (I, however, wasn't able to clear my schedule for it . . .)

The Night I Had a *Spinal Tap* That Didn't Take

Back in 1983, I had a British rock band on my show called Spinal Tap. These three long-haired Englishmen went by the names David St. Hubbins, Nigel Tufnel, and Derek Smalls. Apparently, they were in the midst of their first American tour in a number of years. About midway through the interview, I got the distinct impression that the performers were a bit more eccentric than I had originally thought. As it turned out, the group was in fact an elaborate hoax—Carl Reiner's son, Rob, had just finished making his directorial debut with the film comedy *This Is Spinal Tap*.

Throughout the interview segment, I played everything straight and really believed that these three guys were British musicians in a group that had won praise as "one of England's loudest bands." True to the claim that the group had great punctuality, I can confirm that the boys showed up at our Manhattan soundstage right on time. I think they showed up at *eleven*—Spinal Tap fans will get this joke. The rest of you will just have to see the movie to know what I'm talking about.

I didn't know that the group was a joke until a few days later. Actually, I've been taken in by pranksters a few times over the years. Once there was an old-time singer named Johnny Downs who had a lot of big movies. This guy came on my show and introduced himself as Johnny Downs, and I only found out after the show that the man was in fact a doorman at some building in uptown Manhattan. In the end, it all balances out. The recent DVD release of *This Is Spinal Tap* features a portion of my show's interview with the band back in 1983. It's all in good fun, and my name gets around on every unit they sell . . . so what's the harm?

Hello, Dalí

I used to always take several of the guests from my show to lunch at the Hotel Des Artes across from the WABC television studios (or WJZ TV) after we'd do the program. Once, the brilliant but eccentric Spanish surrealist painter Salvador Dalí was one of my guests, so I took him and two other people for lunch. Thankfully, Dalí had mellowed a bit since the 1940s, when he was arrested for throwing a bathtub through a Macy's shop window after they changed his display design without permission—let me tell you, that would not have gone over too well with the owner of the Hotel Des Artes. Although Salvador usually traveled everywhere with his beautiful and mysterious wife, Gala, she was back at their hotel with a headache.

The lunch was relatively free of incident, and the entire bill came to about $7.95. This was for a complete meal served to four people—aah, *those* were the days. That was a lot of money back then, though. So I said to the waiter, "How about instead of money, I get Mr. Dalí to make a drawing for you on the back of the check?" The waiter said he'd have to go ask the restaurateur, an elegant Frenchwoman whose name I've forgotten. She authorized my request, and the waiter came back with the check. Dalí drew some flowers along with the requisite melting clock and signed his name on the back of the check.

About ten years ago, I ran into that waiter again and he told me that he later sold the check for about $10,000. It's amazing when a piece of paper with a drawing on it can be such a big draw (so to speak!). I'm kind of sorry that I didn't keep the check myself. Ever since the waiter told me his story, I've become a staunch supporter of the fine arts. Do you know of any world-famous painters who might like to appear on my show sometime soon?

GAME 6

7. Which Beatle has also been a successful film producer?

a. John Lennon
b. Paul McCartney
c. George Harrison
d. Ringo Starr

GAME 6 Q6 ANSWER c
When they first appeared on February 9, 1964, they performed five songs in all. The other two were "All My Loving" and "Till There Was You."

GAME 26

7. How many films did Katharine Hepburn and Spencer Tracy make together?

a. Fourteen
b. Twelve
c. Nine
d. Five

GAME 26 Q6 ANSWER b
Fisher and Reynolds, his first wife, had two children, Carrie and Todd. His son was named for Eddie's best friend, Mike Todd. Todd's widow was Elizabeth Taylor. Fisher starred with Reynolds in *Bundle of Joy* (1956) and with Taylor in *Butterfield 8* (1960). He also fathered two daughters with wife number 3, Connie Stevens.

GAME 46

7. Who was *not* a title character in the movie *Bob & Carol & Ted & Alice* (1969)?

a. Natalie Wood
b. Robert Urich
c. Elliott Gould
d. Dyan Cannon

GAME 46 Q6 ANSWER b
The tune was penned by George Harrison, whose marriage to his first wife, Patti Boyd, broke up when she began living with Eric Clapton. The former Mrs. Harrison was the inspiration for Clapton's "Layla." In 1987, Harrison invited Clapton to play lead guitar on his comeback solo album *Cloud Nine*. (By that time, Boyd had left Clapton as well.)

GAME 66

7. Which of the following actors does *not* appear in the 1996 film *Romeo + Juliet*?

a. Leonardo DiCaprio
b. John Leguizamo
c. Claire Danes
d. Ethan Hawke

GAME 66 Q6 ANSWER c
In 1962, *West Side Story* became the only film for which *two* directors were awarded the Oscar for Best Director: Jerome Robbins, who also directed the play, and Robert Wise, who also won for *The Sound of Music*.

GAME 15

6. What was the name of Richie Cunningham's older brother on TV's *Happy Days*?

a. Howard

b. Chuck

c. Arthur

d. Al

GAME 15 Q5 ANSWER b

Max Baer, Jr. played the role of Jethro Clampett, a handsome but simple-minded backwoods boy. Baer also appeared in the films *Macon County Line* (1974) and *The Wild McCullochs* (1975), which he also wrote, produced, and directed.

GAME 35

6. Tom Selleck was Spielberg's first choice for the lead in which film?

a. *Raiders of the Lost Ark* (1981)

b. *Star Wars* (1977)

c. *Schindler's List* (1993)

d. *Saving Private Ryan* (1998)

GAME 35 Q5 ANSWER b

As told in the 1991 documentary *Hearts of Darkness: A Filmmaker's Apocalypse*, director Francis Ford Coppola made the hard decision to replace actor Keitel after only three weeks of shooting. Martin Sheen was brought aboard to play the troubled military assassin Willard. He nearly died from a massive heart attack during the arduous shoot.

GAME 55

6. Which Marx Brothers movie finds Groucho sitting pretty as president of a make-believe country called Fredonia?

a. *Horse Feathers* (1932)

b. *A Night at the Opera* (1935)

c. *Duck Soup* (1933)

d. *Animal Crackers* (1930)

GAME 55 Q5 ANSWER d

In this 1968 Otto Preminger comedy, gangster Jackie Gleason is called out of retirement by Groucho, a mob kingpin named God. The film also features Mickey Rooney, Frankie Avalon, George Raft, and *Batman* villains Frank Gorshin and Cesar Romero.

GAME 75

6. Which World War II film starred Lee Marvin and Mark Hamill?

a. *Hell in the Pacific* (1968)

b. *Force Ten from Navarone* (1978)

c. *The Big Red One* (1980)

d. *The Longest Day* (1962)

GAME 75 Q5 ANSWER c

Directed by Richard Lester, who also directed John and The Beatles in *A Hard Day's Night* (1964) and *Help!* (1965), this film starred Michael Crawford as the lieutenant in charge of a WWII outfit whose mission is to set up a cricket field behind enemy lines. This was Lennon's first public appearance in what became his signature round glasses.

8. Which Beatles album featured the song "Nowhere Man"?

a. *Revolver*

b. *Rubber Soul*

c. *Help!*

d. *Yellow Submarine*

George started Handmade Films to help finance the Monty Python film *Life of Brian* (1978). He also produced *Time Bandits* (1981), *The Long Good Friday* (1982), *Mona Lisa* (1986), and over twenty other movies before selling his interest in Handmade Films in 1994.

---

8. When filming which picture did Humphrey Bogart and Lauren Bacall meet and fall in love?

a. *Key Largo*

b. *To Have and Have Not*

c. *The Big Sleep*

d. *Dark Passage*

They each received Oscar nominations for 1967's *Guess Who's Coming to Dinner*. Hepburn won, while Tracy lost to Rod Steiger for his role in *In the Heat of the Night*.

---

8. Jerry Lewis appeared opposite Tony Curtis in which film?

a. *Boeing, Boeing* (1965)

b. *Way . . . Way Out* (1966)

c. *The Big Mouth* (1967)

d. *Three on a Couch* (1966)

On the short-lived 1973 TV series, Robert Urich played Bob Sanders, but Robert Culp played the role in the film.

---

8. Who narrated Orson Welles' film *Chimes of Midnight*, adapted from the various Falstaff plays?

a. Sir John Gielgud

b. Sir Ralph Richardson

c. Burgess Meredith

d. John Houseman

This retelling of the "star-crossed lovers," directed by Baz Luhrmann, is one of the more radically modernized Shakespeare films to date. DiCaprio and Danes have the title roles, and Leguizamo plays Tybalt. In 2000, Ethan Hawke starred in the modern-dress screen version of *Hamlet*.

5. Jed's son on *The Beverly Hillbillies* was:

a. Abner

b. Jethro

c. Ollie

d. Eb

GAME 15 Q4 ANSWER d
Following in the footsteps of the Nelsons (*The Adventures of Ozzie and Harriet*), whose sons played themselves on the 1944 radio show, Burns and Allen decided to let their son, Ronnie, play himself.

---

5. Which actor was hired and then fired from the lead role in *Apocalypse Now* (1979)?

a. Al Pacino

b. Harvey Keitel

c. Robert DeNiro

d. Jon Voight

GAME 35 Q4 ANSWER b
Comic actor Chris Farley was first cast as the voice of Shrek in this 2001 animated hit, but he died before the movie was made. When Mike Myers took the part, his lovable Scottish accent gave the jolly green ogre a life all his own. *Shrek* received Oscar nominations for Best Adapted Screenplay and Best Animated Feature Film, which it won.

---

5. What was Groucho Marx's final film?

a. *Love Happy*

b. *A Night in Casablanca*

c. *Will Success Spoil Rock Hunter?*

d. *Skidoo*

GAME 55 Q4 ANSWER b
When gangster Bugsy Siegel was murdered, a check from Chico for gambling losses was in his pocket. (According to Groucho, "It was probably a good thing he didn't cash it!")

---

5. John Lennon appeared in which "war" film?

a. *What Did You Do in the War, Daddy?* (1966)

b. *Oh, What a Lovely War* (1969)

c. *How I Won the War* (1967)

d. *Suppose They Gave a War and Nobody Came?* (1970)

GAME 75 Q4 ANSWER c
Fox and Sean Penn headlined a cast that included Ving Rhames, John Leguizamo, and John C. Reilly in the 1989 Brian De Palma war epic.

9. What was The Beatles' first #1 hit in America?

a. "Twist and Shout"

b. "Can't Buy Me Love"

c. "I Want to Hold Your Hand"

d. "She Loves You"

GAME 6 Q8 ANSWER b
Although "Nowhere Man" was featured in the 1968 animated film *Yellow Submarine,* the song is found on the group's 1965 *Rubber Soul* album. The film also includes "When I'm Sixty-Four," from the album *Sgt. Pepper's Lonely Hearts Club Band* (1967), and "Eleanor Rigby" from *Revolver* (1966).

---

9. Which film did *not* feature both Tim Robbins and Susan Sarandon?

a. *The Player* (1992)

b. *Dead Man Walking* (1995)

c. *The Cradle Will Rock* (1999)

d. *Bob Roberts* (1992)

GAME 26 Q8 ANSWER b
Bogey met Bacall on the set of this 1944 film noir classic and it was love at first sight. Bacall was only nineteen years old, while Bogart was forty-four and on his third marriage. Bogart married Bacall in 1945, and they shared a happy life together until Bogart died from cancer in 1957.

---

9. Who co-starred with Anthony Quinn in *Zorba the Greek*?

a. Michael York

b. Alan Bates

c. Richard Chamberlain

d. Richard Harris

GAME 46 Q8 ANSWER a
For a change, Lewis played the subdued character in this bedroom comedy about a playboy bachelor, who must juggle his schedule of flight attendant girlfriends so they don't run into each other.

---

9. Which Shakespearean play did French filmmaker Jean-Luc Godard make a film of in 1987?

a. *As You Like It*

b. *Measure for Measure*

c. *King Lear*

d. *Cymbeline*

GAME 66 Q8 ANSWER b
Gielgud played King Henry IV in this 1966 film; Burgess Meredith played Prince Hal in *Five Kings,* Welles' 1939 theatrical production based on the Falstaff character; and John Houseman was Welles' business partner in the 1930s and 1940s, when the Mercury Theatre took Broadway, radio, and then film by storm.

4. What was the name of George Burns and Gracie Allen's son on their TV show?

a. Robbie
b. Ricky
c. Ralph
d. Ronnie

GAME 15 Q3 ANSWER c
Jerry Mathers played the role of Theodore "Beaver" Cleaver on this TV sitcom, which began its six-season run in 1957. Theodore was also the name of one of the singing Chipmunks (along with Alvin and Simon). Beavers . . . chipmunks . . . I don't know any other rodents named Theodore.

4. Who was supposed to be the voice of Shrek before Mike Myers got the role?

a. Robin Williams
b. Chris Farley
c. Adam Sandler
d. Dana Carvey

GAME 35 Q3 ANSWER c
The producers and writers found they had to change the character too much to fit Lisa's personality. Peri Gilpen was recast in the role. Kudrow scored her break as the ditzy waitress, Ursula, on *Mad About You* in 1993. When *Friends* debuted in 1994, she was cast as Phoebe, Ursula's twin sister.

4. Which Marx Brother was a notorious gambler?

a. Groucho
b. Chico
c. Harpo
d. Gummo

GAME 55 Q3 ANSWER c
The three films are *A Night at the Opera* (1935), *A Day at the Races* (1937), and *A Night in Casablanca* (1946). Not including a little-seen silent film, the brothers teamed up in thirteen movies. Additionally, Groucho, Chico, and Harpo appeared in separate segments of Irwin Allen's 1957 camp classic *The Story of Mankind.*

4. Michael J. Fox appeared in which Vietnam war film?

a. *Born on the Fourth of July* (1989)
b. *Full Metal Jacket* (1987)
c. *Casualties of War* (1989)
d. *Platoon* (1986)

GAME 75 Q3 ANSWER d
What's more, all three films were released by 20th Century Fox. *Catch-22* was yet another war movie released in 1970, adding to the antiwar sentiment of the Vietnam era. *The Dirty Dozen* was released in 1967 and featured Donald Sutherland, one of the future stars of *M*A*S*H.*

10. In 1967, John Lennon and Paul McCartney sang backup vocals for which group?

a. Cream

b. The Who

c. Three Dog Night

d. The Rolling Stones

GAME 6 Q9 ANSWER c
On January 18, 1964, "I Want to Hold Your Hand" broke into *Billboard*'s Top 100 at #45. Within a week, it jumped to #3; the next week, it topped the chart. By the end of March, "She Loves You," "Please Please Me," "Twist and Shout," and "Can't Buy Me Love" filled out the top five slots.

---

10. Which couple appeared together in the most films?

a. Laughton & Lanchester

b. Burton & Taylor

c. Cronyn & Tandy

d. Bogart & Bacall

GAME 26 Q9 ANSWER b
Dead Man Walking was co-written, produced, and directed by Robbins, but starred Sarandon and Sean Penn. Their first (and best-known) co-starring vehicle was *Bull Durham* (1988), which also starred Kevin Costner. Robbins and Sarandon met during the filming of that film.

---

10. In *The Graduate* (1967), what one word of advice is given to Benjamin Braddock at his graduation party?

a. "Plastics"

b. "Women"

c. "Land"

d. "Money"

GAME 46 Q9 ANSWER b
In the 1964 film, Bates plays the tormented British writer who finds a very important friend in Quinn's character—a life-loving Greek peasant.

---

10. Who played Iago to Laurence Fishburne's *Othello* in the 1995 film directed by Oliver Parker?

a. Bob Hoskins

b. Christopher Walken

c. Kenneth Branagh

d. Derek Jacobi

GAME 66 Q9 ANSWER c
This must be one of the strangest Shakespeare adaptations in the world. Molly Ringwald was living in France at the time of filming, so it was easy to get her for the part of Cordelia. What amazes me is how Godard was able to convince Woody Allen, notorious for never wanting to leave Manhattan, to travel overseas for a brief appearance as the Fool.

3. On *Leave it to Beaver*, what was "Beaver" Cleaver's real name?

a. Alvin
b. Wally
c. Theodore
d. Simon

GAME 15 Q2 ANSWER d
After debating over a wide range of names for their new son, Rob and Laura decided on Ritchie. They also gave him the middle name Rosebud, an acronym for Robert, Oscar, Sam, Edward, Benjamin, Ulysses, and David—the names they didn't choose.

3. Which *Friends'* star was originally hired to play *Frasier's* producer, Roz Doyle?

a. Courtney Cox
b. Matthew Perry
c. Lisa Kudrow
d. Jennifer Aniston

GAME 35 Q2 ANSWER c
Hackman was also first in line to play Hannibal Lecter in *The Silence of the Lambs* (1991). Ironically, he was *sixth* in line for the part of "Popeye" Doyle, his Oscar-winning character in *The French Connection*.

3. How many "day" and "night" films did the Marx Brothers make?

a. One
b. Two
c. Three
d. Four

GAME 55 Q2 ANSWER b
Groucho's real name was Julius, Harpo's was Adolf (Arthur), and Zeppo's was Herbert. Gummo, who played the group's straight man on the vaudeville stage, was born Milton. Gummo and Zeppo eventually left the act to become agents.

3. Which war movie was *not* released in 1970?

a. *Patton*
b. *M*A*S*H*
c. *Tora! Tora! Tora!*
d. *The Dirty Dozen*

GAME 75 Q2 ANSWER b
Bob Newhart played the role in Mike Nichols' 1970 adaptation of the Joseph Heller novel. The film starred Alan Arkin as Captain John Yossarian, the B-25 bombardier trying to be declared insane so he can go home. The all-star cast also included Jon Voight, Anthony Perkins, Martin Sheen, Orson Welles, and screenwriter Buck Henry.

11. Which former Beatle recorded an album with Bob Dylan?

a. John Lennon

b. Paul McCartney

c. George Harrison

d. Ringo Starr

GAME 6 Q10 ANSWER d
Lennon and McCartney harmonized on "We Love You," a single released by The Rolling Stones. Mick Jagger returned the favor later that year by joining the chorus on the Fab Four's "All You Need Is Love."

11. To date, which actor has *not* been linked romantically with co-star Diane Keaton?

a. Al Pacino

b. Warren Beatty

c. Steve Martin

d. Mel Gibson

GAME 26 Q10 ANSWER b
The winners are Burton and Taylor with eleven, averaging over a movie a year for the ten years of their first marriage. Laughton and Lanchester come in a close second with ten films in over thirty years of marriage. Tandy and Cronyn shared nine films in their fifty-two years. Bogey and Bacall celebrated five films in twelve years of marriage.

11. Which of The Monkees was the first to quit the group?

a. Mike Nesmith

b. Mickey Dolenz

c. Peter Tork

d. Davey Jones

GAME 46 Q10 ANSWER a
In the opening scene of this film, a family friend gives uninspired college graduate Braddock (Dustin Hoffman) the key to success with this single word of advice. Originally, the filmmakers wanted Robert Redford to play Braddock, who was a blue-eyed blond in the novel. Redford and Hoffman would eventually work together in *All the President's Men*.

11. Which actor directed, wrote, and starred in *Looking for Richard*, a film about Shakespeare's plays?

a. Kevin Spacey

b. Alec Baldwin

c. Kevin Kline

d. Al Pacino

GAME 66 Q10 ANSWER c
Hoskins played a monstrous Iago to Anthony Hopkin's tragic Moor in the 1981 BBC-TV production. Walken played the role as a punk-rocker opposite Raul Julia in a 1991 stage version performed in Central Park. Derek Jacobi played Cassio in the 1965 British film, which starred Sir Laurence Olivier as Othello.

2. On *The Dick Van Dyke Show,* Rob and Laura Petrie's son was:

a. Buddy

b. Robby

c. Alan

d. Ritchie

GAME 15 Q1 ANSWER c

The original Junior was Lanny Rees, who played the role under Jackie Gleason's "Riley." The sitcom lasted only one season (1949/50), but returned three years later with an entirely new cast. William Bendix replaced Gleason, Wesley Morgan took over as Junior. Egbert was the son of Jim Gillis, Riley's friend and coworker.

2. Who did the producers initially want to play the father on *The Brady Bunch*?

a. Robert Reed

b. Jack Lemmon

c. Gene Hackman

d. Ted Knight

GAME 35 Q1 ANSWER b

Lee J. Cobb was also considered for the role, which went to Peter Falk. The character of Columbo first appeared in "Enough Rope," a 1961 segment of *The Sunday Mystery Hour* anthology shows. Bert Freed played the lieutenant. Peter Falk first played the role in the 1968 television adaptation of the play *Prescription: Murder.*

2. What was Chico Marx's real name?

a. Julius

b. Leonard

c. Arthur

d. Herbert

GAME 55 Q1 ANSWER b

After a successful run on Broadway with the George S. Kaufman play *The Cocoanuts*, the Marx Brothers were approached by MGM to do a movie version in 1929. Groucho was a notorious ad-libber. During one stage performance, Kaufman exclaimed, "There must be some mistake. I thought I heard one of the original lines of the play."

2. Which wartime film has a character named Major Major?

a. *Slaughterhouse Five*

b. *Catch 22*

c. *M*A*S*H*

d. *Full Metal Jacket*

GAME 75 Q1 ANSWER b

This 1968 film was John Wayne's salute to the Special Forces. Among other things, it was noted for its realistic sets of Vietnamese villages, which were later used by the Army for training soldiers bound for Vietnam. The other three films came out in 1978.

12. How many Beatles songs made the *Billboard* Top 100 in 1964, the year of their U.S. debut?

a. Five

b. Six

c. Eleven

d. Fourteen

GAME 6 Q11 ANSWER c
In 1988, George, Bob Dylan, Tom Petty, Roy Orbison, and Jeff Lynne recorded *The Traveling Wilburys Volume 1,* the first album by the fictional half-brothers Nelson, Lucky, Charlie T., Jr, Lefty, and Otis Wilbury. Their second album was *The Traveling Wilburys Volume 3.*

12. In which film did real-life couple Woody Allen and Mia Farrow portray a married couple breaking up?

a. *Husbands and Wives*

b. *Alice*

c. *Crimes and Misdemeanors*

d. *Shadows and Fog*

GAME 26 Q11 ANSWER d
Although Keaton has had a number of publicized off-screen relationships with her co-stars, Gibson, with whom she starred in the 1984 film *Mrs. Soffel,* wasn't one of them.

12. As seen in the film *Lenny* (1974), where was comic Lenny Bruce *not* arrested for obscenity?

a. San Francisco, California

b. Chicago, Illinois

c. New York, New York

d. San Diego, California

GAME 46 Q11 ANSWER c
You were thinking it was Mike, right? Actually, it was Peter Tork who quit the group in 1968 to pursue a solo career. Not much was heard from Tork until The Monkees' reunion in the mid-1980s. Their #1 hit song at the time, "That Was Then (This Is Now)," was written by Long Island singer/songwriter Vance Brescia.

12. Which actor does *not* appear in Kenneth Branagh's 1999 film *Hamlet*?

a. Charlton Heston

b. Billy Crystal

c. Michael Keaton

d. Julie Christie

GAME 66 Q11 ANSWER d
Method actor Pacino has long held the Immortal Bard in great esteem, and his 1996 film is about both the study and the performing of Shakespearean plays. Pacino is joined in the film by Alec Baldwin, Kevin Kline, Kevin Spacey, Winona Ryder, and Aidan Quinn, all of whom perform scenes from *Richard III.*

GAME 15

1. On TV's *Life of Riley*, who was Chester Riley's son?

a. Butch
b. Eddie
c. Junior
d. Egbert

The answer to this question is on:

page 198, top frame, right side.

GAME 35

1. Bing Crosby was the first choice to play which TV detective?

a. Ellery Queen
b. Lieutenant Columbo
c. Barnaby Jones
d. "Mac" McMillan

The answer to this question is on:

page 198, second frame, right side.

GAME 55

1. The Marx Brothers first starred in which Hollywood movie?

a. *A Day at the Races*
b. *The Cocoanuts*
c. *Animal Crackers*
d. *A Night at the Opera*

The answer to this question is on:

page 198, third frame, right side.

GAME 75

1. Which film about Vietnam was released while the war was still being fought?

a. *Coming Home*
b. *The Green Berets*
c. *The Deer Hunter*
d. *Go Tell the Spartans*

The answer to this question is on:

page 198, bottom frame, right side.

197

GAME 7

Start Spreading the News

Questions about Frank Sinatra

Turn to page 86 for the first question.

Turn to page 86 for the first question.

GAME 27

Barbra Streisand

The Way Babs Was

Turn to page 86 for the first question.

Turn to page 86 for the first question.

GAME 47

"We Had Faces!"

The Silent Film Era

Turn to page 86 for the first question.

Turn to page 86 for the first question.

GAME 67

Movies of the '30s

From Soup to Screwball

Turn to page 86 for the first question.

Turn to page 86 for the first question.

GAME 15

Kids, Kids, Kids

Children of TV Families

*Turn to page 197
for the first question.*

GAME 14 Q12 ANSWER c
West Side Story (1961), *The Sound of Music* (1965), and *Oliver!* (1968) were all Best Picture winners. *Cabaret* (1972) lost the award to *The Godfather*. More recent musicals nominated for Best Picture are *Moulin Rouge* (2001) and *Beauty and the Beast* (1991), which was the first animated film ever nominated for this award.

GAME 35

Role Play

**Who Was Supposed
to Play That Part?**

*Turn to page 197
for the first question.*

GAME 34 Q12 ANSWER d
Turner again played an investigative type along with Dennis Quaid in *Undercover Blues* (1993). However, she hasn't always garnered such law-abiding roles. She's also played a hitwoman opposite Jack Nicholson in John Huston's *Prizzi's Honor* and a prostitute to Anthony Perkins' sinister minister in Ken Russell's *Crimes of Passion*.

GAME 55

"X Marx the Spot"

Meet the Marx Brothers

*Turn to page 197
for the first question.*

GAME 54 Q12 ANSWER a
Although Baldwin and supermodel Crawford made a great-looking couple in this film, the movie was a box-office disappointment. In *Backdraft*, Baldwin had a tryst with Jennifer Jason Leigh, while *Sliver* had him paired with Sharon Stone. In *Flatliners*, Baldwin co-starred with Julia Roberts, but they weren't involved romantically.

GAME 75

Them's Fightin' Words

War Movies

*Turn to page 197
for the first question.*

GAME 74 Q12 ANSWER c
Drew Barrymore provided the voice of Akima in the animated feature *Titan A.E.* (2000); Cameron Diaz supplied the voice of Princess Fiona in the smash hit *Shrek* (2001); and Meg Ryan was the voice of the sole survivor of Russia's Romanoff family in the animated musical *Anastasia* (1997).

GAME 7	**1.** In 1960, Frank Sinatra made *Billboard's* Top 40 with which children's song? **a.** "Old MacDonald" **b.** "Yankee Doodle" **c.** "This Old Man" **d.** "Frère Jacques"	The answer to this question is on: **page 87, top frame, right side.**
GAME 27	**1.** Streisand recorded a duet with which disco diva? **a.** Gloria Gaynor **b.** Donna Summer **c.** Debbie Harry **d.** Aretha Franklin	The answer to this question is on: **page 87, second frame, right side.**
GAME 47	**1.** Which comic silent film star appears briefly as himself in *Sunset Boulevard* (1950)? **a.** Charlie Chaplin **b.** Buster Keaton **c.** Harold Lloyd **d.** Fatty Arbuckle	The answer to this question is on: **page 87, third frame, right side.**
GAME 67	**1.** How many films did Fred Astaire and Ginger Rogers appear in together? **a.** Five **b.** Seven **c.** Ten **d.** Fourteen	The answer to this question is on: **page 87, bottom frame, right side.**

12. What was the last movie musical to win the Oscar for Best Picture?

a. *West Side Story*

b. *Cabaret*

c. *Oliver!*

d. *The Sound of Music*

GAME 14 Q11 ANSWER a
This 1997 film also features "I Say a Little Prayer." Both songs, which were hits of the 1960s, were written by Burt Bacharach and Hal David, and sung by Dionne Warwick.

---

12. Who played detective V. I. Warshawski in the 1991 film of the same name?

a. Meryl Streep

b. Glenn Close

c. Michelle Pfeiffer

d. Kathleen Turner

GAME 34 Q11 ANSWER a
This was the only film featuring Finney as Hercule Poirot, the Belgian detective. Poirot has been played by Ustinov in three films, and by Suchet on television. Morley appeared in *The Alphabet Murders*, a 1966 Poirot film, but the detective himself was played by Tony Randall.

---

12. Which film paired Cindy Crawford and William Baldwin?

a. *Fair Game* (1995)

b. *Backdraft* (1991)

c. *Flatliners* (1990)

d. *Sliver* (1993)

GAME 54 Q11 ANSWER a
Deneuve, who made her screen debut at age thirteen and is considered one of French cinema's "grandes dames," played an erotic vampire in *The Hunger*.

---

12. Who provided the voice of the Blue Fairy in *A.I.: Artificial Intelligence*?

a. Drew Barrymore

b. Cameron Diaz

c. Meryl Streep

d. Meg Ryan

GAME 74 Q11 ANSWER a
Since its release in December 1997, *Titanic* has grossed over $1.8 billion worldwide to date. The film continues to hold the record for the longest run at the top of the box office with fifteen straight weeks. *Titanic* also won eleven Oscars, including Best Picture.

2. Frank Sinatra won his first Oscar for his role in:

a. *The Man With the Golden Arm* (1955)

b. *Guys and Dolls* (1955)

c. *The Manchurian Candidate* (1962)

d. *From Here to Eternity* (1953)

GAME 7 Q1 ANSWER a

In a conversation with singer Bobby Darin, Sinatra boasted that he could make any song a hit. Darin then bet him that he couldn't make a children's song like "Old MacDonald" a hit. Darin lost the bet.

---

2. What was Barbra Streisand's role in *The Owl and the Pussycat* (1970)?

a. College radical

b. Prostitute

c. College dropout

d. Brooklyn housewife

GAME 27 Q1 ANSWER b

Their #1 hit "No More Tears (Enough is Enough)" was the fourth #1 single for both artists. Streisand's other #1 hits were "The Way We Were," "Love Theme From A Star Is Born (Evergreen)," and "You Don't Bring Me Flowers" with Neil Diamond. Summer's three #1 hits were "MacArthur Park," "Hot Stuff," and "Bad Girls."

---

2. Who was *not* one of the founders of United Artists?

a. Douglas Fairbanks

b. Charlie Chaplin

c. Carl Laemmle

d. D.W. Griffith

GAME 47 Q1 ANSWER b

The Billy Wilder masterpiece starring Gloria Swanson, William Holden, and Erich von Stroheim, also features cameos by Cecil B. DeMille and Hedda Hopper, who appear as themselves.

---

2. Frank Capra won Academy Awards for directing all of these films *except:*

a. *It Happened One Night*

b. *Mr. Deeds Goes to Town*

c. *You Can't Take It With You*

d. *Mr. Smith Goes to Washington*

GAME 67 Q1 ANSWER c

From the 1933 Dolores Del Rio vehicle *Flying Down to Rio*, to 1939's *The Story of Vernon and Irene Castle*, Astaire and Rogers cut many a black-and-white rug together. Then, ten years later, they got together in Technicolor for the first time in Comden and Green's *The Barkleys of Broadway*.

11. In *My Best Friend's Wedding*, what song does Cameron Diaz sing at a karaoke bar?

a. "I Just Don't Know What to Do With Myself"

b. "Walk on By"

c. "I Say a Little Prayer"

d. "Wishin' and Hopin'"

GAME 14 Q10 ANSWER d
Crosby recorded the song with the Williams Brothers in early 1944. Among the brothers was Andy, the thirteen-year-old who would later become known for his version of Henry Mancini's "Moon River."

11. The detective in *Murder on the Orient Express* (1974) was played by:

a. Albert Finney

b. Robert Morley

c. Peter Ustinov

d. David Suchet

GAME 34 Q10 ANSWER a
During the show's last season (1979/80), Selleck played Lance White, James Garner's nearly perfect rival detective.

11. Who starred with David Bowie and Susan Sarandon in Tony Scott's creepy vampire thriller *The Hunger* (1984)?

a. Catherine Deneuve

b. Kathleen Turner

c. Candy Clark

d. Geena Davis

GAME 54 Q10 ANSWER d
The Emmy award-winning actress has four boys. On *Everybody Loves Raymond*, she has a daughter and twin sons. Heaton was born and raised in Cleveland, Ohio, but lives with her family in Los Angeles, where the show is taped.

11. What was the #1 box office moneymaker of the 1990s?

a. *Titanic* (1997)

b. *Jurassic Park* (1993)

c. *Forrest Gump* (1994)

d. *Mrs. Doubtfire* (1993)

GAME 74 Q10 ANSWER d
Amazingly, this show "about nothing" ran from 1990 to 1998. Its colorful cast of characters (headed by Jerry Seinfeld) and often outrageous story lines provided weekly water-cooler conversation and enough *Seinfeld*-isms (including such classics as "shrinkage," "sponge worthy," and "master of one's own domain") to last a lifetime.

3. Which of Sinatra's early movies was a remake of a Marx Brothers film?

a. *Step Lively* (1944)

b. *It Happened in Brooklyn* (1947)

c. *Double Dynamite* (1951)

d. *Till the Clouds Roll By* (1946)

GAME 7 Q2 ANSWER d
Sinatra had been a singing lead in romantic comedies when his vocal cords hemorrhaged in 1952. He pleaded for the nonsinging supporting role of Private Angelo Maggio in *From Here to Eternity*, taking it away from Eli Wallach. The movie launched Sinatra's new career as a dramatic actor.

3. Which actor does Barbra Streisand's character kill in the 1987 film *Nuts*?

a. Leslie Nielsen

b. Karl Malden

c. Eli Wallach

d. Richard Dreyfuss

GAME 27 Q2 ANSWER b
Streisand played Doris, a good-hearted hooker, opposite George Segal's mild-mannered Felix in this film. She was college dropout Judy Maxwell in *What's Up, Doc?* (1972), college radical Katie Morowsky in *The Way We Were* (1973), and housewife "Henry" Robbins who gets involved with loan sharks in *For Pete's Sake* (1974).

3. Which was the first movie actually made in Hollywood?

a. *The Gold Seekers*

b. *The Squaw Man*

c. *Man's Lust for Gold*

d. *In Old California*

GAME 47 Q2 ANSWER c
Along with Fairbanks, Chaplin, and Griffith, "America's Sweetheart," Mary Pickford, was the fourth artist involved with this independent film distribution company, which was formed in 1919. Laemmle was the father of Universal Pictures, which specialized in monster movies like *Dracula* with Bela Lugosi and *Frankenstein* with Boris Karloff.

3. Which actor was *not* one of Judy Garland's companions in *The Wizard of Oz*?

a. Ray Bolger

b. Buddy Ebsen

c. Bert Lahr

d. Jack Haley

GAME 67 Q2 ANSWER d
Along with these three Oscars (his only winners), Capra received a Best Director nomination for *Mr. Smith Goes to Washington* (he lost to Victor Fleming for *Gone With the Wind*). He was also nominated for his directorial work on the 1933 film *Lady for a Day* and the 1947 classic *It's a Wonderful Life*.

10. What song does Bing Crosby sing in *Going My Way* (1944)?

a. "High Hopes"

b. "White Christmas"

c. "Getting to Know You"

d. "Swinging on a Star"

In this delightfully eccentric film from writer/director Terry Gilliam, Williams is a delusional streetperson on a quest for the Holy Grail in modern-day New York. He sings the song to his date, Lydia, who is played by Amanda Plummer.

---

10. Which future television detective portrayed a private eye on *The Rockford Files*?

a. Tom Selleck

b. Don Johnson

c. Dennis Franz

d. Bruce Willis

After injuring his hand, Sinatra had to give up the role of Detective Harry Callahan. The studios also approached John Wayne and Paul Newman, but Clint Eastwood got the part. Eastwood and *Dirty Harry* director Don Siegel also worked together on the 1979 film *Escape From Alcatraz*.

---

10. How many children does Patricia Heaton, who plays Debra Barone on *Everybody Loves Raymond*, have in real life?

a. One

b. Two

c. Three

d. Four

Actually, all four of these actresses starred in this 1998 film about a writer (Kenneth Branagh), who has a mid-life crisis, divorces his wife, and seeks out exciting affairs with beautiful women.

---

10. Which '90s sitcom introduced us to Pigman, a baby named Seven, and a holiday called Festivus?

a. *Roseanne*

b. *The Larry Sanders Show*

c. *The Simpsons*

d. *Seinfeld*

Sting's sixth solo album *Brand New Day* has been his most successful to date, selling over 8 million copies. Mick Jagger's newest solo album *Goddess in the Doorway* and James Taylor's *October Road* were released in 2002. Paul Simon's latest album, *You're the One*, was released in 2000.

4. The first MGM musical starring Frank Sinatra was:

a. *High Society*

b. *On the Town*

c. *Anchors Aweigh*

d. *Take Me Out to the Ball Game*

GAME 7 Q3 ANSWER a
With words and music by Sammy Cahn and Jules Styne, *Step Lively* (1943) was a musical remake of the Marx Brothers backstage comedy *Room Service* (1938). Incidentally, Sinatra starred with Groucho Marx in the 1951 film *Double Dynamite*.

---

4. In which movie did Barbra Streisand spend most of her time dressed as a boy?

a. *Funny Girl* (1968)

b. *The Mirror Has Two Faces* (1996)

c. *Yentl* (1983)

d. *The Prince of Tides* (1991)

GAME 27 Q3 ANSWER a
Best known in the '80s for his comic roles in the *Naked Gun* spoofs, Nielsen plays an impressive dramatic role in this film, which stars Streisand as a high-class prostitute. In self defense, Streisand kills Nielsen—a "client" who turns violent. Malden is Streisand's sexually abusive stepfather, Wallach plays her psychiatrist, and Dreyfuss is her lawyer.

---

4. Which film starred Buster Keaton?

a. *The Great Dictator* (1940)

b. *The General* (1927)

c. *Sons of the Desert* (1933)

d. *The Freshman* (1925)

GAME 47 Q3 ANSWER d
D.W. Griffith made this Biograph Company film in March of 1910; two months later, he released *The Gold Seekers*. His *Man's Lust for Gold* came out in 1912. Cecil B. DeMille's *The Squaw Man* was made in 1914, and remade into a talkie in 1931.

---

4. Which John Steinbeck novel was made into a film in 1939?

a. *Of Mice and Men*

b. *The Grapes of Wrath*

c. *Tortilla Flat*

d. *Cannery Row*

GAME 67 Q3 ANSWER b
Buddy Ebsen was, in fact, supposed to play the Tin Man, but discovered he was allergic to the metallic make-up that was used for the role. Jack Haley got the part instead.

9. In *The Fisher King* (1991), Robin Williams sings:

a. "Hooray for Captain Spaulding"

b. "The Teddy Bear's Picnic"

c. "Lydia the Tatooed Lady"

d. "Who's Afraid of the Big Bad Wolf?"

GAME 14 Q8 ANSWER a

The song is first sung by a full busload of passengers; but later in the film, Gable sings it solo as he's driving to the motel where he left Claudette Colbert. He also sings "Who's Afraid of the Big Bad Wolf?" in this movie.

---

9. Before Clint Eastwood was cast, who was slated for the lead role in *Dirty Harry* (1972)?

a. John Wayne

b. Charles Bronson

c. Frank Sinatra

d. Marlon Brando

GAME 34 Q8 ANSWER b

Benigni played Clouseau's illegitimate son, Chief Inspector Jacques Gambrelli, in *Son of the Pink Panther* (1993). Sellers—the most well-known Clouseau—originated the role in *The Pink Panther* (1964), Arkin was the detective in *Inspector Clouseau* (1968), and Moore played the part as a cameo in *Curse of the Pink Panther* (1983).

---

9. Who played a neurotic supermodel hypochondriac in Woody Allen's comedy *Celebrity*?

a. Charlize Theron

b. Winona Ryder

c. Bebe Neuwirth

d. Melanie Griffith

GAME 54 Q8 ANSWER b

This beautiful Victoria's Secret model showed screen appeal in *Coyote Ugly* (2000), so the folks in Hollywood wanted to see if she had scream appeal as well. My guess is that Tyra did some screaming after reading some of the film's reviews.

---

9. Which world-class singer felt millennial in his song "A Thousand Years," the first track on his 1999 album?

a. Mick Jagger

b. Sting

c. Paul Simon

d. James Taylor

GAME 74 Q8 ANSWER d

Lee continues to push American independent cinema into brave and sometimes alarming places. *Summer of Sam* takes place during the sweltering summer of 1977, when serial killer David Berkowitz terrorized New York City.

5. Which film did *not* pair Frank Sinatra with Kathryn Grayson?

a. *Anchors Aweigh*

b. *It Happened in Brooklyn*

c. *The Kissing Bandit*

d. *Take Me Out to the Ball Game*

GAME 7 Q4 ANSWER c
Anchors Aweigh (1945) was the first film in which Sinatra and Gene Kelly donned sailor suits to sing and dance. This is also the film in which Kelly dances with Jerry, the famous cartoon mouse.

5. What song did Barbra Streisand sing in the movie *Yentl* (1983)?

a. "Papa Don't Preach"

b. "Papa, Can You Hear Me?"

c. "Papa was a Rolling Stone"

d. "Oh My Papa"

GAME 27 Q4 ANSWER c
Based on a short story by Isaac Bashevis Singer, *Yentl* takes place in Eastern Europe at the turn of the twentieth century. Streisand plays a young Jewish woman who disguises herself as a boy to gain admittance to a Yeshiva, so she can study the Talmud.

5. Who played the "Tin Man" in the 1925 silent version of *The Wizard of Oz*?

a. Stan Laurel

b. Oliver Hardy

c. Harold Lloyd

d. Ben Turpin

GAME 47 Q4 ANSWER b
This was one of those rare Civil War-era films in which the bad guys are Union and the good guy is a would-be Confederate. Joseph Frank Keaton VI was nicknamed "Buster" by Harry Houdini, who saw the young Keaton take a big tumble, or "buster," down a flight of steps and rise unharmed.

5. Ten years before Humprey Bogart played Sam Spade, who starred as the detective in the 1931 *Maltese Falcon*?

a. Warren William

b. Ricardo Cortez

c. John Barrymore

d. Edward G. Robinson

GAME 67 Q4 ANSWER a
To date, *Of Mice and Men* has been made into four movies for the silver screen. The first version, which came out in 1939, starred Lon Chaney, Jr. and Burgess Meredith. *The Grapes of Wrath* came out in 1940, *Tortilla Flat* in 1942, and *Cannery Row* in 1982.

8. In *It Happened One Night* (1934), Clark Gable sings:

a. "Man on the Flying Trapeze"
b. "Brother, Can You Spare a Dime?"
c. "In the Good Old Summertime"
d. "Bicycle Built for Two"

GAME 14 Q7 ANSWER b
As "Dave Bowman" removes its memory modules, HAL, the Heuristic Algorithmic Logarithm computer, regresses, eventually singing the strains of "Bicycle Built for Two." Five years later, Douglas Rain, the voice of the HAL 9000, reprised his ominous computer voice for Woody Allen's *Sleeper* (1973).

---

8. Who has never played Inspector Jacques Clouseau?

a. Peter Sellers
b. Roberto Benigni
c. Roger Moore
d. Alan Arkin

GAME 34 Q7 ANSWER d
"Boss" Hogg, played by Sorrell Brooke, was the local politician on TV's *The Dukes of Hazzard.* Jackie Gleason was Buford T. Justice in *Smokey and the Bandit,* Joe Don Baker was Buford Pusser in *Walking Tall,* and Clifton James played J.W. Pepper in *Live and Let Die* and *The Man With the Golden Gun.*

---

8. Which supermodel starred in *Halloween: Resurrection* (2002), the eighth film in the *Halloween* series?

a. Kate Moss
b. Tyra Banks
c. Cindy Crawford
d. Naomi Campbell

GAME 54 Q7 ANSWER d
Wuhrer appeared on *Remote Control,* and Electra replaced McCarthy on *Singled Out.* Anderson wasn't a game show hostess, but she did play Lisa, the "Tool Time" girl, on Tim Allen's *Home Improvement.*

---

8. Spike Lee began the 1990s with his film about jazz, *Mo' Better Blues.* What was the last film he directed in the 1990s?

a. *Bamboozled*
b. *Girl 6*
c. *Clockers*
d. *Summer of Sam*

GAME 74 Q7 ANSWER c
Performing as Mother Love Bone in the late '80s, Pearl Jam became a complete unit with the addition of enigmatic lead singer/lyricist Eddie Vedder. The group's five albums released in the '90s were: *Ten* (1991); *Vs.* (1993); *Vitality* (1994); *No Code* (1996); and *Yield* (1998). They began the 21st century with a new album, *Binaural* (2000).

6. In which film does Frank Sinatra play a would-be presidential assassin?

a. *The Man With the Golden Arm*

b. *The Manchurian Candidate*

c. *Kings Go Forth*

d. *Suddenly*

GAME 7 Q5 ANSWER d
This 1949 Busby Berkeley MGM musical featured Esther Williams as Miss K.C. Higgins, the new owner of a baseball team on which Sinatra and Kelly play. Of course, the filmmakers still found a way to get Williams into a hotel pool for one of her legendary choreographed swimming extravaganzas.

---

6. What film follows Barbra Streisand's character through three decades?

a. *The Way We Were* (1973)

b. *Funny Lady* (1968)

c. *A Star Is Born* (1976)

d. *The Mirror Has Two Faces* (1996)

GAME 27 Q5 ANSWER b
"Papa Don't Preach," was a hit for Madonna; "Papa was a Rolling Stone," was sung by The Temptations; and "Oh My Papa," was recorded by my friend Eddie Fisher (Carrie's dad).

---

6. What was the first silent film serial?

a. *The Perils of Pauline*

b. *What Happened to Mary?*

c. *The Adventures of Kathlyn*

d. *The Fatal Ring*

GAME 47 Q5 ANSWER b
Both Laurel and Hardy had significant careers in silent films before officially teaming up in the two-reeler *Duck Soup* (1927). Contrary to perception, thin Stanley was 3" *shorter* than the 6'1" Ollie.

---

6. What determined the roles of Douglas Fairbanks, Jr. and Cary Grant in *Gunga Din*?

a. A fifty-yard race

b. A boxing match

c. An arm wrestle

d. A coin toss

GAME 67 Q5 ANSWER b
The film, also known as *Dangerous Female*, starred the Valentino-esque Cortez (who was actually Austrian-born Jacob Krantz). He was also the first (and only) actor to have his name appear above Greta Garbo's in 1926's *The Torrent*, her first American film.

7. In *2001: A Space Odyssey*, the computer HAL sings:

a. "Mary Had a Little Lamb"

b. "Bicycle Built for Two"

c. "Take Me Out to the Ballgame"

d. "Row, Row, Row Your Boat"

GAME 14 Q6 ANSWER b
Nicholson actually appeared in the original "nonmusical" version of this movie as a masochistic dental patient. In *Tommy*, he had a singing role as A. Quackson, a mental health specialist. He also had a minor part in *On a Clear Day You Can See Forever*, and in *Head*, he played himself in an uncredited role.

7. Which character was *not* a Southern sheriff?

a. Buford T. Justice

b. Buford Pusser

c. J.W. Pepper

d. Jefferson Davis Hogg

GAME 34 Q6 ANSWER b
According to the show's theme song, "He kept his eye on the sparrow," but Robert Blake's character Tony Baretta had a pet cockatoo named Fred. TV detective *Honey West* kept an ocelot named Bruce. *Magnum, P.I.* lived with two dobermans named Apollo and Zeus.

7. Which actress/model was *not* a sidekick on an MTV game show?

a. Kari Wuhrer

b. Jenny McCarthy

c. Carmen Electra

d. Pam Anderson

GAME 54 Q6 ANSWER b
Reactionary liberal Maude was married to Walter, her fourth husband. Maude's divorced daughter Carol lived with them. Shirley was a young widow with five musical kids. Alice Hyatt was also a widow with one *non-musical* kid. Kate Tanner was married to Willy, but played Earth mother to ALF (a.k.a. Gordon Schumway on Melmac).

7. How many studio albums did rock group Pearl Jam release in the 1990s?

a. Three

b. Four

c. Five

d. Six

GAME 74 Q6 ANSWER b
Sean Penn's first film as writer/director was *The Indian Runner*, released in 1991 and featuring actors David Morse and Viggo Mortensen. After starring in *The Crossing Guard* (1995), Jack Nicholson also starred in Penn's third film, *The Pledge* (2001). Although Penn starred in *Dead Man Walking*, the movie was written and directed by Tim Robbins.

Even Stars Can Lose Their Way

When I was a kid, I remember learning how sailors in centuries gone by would look at the stars in the night sky to help navigate their way back home. Many of us have looked at *movie* stars in the same way. We look to the beautiful people on the big screen to show us reflections of who we are, where we've been, where we're going, and how we might get there. But what about the stars themselves? Who guides them, protects them, showers light on them? All too often, stars end up alone. Yes, my friends, I'm sorry to say that one of the saddest lessons I've learned in my over fifty years of show business is that a star's life is not always bright. What often seems to the public to be a charmed and glamorous existence can be extinguished as easily as a weak wick on a stubby candle.

Of the truly talented folks whom I have seen fall upon hard times, I was always particularly upset about what happened to the beautiful movie actress Veronica Lake. She was a wonderful performer, starring in such first-class Hollywood motion pictures as Preston Sturges's *Sullivan's Travels,* and others like *The Blue Dahlia, This Gun for Hire, I Married a Witch, I Wanted Wings, So Proudly We Hail!,* and *The Glass Key.* In 1944, the United States government gave her the Congressional Medal of Honor for the selling of war bonds. Five or six years later, the government came to her house and physically put her out on the streets because of back income tax that was still owed. Life can be cruel. She was one of the only guests on my show whom I would pay to appear—it was really my way of giving her some money to pay for the hotel she was living in and to get through the day-to-day expenses. It's a real shame when those performers who have given so many so much, are left with so little for themselves.

My Office; or, How I Learned to Stop Worrying and Love the Clutter

My first office was at 220 West 42nd Street, then 152 West 42nd Street, then 147 West 42nd Street . . . are you starting to see a pattern? That's right, I've always had offices near 42nd Street in the Times Square area. I love that part of the city. It's near all the Broadway shows, great restaurants, fun and exciting nightlife, and all that glittery neon that seems to stretch on forever into the evening sky.

I've discovered some interesting things about my offices over the years. For example, I learned that my first office building was called the Hotel Knickerbocker before it was converted into an office building. The shoeshine man at the time told me that my suite was once the private residence of opera legend Enrico Caruso. I was very thrilled to learn that I and my rotary phone and standard typewriter were sitting where the Great Caruso had lived.

Have you seen my office? It's an amazing thing—TV and newspaper articles have been written about it. Nearly everything I've ever received or collected during my career remains in my office. Over the years, I think my passion for collecting inadvertently created the nostalgia craze and the still booming business of collectibles. When I was a kid, I used to collect old sheet music from the popular Tin Pan Alley era—the songs that were popular in the '20s and '30s. I also bought hard-to-find 78 RPMs in the flea market shops for a penny. I still go to nostalgia shows whenever I can.

These days, I've got office space at 300 West 43rd Street. I joke sometimes that there's so much stuff in my office, if you looked hard enough you'd find another office in there somewhere. Maybe that's where my next office will be located . . .

7. In *High Society*, the 1956 musical remake of *The Philadelphia Story*, Frank Sinatra plays whose role?

a. Jimmy Stewart's

b. Cary Grant's

c. John Howard's

d. Bing Crosby's

GAME 7 Q6 ANSWER d
Sinatra withdrew this little-known black-and-white thriller from circulation when rumors surfaced that Lee Harvey Oswald viewed it shortly before assassinating JFK.

7. Identify the mismatched Streisand song and movie:

a. "Evergreen" and *A Star Is Born*

b. "How Lucky Can You Get" and *Funny Lady*

c. "People" and *Hello, Dolly!*

d. "No Wonder" and *Yentl*

GAME 27 Q6 ANSWER a
The Sydney Pollack film, which begins in the late 1930s, follows Streisand's character from her radical college days through her politically active adult life.

7. Which ex-silent film actor appeared with Judy Garland in *In the Good Old Summertime* (1949)?

a. Harold Lloyd

b. Charlie Chaplin

c. Fatty Arbuckle

d. Buster Keaton

GAME 47 Q6 ANSWER b
The twelve-parter starring Mary Fuller first appeared in late July 1912. Kathlyn Williams' thirteen-part serial premiered in 1913. Pearl White starred in the twenty-episode *Pauline* series, which debuted in 1914. She also starred in the twenty-part *Ring* series, which began in 1917.

7. In *The Thin Man* (1934), Nick and Nora Charles are aided in their detective capers by their dog:

a. Falla

b. Asta

c. Colette

d. Chaucer

GAME 67 Q6 ANSWER d
Grant and Fairbanks both enjoyed working on *Gunga Din* (1939), and until Grant's death, the two actors always addressed each other as their characters—Cutter and Ballantine. With today's movies so dependent on the bottom line, it's nice to remember a time when a coin toss could actually make such an important determination.

GAME 14

6. Jack Nicholson appeared in all of these movie musicals *except:*

a. *Tommy* (1975)

b. *Little Shop of Horrors* (1986)

c. *On a Clear Day You Can See Forever* (1970)

d. *Head* (1968)

GAME 14 Q5 ANSWER c
Based on the Comden and Green Broadway musical, this Vincente Minnelli-directed film was to be Holliday's last. The famous ditsy blonde of *Adam's Rib* (1949) and *Born Yesterday* (1950) played telephone operator Ella Peterson.

GAME 34

6. What kind of pet did TV detective *Baretta* have?

a. A sparrow

b. A cockatoo

c. A doberman pinscher

d. An ocelot

GAME 34 Q5 ANSWER c
Bochco also produced *Cop Rock*, *Hooperman*, *Brooklyn South*, *Murder One*, and *Philly* among others. In addition, Bochco wrote a number of the original *Columbo* movies, including the first regular episode, *Columbo: Murder by the Book*, directed by Steven Spielberg.

GAME 54

6. Name the divorced TV mom:

a. Alice Hyatt of *Alice*

b. Maude Findlay of *Maude*

c. Kate Tanner of *ALF*

d. Shirley Partridge of *The Partridge Family*

GAME 54 Q5 ANSWER d
At sixteen years old, the future star of *An Officer and a Gentleman* applied for Israeli citizenship and spent three months in basic training before returning to the United States.

GAME 74

6. What was the second film that actor Sean Penn wrote and directed?

a. *The Indian Runner*

b. *The Crossing Guard*

c. *The Pledge*

d. *Dead Man Walking*

GAME 74 Q5 ANSWER c
Michael Keaton torments Melanie Griffith and Matthew Modine in *Pacific Heights* (1990); Richard Gere plays a dirty cop who torments Andy Garcia and wife Nancy Travis in *Internal Affairs* (1990); and Don Johnson is a smooth-talking psychotic who plays mind games with his lawyer, Rebecca DeMornay, in *Guilty as Sin* (1993).

8. Frank Sinatra recorded duets with all of these singers *except:*

a. Donna Summer

b. Carly Simon

c. Linda Ronstadt

d. Nancy Sinatra

GAME 7 Q7 ANSWER a

Sinatra plays reporter Mike Connor of *Spy* magazine. *High Society* featured the music of Cole Porter and a rousing performance by "Satchmo" himself, the wonderful Louis Armstrong.

---

8. Barbra Streisand recorded duets with all of these singers *except:*

a. Bryan Adams

b. Neil Diamond

c. Barry Gibb

d. Smokey Robinson

GAME 27 Q7 ANSWER c

Many songs from *Hello, Dolly!* became big hits, including the title song. "People," however, was from Barbra's first hit movie, *Funny Girl.*

---

8. In which classic Charlie Chaplin movie does the Little Tramp eat his own shoe?

a. *City Lights* (1931)

b. *The Gold Rush* (1925)

c. *Modern Times* (1936)

d. *Easy Street* (1917)

GAME 47 Q7 ANSWER d

This remake of *The Shop Around the Corner* (most recently remade as *You've Got Mail* with Tom Hanks and Meg Ryan), starred Judy Garland and Van Johnson. Johnson, Keaton, and S.Z. "Cuddles" Sakall join in singing the title song. In the last scene, playing Judy Garland's little daughter, is none other than Judy Garland's own daughter Liza Minnelli.

---

8. The 1939 film *Stagecoach* made young John Wayne a star. Which role did he play?

a. Dallas

b. Curly

c. Buck

d. The Ringo Kid

GAME 67 Q7 ANSWER b

This adorable wirehaired terrier's original name was Skippy. After the first *Thin Man* movie became a hit, the character of Asta the dog was so popular that Skippy took on the name of Asta in real life. Asta also starred as Mr. Smith in *The Awful Truth* (1937) and as George the dog in *Bringing Up Baby* (1938).

GAME 14

5. Who starred opposite Judy Holliday in *Bells Are Ringing* (1960)?

a. Paul Douglas
b. Jack Lemmon
c. Dean Martin
d. Peter Lawford

GAME 14 Q4 ANSWER b
Although it is rarely seen, *Song of the South* holds the distinction of being the first Disney film featuring a live actor. James Baskett won a special Oscar for his portrayal of Uncle Remus.

GAME 34

5. Steven Bochco produced all of the following police shows *except*:

a. *Hill Street Blues*
b. *NYPD Blue*
c. *The Rockford Files*
d. *Delvecchio*

GAME 34 Q4 ANSWER d
Pete Malloy was the character played by Martin Milner in *Adam-12*, which, like *Dragnet*, was developed and produced by Jack Webb—Joe Friday himself. Webb occasionally directed episodes of *Dragnet, Adam-12,* and *Emergency!*—another show he created.

GAME 54

5. Which actress joined the Israeli Army following high school?

a. Sandra Bullock
b. Natalie Portman
c. Kirstie Alley
d. Debra Winger

GAME 54 Q4 ANSWER a
Shelley Hack played Tiffany Welles, replacing Kate Jackson's Sabrina Duncan during the 1979/80 season. Hack was replaced by Tanya Roberts as Julie Rogers. Jaclyn Smith played Kelly Garrett for the show's entire five-year run.

GAME 74

5. In *Unlawful Entry* (1992), who plays the police officer who menaces Kurt Russell and Madeleine Stowe?

a. Michael Keaton
b. Richard Gere
c. Ray Liotta
d. Don Johnson

GAME 74 Q4 ANSWER b
Hook (1991), the story of Peter Pan's return to Neverland, had more cameos than good reviews. Williams played the grown-up Peter Pan with Roberts as the fairy Tinkerbelle. Paltrow was Wendy, and Hoffman was cast as Hook. Bob Hoskins, Phil Collins, Dame Maggie Smith, David Crosby, and Glenn Close also appeared in the film.

GAME 7

9. Frank Sinatra appeared opposite all of these actresses *except:*

a. Gina Lollabrigida

b. Leslie Caron

c. Natalie Wood

d. Debbie Reynolds

GAME 7 Q8 ANSWER a

He and his boot-wearing daughter Nancy Sinatra had a #1 hit with "Somethin' Stupid" in 1967. Carly Simon sang with Sinatra on his *Duets* album (1993), and Linda Ronstadt joined him on *Duets II* (1994).

GAME 27

9. Who played the left-wing student who loses girlfriend Barbra Streisand in *The Way We Were* (1973)?

a. Tommy Lee Jones

b. Peter Riegert

c. James Woods

d. Robert Redford

GAME 27 Q8 ANSWER d

In 1978, Barbra complained to old high school friend Neil Diamond that "You Don't Bring Me Flowers." She became "A Woman in Love" with Barry Gibb in 1980, and told Bryan Adams that "I've Finally Found Someone" in 1996.

GAME 47

9. Which of the following films was Rudolph Valentino's last?

a. *Son of the Sheik*

b. *The Sheik*

c. *The Four Horsemen of the Apocalypse*

d. *Eyes of Youth*

GAME 47 Q8 ANSWER b

The scene in which the Lone Prospector (Chaplin) and Big Jim McKay (Mark Swain) share a boot for supper took over sixty takes to suit Chaplin, who directed this silent film classic. The boot was made of licorice. Chaplin reissued the movie in 1942 with added music and his own voiceover narration.

GAME 67

9. What 1934 screwball comedy centers on a road trip?

a. *The Hitchhiker*

b. *Bus Stop*

c. *You Can't Run Away From It*

d. *It Happened One Night*

GAME 67 Q8 ANSWER d

Dallas was played by Claire Trevor; Curly, by George Bancroft; and Buck, by Andy Devine.

4. Which Disney film features the song "Zip-a-Dee-Doo-Dah"?

a. *Cinderella* (1950)

b. *Song of the South* (1946)

c. *The Three Caballeros* (1945)

d. *Snow White and the Seven Dwarfs* (1937)

GAME 14 Q3 ANSWER c
To date, this album has sold over 30 million copies—including the eight-track version, of course. Six songs from the album hit #1, including the Bee Gees' chart toppers "Night Fever" and "Stayin' Alive."

4. On *Dragnet*, who was *not* one of Sergeant Joe Friday's partners?

a. Officer Bill Gannon

b. Officer Frank Smith

c. Sergeant Ed Jacobs

d. Officer Pete Malloy

GAME 34 Q3 ANSWER c
Sort of an updated *Mod Squad*, this show about young-looking, big-city cops who could pass as high school or college students also starred Holly Robinson, Peter DeLuise (Dom's son), and Richard Grieco. Grieco's character, Dennis Booker, was spun off to his own series on Fox in 1989.

4. Who was *not* one of *Charlie's Angels* during its final 1981 season?

a. Shelley Hack

b. Tanya Roberts

c. Cheryl Ladd

d. Jaclyn Smith

GAME 54 Q3 ANSWER b
Pert played Alice when *The Honeymooners* was a recurring 10- to 15-minute sketch on *Cavalcade of Stars* (1951 to 1952). She also played Shirley Jones' mother in the 1962 film *The Music Man*. In 1967, she got to play Mrs. Gibson, Alice Kramden's mother, in a musical *Honeymooners* episode on *The Jackie Gleason Show*.

4. Julia Roberts, Gwyneth Paltrow, Robin Williams, and Dustin Hoffman appeared in a film directed by:

a. Sydney Pollack

b. Steven Spielberg

c. Mike Nichols

d. Robert Altman

GAME 74 Q3 ANSWER c
Whitney Houston sang the hit song on the soundtrack, but it was written and originally released by Dolly Parton herself in 1974. Parton recorded the love song again for the soundtrack of *The Best Little Whorehouse in Texas* (1982).

10. Which film did *not* feature both Frank Sinatra and Shirley MacLaine?

a. *Can-Can* (1960)

b. *Ocean's Eleven* (1960)

c. *Some Came Running* (1958)

d. *Pal Joey* (1957)

GAME 7 Q9 ANSWER b
Sinatra co-starred with Gina Lollabrigida in *Never So Few* (1959), Debbie Reynolds in *The Tender Trap* (1955), and Natalie Wood in *Kings Go Forth* (1958).

10. Which British rocker appeared in Barbra Streisand's 1984 music video, "Emotion"?

a. Ray Davies

b. Roger Daltrey

c. Mick Jagger

d. David Bowie

GAME 27 Q9 ANSWER c
Ironically, in real life, Streisand is perhaps Hollywood's most visible left-wing liberal while James Woods has emerged as a staunch right-wing conservative.

10. What fellow silent film star acted with Chaplin at the end of *Limelight* (1952)?

a. Harold Lloyd

b. Harry Langdon

c. Buster Keaton

d. Douglas Fairbanks

GAME 47 Q9 ANSWER a
Valentino died suddenly of peritonitis in 1926, a mere eight days after the premiere of *Son of the Sheik* in New York. His fans knew him as "The Great Lover," but Valentino's real name was actually Rodolpho Alfonzo Rafaelo Pierre Filibert Guglielmi di Valentina d'Antonguolla.

10. In *Bringing Up Baby* (1938), what song soothes Katherine Hepburn's pet leopard Baby?

a. "I Can't Give You Anything But Love"

b. "Lover"

c. "All of Me"

d. "All or Nothing at All"

GAME 67 Q9 ANSWER d
Starring Claudette Colbert and Clark Gable, *It Happened One Night* is considered a pioneer screwball comedy, and was the first film to win all five major Oscars: picture, actor, actress, director, and screenplay. *You Can't Run Away From It* was a 1956 musical version of the same story.

3. Which of the following movies has the biggest selling soundtrack to date:

a. *South Pacific* (1958)

b. *Fiddler on the Roof* (1971)

c. *Saturday Night Fever* (1977)

d. *Footloose* (1984)

GAME 14 Q2 ANSWER b
In 1964, Andrews, who starred in *My Fair Lady* on Broadway, lost the film role to Audrey Hepburn (the studios didn't want to take a risk with a newcomer). She made *Mary Poppins* instead, and proved the studios wrong.

3. *21 Jump Street* was the launching pad for which actor?

a. Robin Givens

b. Leonardo DiCaprio

c. Johnny Depp

d. Tea Leoni

GAME 34 Q2 ANSWER d
This series was also one of the first to feature an African-American performer as a regular (Nipsey Russell played Officer Dave Anderson). The show ran from 1961 to 1963.

3. Who played Alice Kramden in the first *Honeymooners* sketches?

a. Audrey Meadows

b. Pert Kelton

c. Joyce Randolph

d. Sheila MacRae

GAME 54 Q2 ANSWER d
The other original angels were played by Jaclyn Smith (Kelly) and Kate Jackson (Sabrina). Cheryl Ladd joined the cast in 1977, replacing Fawcett's character as her sister Kris.

3. Who wrote the 1992 song from *The Bodyguard*, "I Will Always Love You"?

a. Whitney Houston

b. Diana Ross

c. Dolly Parton

d. Willie Nelson

GAME 74 Q2 ANSWER c
In the autobiographical *This Boy's Life*, DeNiro plays Dwight Hansen, the abusive, alcoholic stepfather of Tobias Wolf. Dwight's version of proper parenting is to shout "Shut yer pie hole!" and hit young Tobias. In the 2000 comedy *Meet the Parents*, a very frustrated Ben Stiller yells the same phrase at an annoying flight attendant.

11. Which "numbered" Dean Martin/Frank Sinatra flick did *not* feature Sammy Davis, Jr.?

a. *4 for Texas* (1963)

b. *Ocean's Eleven* (1960)

c. *Robin and the 7 Hoods* (1964)

d. *Sergeants 3* (1962)

GAME 7 Q10 ANSWER d
Frank's co-stars in *Pal Joey* were Kim Novak and Rita Hayworth. Little Shirley MacLaine Beatty showed up uncredited as a drunk girl in *Ocean's Eleven*, so Francis Albert Sinatra showed up in small roles in MacLaine's *Around the World in Eighty Days* and *Cannonball Run II*.

---

11. Who has Barbra Streisand *not* been linked to romantically over the years?

a. Don Johnson

b. Andre Agassi

c. Peter Jennings

d. Mandy Patinkin

GAME 27 Q10 ANSWER b
Who? That's right—Roger Daltrey, the leather-voiced lead vocalist of The Who, appeared as Streisand's bespectacled and distracted bookworm husband. I thought they made a cute couple, but he's no James Brolin!

---

11. Which of Alfred Hitchcock's silent films featured the first of his now-famous "cameos"?

a. *The Lodger* (1926)

b. *The Pleasure Garden* (1925)

c. *The Manxman* (1929)

d. *Blackmail* (1929)

GAME 47 Q10 ANSWER c
Although Chaplin had been able to make a successful transition from the silent films to sound, Keaton had all but lost his reputation. As the years passed, however, Keaton would be rediscovered as an important pioneer of film craft and technique. His film *Sherlock, Jr.* (1924) had a huge influence on Woody Allen's *The Purple Rose of Cairo* (1985).

---

11. Which of the following Hollywood monster movies was *not* released in the 1930s?

a. *Dracula*

b. *Frankenstein*

c. *The Wolf Man*

d. *The Mummy*

GAME 67 Q10 ANSWER a
In her one and only screwball comedy, Katherine Hepburn is a wonderfully wacky heiress who disrupts zoologist Cary Grant's search for the missing "intercostal clavicle" to his dinosaur.

2. Julie Andrews' first starring role was in which film?

a. *The Sound of Music*

b. *Mary Poppins*

c. *Thoroughly Modern Millie*

d. *My Fair Lady*

GAME 14 Q1 ANSWER a
Verdon was both wife and inspiration to Fosse, who gave her the lead in the Broadway show *Sweet Charity*. MacLaine played the role in the 1969 movie. Liza Minnelli starred in Fosse's 1972 film musical *Cabaret*, for which she won the Best Actress Oscar. Ann Reinking appeared in Fosse's 1979 autobiographical film *All That Jazz*.

2. What was the first sitcom about police officers?

a. *Barney Miller*

b. *Police Squad!*

c. *Holmes and Yoyo*

d. *Car 54, Where Are You?*

GAME 34 Q1 ANSWER c
Allyce Beasley played Ms. Agnes DiPesto, the rhyming receptionist at the Blue Moon Detective Agency, owned by Maddie Hayes (Cybill Shepherd). Mildred Krebs (Doris Roberts) was *Remington Steele*'s secretary on CBS, and Sam (Mary Tyler Moore) answered phones for NBC's *Richard Diamond, Private Eye*.

2. Who was Farrah Fawcett's character on *Charlie's Angels*?

a. Kris Munroe

b. Kelly Garrett

c. Sabrina Duncan

d. Jill Munroe

GAME 54 Q1 ANSWER d
Although much of *Bosom Buddies* took place in the Susan B. Anthony, an affordable hotel for women, this *Some Like it Hot*-inspired sitcom focused on two men in drag, played by Tom Hanks—in his only starring television series to date—and Peter Scolari, who went on to play Michael, the young TV producer in *Newhart*.

2. In *This Boy's Life* (1993), who plays Leonardo DiCaprio's stepfather?

a. Al Pacino

b. Johnny Depp

c. Robert DeNiro

d. Alan Thicke

GAME 74 Q1 ANSWER b
This updated version of *Les Liaisons Dangereuses* for the high school set, also starred Ryan Phillippe and Oscar winner Louise Fletcher. This story was also told in the 1988 film *Dangerous Liaisons*, starring Glenn Close and John Malkovich, and again in 1989's *Valmont*, starring newcomer Annette Bening.

12. Which was *not* a nickname for Frank Sinatra?

a. "Old Blue Eyes"

b. "The Voice"

c. "The Chairman of the Board"

d. "The Skinny Kid from Brooklyn"

GAME 7 Q11 ANSWER a
Although Davis showed up as a wino in another "4" picture, *Convicts 4* (a 1962 Ben Gazzara starrer), he did not appear in the 1963 Martin/Sinatra *4 for Texas*. Rounding out the 4 in this Western romp were Anita Ekberg and Ursula Andress.

12. To date, which of the following actors has starred in two movies with Barbra Streisand?

a. George Segal

b. Ryan O'Neal

c. Robert Redford

d. Richard Dreyfuss

GAME 27 Q11 ANSWER d
Mandy Patinkin co-starred along with Amy Irving (the *first* Mrs. Spielberg) in Streisand's marvelous film *Yentl* (1983). He is a loving husband and father who actually quit the CBS-TV show *Chicago Hope* so he could spend more time with his family. In my book, he's a real *mensch*.

12. Which legendary filmmaker gave Charlie Chaplin the idea for his 1947 movie, *Monsieur Verdoux*?

a. Billy Wilder

b. Erich von Stroheim

c. Orson Welles

d. Jean Renoir

GAME 47 Q11 ANSWER a
In this classic thriller, Hitchcock is first seen with his back to the camera in a newsroom and again as a member of an angry mob. The director's appearance in his own films became a great promotional novelty over the years. In his last film, *Family Plot* (1976), his silhouette makes a cameo from behind a glass door.

12. Who played the husband of Cathy (Merle Oberon) in the 1939 film *Wuthering Heights*?

a. Laurence Olivier

b. Edgar Linton

c. David Niven

d. Leslie Howard

GAME 67 Q11 ANSWER c
Did you know a Spanish version of *Dracula* was shot at night on the same sets used during the day to make the Bela Lugosi version? Or that *Frankenstein* and *Dracula* were both released in 1931? Or that Boris Karloff appeared both in *Frankenstein* and *The Mummy* (1933), while Lugosi appeared with Lon Chaney, Jr. in 1941's *The Wolf Man*? Well, now you do.

GAME 14

1. Bob Fosse directed movies featuring all of these actresses *except:*

a. Gwen Verdon

b. Ann Reinking

c. Shirley MacLaine

d. Liza Minnelli

The answer to this question is on:

page 184, top frame, right side.

GAME 34

1. The receptionist's first name on *Moonlighting* was:

a. Maddie

b. Mildred

c. Agnes

d. Sam

The answer to this question is on:

page 184, second frame, right side.

GAME 54

1. Which show was *not* centered on an unmarried woman living alone in the city?

a. *Felicity*

b. *That Girl*

c. *Suddenly Susan*

d. *Bosom Buddies*

The answer to this question is on:

page 184, third frame, right side.

GAME 74

1. Which actress did *not* appear in 1999's *Cruel Intentions*?

a. Reese Witherspoon

b. Tara Reid

c. Selma Blair

d. Sarah Michelle Gellar

The answer to this question is on:

page 184, bottom frame, right side.

183

GAME 8

Memory Lane Grab Bag

Turn to page 100 for the first question.

GAME 7 Q12 ANSWER d
Everyone knows "The Skinny Kid" was from Hoboken, New Jersey. For the record, I am known as "The Dynamo from the Bronx." My mirror calls me that all the time.

GAME 28

Memory Lane Grab Bag

Turn to page 100 for the first question.

GAME 27 Q12 ANSWER b
O'Neal and Streisand starred together in Peter Bogdanovich's 1972 throwback to screwball comedy *What's Up Doc?* and again in 1979's *The Main Event*. Redford was her leading man in *The Way We Were* (1973). Segal starred with Barbra in *The Owl and the Pussycat* (1970), and Dreyfuss was her co-star in *Nuts* (1987).

GAME 48

Memory Lane Grab Bag

Turn to page 100 for the first question.

GAME 47 Q12 ANSWER c
During a friendly dinner in 1946, Welles suggested to Chaplin that he break away from the "little tramp" persona by making a modern version of the Bluebeard story. Chaplin was always irritated that he had to put Welles' name in the screen credits as "Idea suggested by Orson Welles."

GAME 68

Memory Lane Grab Bag

Turn to page 100 for the first question.

GAME 67 Q12 ANSWER c
In this haunting film, Cathy loves the passionate Heathcliff, played by Sir Laurence Olivier. But Cathy's desire for a respectable station in life causes her to reject Healthcliff in favor of marriage to the wealthy and civilized Edgar Linton, played by David Niven.

GAME 14

Musicals and Singers

And Those Who Shouldn't Sing

Turn to page 183 for the first question.

GAME 13 Q12 ANSWER a

Funny Girl lost the Best Original Music Score in 1968 to *Oliver!* Of the choices listed, only *The Sound of Music* won Best Picture.

GAME 34

The Right to Remain Silent

Where's a Good Detective When You Need One?

Turn to page 183 for the first question.

GAME 33 Q12 ANSWER d

This 1969 film portrays Fonda and Hopper as a couple of unconventional, long-haired hippie bikers. With money gained from a Mexican drug deal, they journey eastward on their choppers from Los Angeles through the American Southwest on their way to Mardis Gras. Personally, I prefer the subway and a Broadway show for fun.

GAME 54

Ladies Night

Name the Actress

Turn to page 183 for the first question.

GAME 53 Q12 ANSWER c

This NBC comedy, which ran from 1990 to 1997, involved a wacky cast of characters who wandered in and out of a small commuter airport on the island of Nantucket.

GAME 74

At Century's End

The '90s and Beyond

Turn to page 183 for the first question.

GAME 73 Q12 ANSWER c

Straight Arrow was a Western written for kids that ran on the radio from 1948 to 1951. As a Comanche orphan raised by whites, Straight Arrow (played by Howard Culver) chose the name Steve Adams as his white man disguise. (Note that both names share the same initials.)

GAME 8

1. For which film did Joan Crawford win the Best Actress Oscar in 1945?

a. *Leave Her to Heaven*

b. *Love Letters*

c. *Mildred Pierce*

d. *The Valley of Decision*

The answer to this question is on:

page 101, top frame, right side.

GAME 28

1. On the sitcom *One Day at a Time*, the daughters' names were Barbara and:

a. Julie

b. Sara

c. Jackie

d. Ann

The answer to this question is on:

page 101, second frame, right side.

GAME 48

1. Which child actor played Murphy Brown's son, Avery, in the show's final 1998 season?

a. Haley Joel Osment

b. Elijah Wood

c. Jonathan Taylor Thomas

d. Lucas Haas

The answer to this question is on:

page 101, third frame, right side.

GAME 68

1. Which ventriloquist provides the voice of Tigger in the "Winnie-the-Pooh" movies and TV shows?

a. Edgar Bergen

b. Jay Johnston

c. Señor Wences

d. Paul Winchell

The answer to this question is on:

page 101, bottom frame, right side.

12. Which Oscar-nominated musical did *not* win the award for Best Score?

a. *Funny Girl* (1968)

b. *Mary Poppins* (1964)

c. *Hello, Dolly!* (1969)

d. *The Sound of Music* (1965)

GAME 13 Q11 ANSWER b
Sonny Curtis, one of the guitarists for the Crickets, wrote and sang "Love Is All Around" for *The MTM Show*. Curtis often played with the Everly Bothers, who recorded his song "Walk Right Back." Among other contributions, Curtis wrote "I Fought the Law," a big hit for The Bobby Fuller Four in 1965.

---

12. In *Easy Rider,* what is the ultimate destination of motorcyclists Peter Fonda and Dennis Hopper?

a. Los Angeles

b. Mexico

c. Woodstock

d. New Orleans

GAME 33 Q11 ANSWER d
This 1981 film starred James Brolin and Margot Kidder, who inhabited the house, and Rod Steiger as a priest who tries to banish the house's evil.

---

12. What was the name of the airline owned and run by Joe and Brian Hacket on *Wings*?

a. Aero Mass

b. Nantucket Air

c. Sandpiper Air

d. Whisperjet Air

GAME 53 Q11 ANSWER c
This family drama series premiered in January 1999, and features former *M*A*S*H* star Mike Farell as the widowed father and veterinarian. The show's use of The Beatles' "In My Life" as its theme song has made the 1965 song very popular with yet another generation.

---

12. On which radio show did a Comanche Indian disguise himself as white cattle rancher Steve Adams?

a. *The Cisco Kid*

b. *Red Ryder*

c. *Straight Arrow*

d. *The Tom Mix Ralston Straightshooters*

GAME 73 Q11 ANSWER b
Those listening to *Arthur Godfrey and His Friends* on October 19, 1952, had the shock of hearing Godfrey fire singer LaRosa just minutes into the program. Legend has it that Godfrey felt the young singer was getting too big for his britches and acting ungrateful.

2. Which *Saturday Night Live* episode has Lorne Michaels sworn publicly never to air again?

a. The George Carlin episode

b. The Richard Pryor episode

c. The Lili Tomlin episode

d. The Milton Berle episode

GAME 8 Q1 ANSWER c

That year, Joan Crawford was up against some wonderful actresses: Gene Tierney in *Leave Her to Heaven;* Jennifer Jones in *Love Letters;* Greer Garson in *The Valley of Decision;* and Ingrid Bergman in *The Bells of St. Mary's.* I think Crawford was truly magnificent in her role, though, and deserved to win for that powerhouse performance.

---

2. Which of the following Academy Award winners used sign language in her acceptance speech?

a. Sally Field

b. Louise Fletcher

c. Shirley MacLaine

d. Marlee Matlin

GAME 28 Q1 ANSWER a

Ann Romano (Bonnie Franklin) was the divorced mother of Julie and Barbara Cooper (MacKenzie Phillips and Valerie Bertinelli). The show ran from 1974 to 1984, ending with mother and daughter, Ann and Barbara, marrying an architect and his dental student son.

---

2. What are the first words spoken in the 1968 film *2001: A Space Odyssey*?

a. "My God, it's full of stars."

b. "The dawn of man"

c. "Here you are, sir. Main level, please."

d. "Do you read me, Hal?"

GAME 48 Q1 ANSWER a

Before his Oscar-nominated performance opposite Bruce Willis in *The Sixth Sense* (1999), Haley Joel Osment was also seen by millions of filmgoers as Tom Hanks' young son, Forrest, Jr., in *Forrest Gump* (1994). Before then, at age four, he appeared in a 1992 Pizza Hut commercial.

---

2. Who got her start on TV in 1955 playing dummy Jerry Mahoney's girlfriend?

a. Mary Tyler Moore

b. Julie Andrews

c. Carol Burnett

d. Candace Bergen

GAME 68 Q1 ANSWER d

Although Winchell has dedicated most of the past forty years to medical research (he developed one of the first artificial hearts in 1963), he has regularly done cartoon voice work, as well.

11. *The Mary Tyler Moore Show* theme song was written by a former member of what group?

a. The Four Seasons

b. Buddy Holly and the Crickets

c. The Beach Boys

d. Gary Puckett and the Union Gap

GAME 13 Q10 ANSWER b
Ben was the pet rat of loner Willard in the original horror story. In *Ben*, the 1972 sequel, little David Garrison owned him.

11. *The Amityville Horror* is based on the true story of a house in which state?

a. Texas

b. Maine

c. California

d. New York

GAME 33 Q10 ANSWER c
This '80s group featured Yes guitarist virtuoso Steve Howe and bassist/singer John Wetton from King Crimson. Their big hits were "Only Time Will Tell" and "Heat of the Moment."

11. On NBC's *Providence*, what is the name of Joanie Hansen's trendy pet food store?

a. The Pet Café

b. Come 'n Get It Café

c. The Barkery

d. Café Chihuahua

GAME 53 Q10 ANSWER b
Among the many awards this comedy series has received since its 1998 debut, are Emmys for Outstanding Lead Actor in a Comedy Series (Eric McCormack), Outstanding Supporting Actress (Megan Mullally), Outstanding Supporting Actor (Sean Hayes), and Outstanding Comedy Series.

11. Which popular radio show personality fired up-and-comer Julius LaRosa live on the air?

a. Major Edward Bowes

b. Arthur Godfrey

c. Fred Allen

d. Milton Berle

GAME 73 Q10 ANSWER a
Introduced as the first show of a summer series, this story was a creepy version of *Dracula* (perhaps the closest to the novel of any dramatic production performed to date). *Treasure Island* ran the second week. On Halloween of that year, Welles shocked the world with *The War of the Worlds*.

GAME 8

3. What's the last picture shown in *The Last Picture Show* (1971)?

a. *Father of the Bride* (1950)

b. *Stagecoach* (1939)

c. *Red River* (1948)

d. *The Grapes of Wrath* (1939)

GAME 8 Q2 ANSWER d
Allegedly, the late "Mr. Television" threw his weight around so arrogantly during the week's rehearsals that nearly the entire cast and crew couldn't wait for the show to air and be done with.

GAME 28

3. Who was announcing nominees at the 1974 Oscars when a man ran naked across the stage?

a. Burt Reynolds

b. Clint Eastwood

c. David Niven

d. Angie Dickinson

GAME 28 Q2 ANSWER b
Fletcher, who won the Best Actress Oscar for her unforgettable performance as Nurse Ratched in 1975's *One Flew Over the Cuckoo's Nest,* signed her speech for her deaf parents.

GAME 48

3. To date, how many lead vocalists have been in the Australian heavy metal band AC/DC?

a. One

b. Two

c. Three

d. Four

GAME 48 Q2 ANSWER c
Though over two hours long, this film has only about forty minutes of dialogue. (Kubrick was a great admirer of the subtle art of silent films.) The last words of *2001:* "Its origin and purpose—still a total mystery," are in reference to the mysterious black monolith on which the film is based.

GAME 68

3. What was the name of Señor Wences's "hand" puppet?

a. Charlie McCarthy

b. Jerry Mahoney

c. Johnny

d. Pedro

GAME 68 Q2 ANSWER c
Ventriloquist Paul Winchell and his dummies Jerry Mahoney and Knucklehead Smith had a half-hour Saturday morning show on NBC from 1954 to 1956. Burnett played the dummy's girlfriend for thirteen episodes.

10. Michael Jackson's hit "Ben" was the theme to the *sequel* of what movie?

a. *Benji* (1975)

b. *Willard* (1971)

c. *Private Benjamin* (1980)

d. *Gentle Giant* (1967)

GAME 13 Q9 ANSWER b
This 1937 film was the first for Hope at Paramount and the last for Fields. Hope played the host of a radio program that was broadcast from an ocean liner. Shirley Ross played his first ex-wife.

---

10. Which band did *not* originate in its geographical name?

a. Kansas

b. Chicago

c. Asia

d. Boston

GAME 33 Q9 ANSWER c
The Carter Family, who can be credited with pioneering modern country music back in the 1920s, hails from Virginia.

---

10. Grace of NBC's *Will & Grace* runs a(n):

a. Vintage clothing store

b. Interior decorating business

c. Antique shop

d. Employment agency

GAME 53 Q9 ANSWER c
Taxi's comic cast of characters weren't *really* cab drivers—they just worked at the Manhattan-based company (with the boss from hell, played by Danny DeVito) until their shot at something better came along. The series merited a number of writing and acting Emmys during its 1978 to 1983 run, including three for Outstanding Comedy Series.

---

10. Which story was the first one performed on Orson Welles' *Mercury Theatre On the Air* in July 1938?

a. *Bram Stoker's Dracula*

b. *Heart of Darkness*

c. *The War of the Worlds*

d. *Treasure Island*

GAME 73 Q9 ANSWER c
Simple but reliable, Shrevie had a habit of repeating his words, like "Are you sure you seen 'em leave the building, are you sure you seen?" Legend has it that Shrevie was specifically brought in for those episodes that the writers were trying to stretch to hit the show's half-hour mark. Ah, show business . . .

4. Where did Janet and Chrissie first find Jack Tripper on TV's *Three's Company*?

a. In a restaurant

b. At a bar

c. At the movies

d. In their bathtub

Peter Bogdanovich's poignant telling of the Larry McMurtry novel is about the ending of all things, whether they be movies or love affairs or innocence or life itself. Best Supporting Actor Ben Johnson died soon after making this film, which also introduced the world to Cybil Shepherd. Incidentally, *Father of the Bride* is the first picture seen in this movie.

4. Which of the following actors has *not* yet won an Oscar?

a. Martin Sheen

b. Michael Caine

c. Sean Connery

d. Charlton Heston

Niven's shocked but memorable reaction to Robert Opal, the "Oscar Streaker," resulted in the line, *"The only laugh that man will ever get in his life is by stripping . . . and showing his shortcomings."* As Opal crossed the stage, he flashed a peace sign, and the cameras had to cut away to avoid full frontal nudity.

4. Who did *not* perform at The Band's farewell concert in the 1978 film *The Last Waltz*?

a. Judy Collins

b. Neil Diamond

c. Stephen Stills

d. Joni Mitchell

The band's first singer was Dave Evans, who sang with the group from 1973 to 1975. However, the group did not record its first album (*High Voltage*) until 1975, at which time Bon Scott was the lead singer. After Scott died in 1980, Brian Johnson joined the group and debuted as lead vocalist on the now-classic album *Back in Black*.

4. Which variety show headed by a musical couple came first?

a. *Make Your Own Kind of Music*

b. *The Captain & Tennille Show*

c. *The Sonny & Cher Comedy Hour*

d. *Donny and Marie*

Along with puppets Johnny (his hand) and Pedro (a gravel-voiced head in a box), Señor Wences—a former matador, juggler, and acrobat—made frequent appearances on Ed Sullivan and Milton Berle's shows. (Speaking of ventriloquists, I've always wondered how Edgar Bergen was able to gain fame doing his ventriloquism on the radio.)

9. Which cast member sang the Oscar winner "Thanks for the Memory" in *The Big Broadcast of 1938*?

a. W.C. Fields

b. Bob Hope

c. Dorothy Lamour

d. Martha Raye

Written by Jay Livingston and Ray Evans, "Mona Lisa" was sung only in Italian in this 1950 film. "I Love Paris" was featured in the Oscar-winning *An American in Paris* (1951). "High Hopes," from *A Hole in the Head* starring Frank Sinatra, won in 1959, while "The Shadow of Your Smile" was the winner from *The Sandpipers* (1965).

---

9. Which group does *not* hail from Georgia?

a. R.E.M.

b. Indigo Girls

c. The Carter Family

d. The B-52s

James Taylor was the first outside performer to record on The Beatles' fledgling Apple Records in 1968. His debut album, *James Taylor,* included his classic "Carolina In My Mind," for which Paul McCartney played bass and George Harrison sang backup.

---

9. The crew on the ABC sitcom *Taxi* worked at:

a. Louie's Cab Company

b. DiPalma's Cab Company

c. Sunshine Cab Company

d. Sunny Cab Company

Much of the popularity of this ABC television series, which ran from 1985 to 1989, came from the sexual tension between Maddie Hayes (Cybill Shepherd) and David Addison (Bruce Willis). The series ended shortly after the two characters "got together."

---

9. What was the name of Lamont Cranston's cab driver on *The Shadow*?

a. Ned

b. Ralph

c. Shrevie

d. Terry

The show said it best: "The Shadow is, in reality, Lamont Cranston, wealthy man about town. Years ago in the Orient, Cranston learned a strange and mysterious secret. The ability to cloud mens' minds so that they cannot see him."

GAME 8

5. Which actress did *not* portray a deaf person in the following films?

a. Holly Hunter in *The Piano*

b. Jane Wyman in *Johnny Belinda*

c. Marlee Maitlin in *Children of a Lesser God*

d. Patty Duke in *The Miracle Worker*

GAME 8 Q4 ANSWER d
Jack had fallen asleep in the tub during a party the girls held the night before. Though critics hated this show when it first debuted in 1978, audiences loved it and made it a huge hit. Based on a BBC sitcom called *Man About the House*, this show made both John Ritter and Suzanne Somers household names.

GAME 28

5. Who refused Marlon Brando's Oscar for *The Godfather* on his behalf at the 1973 Academy Awards?

a. Sacheen Littlefeather

b. Julie Moon

c. Wanda Wintergrove

d. Rain Cloudwalker

GAME 28 Q4 ANSWER a
Caine has won two Best Supporting Actor awards: one for *Hannah and Her Sisters* (1986) and another for *The Cider House Rules* (1999). Connery (who appeared with Caine in 1975's *The Man Who Would Be King*) was awarded the Best Supporting Actor Oscar in 1987 for *The Untouchables*. Charlton Heston won Best Actor for *Ben Hur* (1960).

GAME 48

5. Who was the first to play at the Woodstock festival in 1969?

a. The Who

b. Santana

c. Crosby, Stills & Nash

d. Richie Havens

GAME 48 Q4 ANSWER a
Though Judy Collins did not perform at the concert, Stephen Stills (the man who immortalized her in the Crosby, Stills & Nash song "Suite: Judy Blue Eyes") did play onstage towards the end of the show. Judy received the first of several Grammy nominations in 1967 for her recording of "Both Sides Now," which was, in fact, written by Joni Mitchell.

GAME 68

5. In *Diner*, Steve Gutenberg's fiancée must pass a trivia test about which type of professional sports team?

a. Football

b. Baseball

c. Basketball

d. Hockey

GAME 68 Q4 ANSWER a
Make Your Own Kind of Music (1971) starred siblings Karen and Richard Carpenter, and featured trumpeter Al Hirt and Mark Lindsay, formerly of Paul Revere and the Raiders. *The Sonny & Cher Comedy Hour Show* debuted later that summer. *Donny and Marie* debuted in January 1976, and *The Captain & Tennille Show* first aired that September.

8. Which Oscar-winning song is from the Alan Ladd film *Captain Carey, U.S.A.*?

a. "Mona Lisa"

b. "I Love Paris"

c. "The Shadow of Your Smile"

d. "High Hopes"

GAME 13 Q7 ANSWER b
During the film's shooting, director Carol Reed came across Anton Karas and his zither in a tavern in Vienna. Karas wrote the score, and played the entire soundtrack of the film on a single instrument.

---

8. Which of these "state" songs was on James Taylor's first album?

a. "Sweet Home Alabama"

b. "Carolina In My Mind"

c. "Mississippi Queen"

d. "Georgia (On My Mind)"

GAME 33 Q7 ANSWER b
The location comes straight from the lyrics of her autobiographical song "Coal Miner's Daughter." Loretta, who was the second of eight children, was also a mother of four by age seventeen. Singer Crystal Gayle is her younger sister.

---

8. On *Moonlighting*, the name of Maddie's detective agency was:

a. Full Moon

b. Moonlight

c. Blue Moon

d. Light of the Moon

GAME 53 Q7 ANSWER d
Berry Gordy originally hired Marvin Gaye in 1960 as a session drummer and vocalist for the Motown label. After marrying Gordy's sister in 1961, Gaye was offered a solo recording contract, which launched his successful singing career. His chart toppers included such songs as "What's Going On," "Ain't That Peculiar," and "Mercy, Mercy Me."

---

8. What was the real name of *The Shadow*?

a. Lamont Cranston

b. Bill Powers

c. Richard Diamond

d. Sam Spade

GAME 73 Q7 ANSWER b
Agnes Moorehead gave such an impressive performance in this classic 1938 radio broadcast that she was invited back to *Suspense* a few years later to reprise her role in a new performance. Barbara Stanwyck played the same role in the film version.

GAME 8

6. Which 1940s Preston Sturges film inspired the Coen Brothers' *O Brother, Where Art Thou?*

a. *The Great McGinty*

b. *Sullivan's Travels*

c. *The Lady Eve*

d. *Unfaithfully Yours*

GAME 8 Q5 ANSWER a

In an interesting twist, Holly Hunter's character can hear perfectly well, but has decided to mute herself from all speech and communicate only through her piano.

GAME 28

6. Which actor from the film *Ordinary People* was *not* nominated for an Academy Award?

a. Judd Hirsch

b. Donald Sutherland

c. Timothy Hutton

d. Mary Tyler Moore

GAME 28 Q5 ANSWER a

Sacheen Littlefeather, whose real name is Maria Cruz, is a California native of Yaqui ancestry. Ever disdainful of any awards ceremonies, Brando used the occasion of the Oscars to protest what he felt was Hollywood's insensitive and racist treatment of Native Americans in film.

GAME 48

6. In which U.S. city was Jim Morrison charged with obscenity and indecent exposure in 1969?

a. Miami, Florida

b. San Francisco, California

c. New York, New York

d. New Haven, Connecticut

GAME 48 Q5 ANSWER d

A quiet and sensitive folk singer, Richie Havens got the festival off to the right start with an impassioned performance of his song "Freedom." On the last day of the show, the final performer of the festival was Jimi Hendrix, who wowed the audience of 500,000 with his electrifying interpretation of "The Star Spangled Banner."

GAME 68

6. Which film star did *not* write a best-selling fiction title?

a. Tom Tryon

b. Robert Shaw

c. Carrie Fisher

d. Charlton Heston

GAME 68 Q5 ANSWER a

The questions are all about the Baltimore Colts. Gutenberg's fiancée gets only a 63 (65 is passing). Baltimore's football team is now the Ravens, named for Edgar Allan Poe's famous poem.

7. Which film's score is played on a zither?

a. *The Wrong Man* (1956)
b. *The Third Man* (1949)
c. *The Thin Man* (1934)
d. *The Invisible Man* (1933)

GAME 13 Q6 ANSWER c
Camelot won for Best Score, but it was "Talk to the Animals" from *Doctor Dolittle* that won for the Best Song. Meanwhile, "The Look of Love" from *Casino Royale* was also nominated for Best Song that year. No music from *The Graduate* was nominated.

7. Where in Kentucky was country singer Loretta Lynn born?

a. Louisville
b. Butcher Hollow
c. Ashland
d. Lexington

GAME 33 Q6 ANSWER b
The rocket ship they accidentally launch first goes to New Orleans, where the boys pick up some hitchhiking crooks, and then ends up in Venus, which is populated by beauty contestants.

7. Singer Marvin Gaye was hired by Motown Records as a:

a. Solo singing artist
b. Receptionist
c. Pianist
d. Drummer

GAME 53 Q6 ANSWER c
Collins plays Reverend Eric Camden on *7th Heaven*, Christopher was *M*A*S*H's* Father Mulcahy, and Tom Bosley led *The Father Dowling Mysteries*. Ritter, who played Reverend Fordwick from 1972 through 1975, also played the minister who married Ted and Georgette on *The Mary Tyler Moore Show*.

7. Which actress overhears a murderous phone call in the classic Lucille Fletcher radio play *Sorry, Wrong Number*?

a. Barbara Stanwyck
b. Agnes Moorehead
c. Lucille Ball
d. Ruth Warrick

GAME 73 Q6 ANSWER a
As he changed in the late '30s from talented Broadway director to host of radio's *Mercury Theatre on the Air*, Welles became widely known to radio listeners as a self-proclaimed "obedient servant." Welles was anything but obedient, however, when he frightened most of the country in 1939 with his notorious "War of the Worlds" radio broadcast.

What Makes Me Laugh?

I always wanted to be a gag writer when I was a kid. Listening to Bob Hope and Jack Benny, I used to jot down jokes that I heard over the radio. When I think of how I used to try to scribble down one-liners night after night, I'm reminded of that old joke—I think Rudy Vallee told it to me first. It goes something like this: Milton Berle was once at a nightclub watching a comedian, and he laughed so hard that he dropped his pencil!

Rudy Vallee also told me he was once at a nightclub recording somebody's act. He paid twenty bucks just to get into the club. When he got home later that night, he was absolutely mortified to learn that his hidden tape recorder hadn't been working!

I don't laugh too easily. I'm a really easy-going guy and a sentimental fella, but it takes a lot to make me laugh. If I had to name the comedian who made me laugh the most, it would be a tossup between Rodney Dangerfield and Red Skelton. I love both those guys, but Red Skelton used to come on my show and break me up. When I look back, it's strange that he would crack me up because he would always talk about things other than comedy. He would come on to talk about his album *Red Skelton Conducts . . .* and things like that.

After one show, Red showed me something that probably only a few people were aware of. I had asked him, "Red, when you fall in your act, do you really fall?" Red's routines in those days featured a lot of pratfalls, and they were always hard, rough, and knockdown, and looked like they really hurt. Red proceeded to roll up his pants leg and I saw that his leg was completely covered with black and blue marks. When he fell in the act, it was an honest drag-out fall onto hard floors. Talk about getting into your work!

That was Red, though. He was very truthful, he never used stunt doubles, and he was always absolutely honest with his beloved audience.

Speaking of comedians, over the years, I have also come to greatly respect and admire Jackie Mason. I had Jackie on my show at least twenty times, and each time, he would put me down. But that's his routine, his schtick if you will. He's still a funny man, probably the funniest man in the world—and he never uses anybody else's material. If you want original humor, he's the guy. He never tells anybody else's jokes. And he's fairly fearless, as the world learned when he gave Ed Sullivan the finger during his appearance on the show in the early '60s. Apparently, Jackie had been scheduled for a ten-minute routine, and had prepared for such. Then suddenly, Ed gave him word—live on television—to cut the routine to three minutes. Some people just don't like to be told what to do. Luckily, Jackie and I never had any problems like that.

People often ask me what I think about the all-too-common use of profanity in today's comedy acts. I really believe that the curse word has become the crutch of the lazy comic. Listen to Bill Cosby, Bob Newhart, Mort Sahl, Soupy Sales, Shecky Greene, Woody Allen, Jonathan Winters, and Nichols and May—they're all brilliant comics, and they hardly ever fall back on profanity. Too many comics have resorted to cursing as a way of either stretching a short routine to run longer or getting quick laughs based more on shock than on legitimate cleverness. In their time, comics such as Lenny Bruce, George Carlin, and Richard Pryor at least used profanity in ways that clearly sprung from thought. If you take milk from a cow and you drink it for nourishment, you keep yourself alive. If you take milk from the cow and spill it all over the ground, you won't get any healthier . . . and you'll be wasting the cow's time.

7. What was the name of the *Saturday Night Live* singing group, fronted by **John Belushi**, that sang "King Bee?"

a. The Blues Brothers
b. The Bicycle Warriors
c. The Killer Bees
d. The Landsharks

GAME 8 Q6 ANSWER b
In this classic 1942 film, Joel McCrea plays a burnt out and disillusioned Hollywood director who wants to help his fellow man by making a movie about the lives of hobos called *O Brother, Where Art Thou?* Sixty years later, the Coen Brothers picked up the cue and turned in a version of Homer's *Odyssey*, Appalachian-style.

7. "Monty Python" regular Eric Idle made a film in 1978 about a make-believe British rock group called:

a. The Rigbies
b. The Reefers
c. The Rutles
d. The Rubles

GAME 28 Q6 ANSWER b
In this 1980 film filled with excellent performances, I've always felt that Donald Sutherland's sensitive portrayal of the troubled family's father should have at least received a nomination. Judd Hirsch was nominated for Best Supporting Actor along with Timothy Hutton, and Mary Tyler Moore was nominated for Best Actress. Hutton was the only winner.

7. Who played rocker Jerry Lee Lewis in *Great Balls of Fire* (1989)?

a. Alec Baldwin
b. Dennis Quaid
c. Michael Keaton
d. Johnny Depp

GAME 48 Q6 ANSWER a
Morrison had recently seen a play in New York by The Living Theatre called *Paradise Now*, which featured full frontal nudity on stage. It's been suggested that Morrison might have attempted to expose himself during a Doors concert in the same way.

7. Which film does *not* revolve around a bowler?

a. *The Big Lebowski* (1998)
b. *Strike Zone* (1999)
c. *Kingpin* (1996)
d. *Greedy* (1994)

GAME 68 Q6 ANSWER d
To date, Heston has written only his memoirs. Tom Tryon, known for his performance in *The Cardinal* (1963), wrote *Crowned Heads* and *Harvest Home* in the early '70s. Robert Shaw wrote *The Man in the Glass Booth*, made into a film in 1975. Carrie Fisher's *Postcards From the Edge* (1990) was made into a film starring Meryl Streep and Shirley MacLaine.

6. Which of the following 1967 movies received the Oscar for Best Score?

a. *The Graduate*
b. *Doctor Dolittle*
c. *Camelot*
d. *Casino Royale*

GAME 13 Q5 ANSWER d
Producers liked the 1984 Huey Lewis hit "I Want a New Drug" and approached Parker that same year to come up with a song that sounded like it. "I Want a New Drug" peaked on the charts at #6, while "Ghostbusters" hit #1. Lewis sued Parker for plagiarizing the song; the case was settled out of court.

6. In *Abbott and Costello Go to Mars* (1953), where do the boys travel?

a. Mars
b. Venus
c. The Moon
d. Las Vegas

GAME 33 Q5 ANSWER b
In 1974, drummer Neil Peart joined Rush, a band started five years earlier by members Geddy Lee and Alex Lifeson along with drummer John Rutsey. Their best-selling 1981 album, *Moving Pictures,* includes the song "Tom Sawyer" with lyrics written by Peart.

6. Who played the Reverend Matthew Fordwick on *The Waltons*?

a. Stephen Collins
b. William Christopher
c. John Ritter
d. Tom Bosley

GAME 53 Q5 ANSWER a
In this 1993 tearjerker, DeVito is a widower who is trying to balance his grief with the desire to be a better dad to his two sons. The actor, himself a father of three, kept his beautician's license renewed for many years in case he didn't make it as a performer. Keep an eye out for *Seinfeld* star Julia-Louis Dreyfus in this film.

6. Who would always sign off his radio programs as "Your obedient servant"?

a. Orson Welles
b. Bob Hope
c. Arthur Godfrey
d. Jimmy Durante

GAME 73 Q5 ANSWER c
Many of these Camel radio commercials included testimonials from medical doctors who actually praised the positive physical effects of cigarette smoking. Famous radio and television personality Arthur Godfrey, a smoker, ultimately began publicly condemning cigarette sponsors after he was diagnosed with lung cancer.

8. How many *Rocky* films have been made to date?

a. Three

b. Four

c. Five

d. Six

Belushi and sidekick Dan Aykroyd often brought their love of Chicago blues to the show in live performances. The Killer Bees were later transformed into The Blues Brothers, one of *SNL's* most popular set of characters.

---

8. Which film starring Gene Hackman was written and directed by Francis Coppola?

a. *The French Connection* (1971)

b. *The Heist* (2001)

c. *Mississippi Burning* (1988)

d. *The Conversation* (1974)

The Rutles were made to look, act, and sound just like the Fab Four. This film had its beginnings in a skit from TV's *Saturday Night Live* and features cameos by *SNL* members Bill Murray, John Belushi, Dan Aykroyd, Gilda Radner, and pop stars Paul Simon and Mick Jagger.

---

8. What 1950s comic did his stand-up routine with a folded newspaper under his arm?

a. Mort Sahl

b. Shecky Greene

c. Jonathan Winters

d. Soupy Sales

Although Dennis Quaid lip-synched to Jerry Lee's vocals, he is a dynamite piano player and actually played the music in the film. Alec Baldwin co-starred as Jerry Lee's fiery evangelist cousin Jimmy Swaggart.

---

8. In Abbott and Costello's "Who's on First?" sketch, what's the name of the pitcher?

a. "Because"

b. "I Don't Know"

c. "Today"

d. "Tomorrow"

Featured as competitive bowlers in the other films were actors Jeff Bridges, John Goodman, and Steve Buscemi in *The Big Lebowski*, Woody Harrelson and Bill Murray in *Kingpin*, and Michael J. Fox in *Greedy*.

5. Who sang the theme song from *Ghostbusters* (1984)?

a. Huey Lewis and the News

b. The Busboys

c. Oingo Boingo

d. Ray Parker, Jr.

GAME 13 Q4 ANSWER c
Sinatra sang "All the Way" (*The Joker Is Wild*), "High Hopes" (*A Hole in the Head*), and the theme from *Three Coins in the Fountain*. Day sang "Secret Love" (*Calamity Jane*) and "Que Sera Sera" (*The Man Who Knew Too Much*). Dion sang the themes from *Beauty and the Beast* and *Titanic;* Madonna's songs were from *Evita* and *Dick Tracy*.

---

5. Which band hails from Canada?

a. AC/DC

b. Rush

c. The Scorpions

d. Dexy's Midnight Runners

GAME 33 Q4 ANSWER a
This 1946 Danny Kaye milkman-turned-prizefighter musical fairy tale was a remake of a 1936 Harold Lloyd film *The Milky Way*. Both films were fun.

---

5. In which film is Danny DeVito a horror-movie host?

a. *Jack the Bear* (1993)

b. *Death to Smoochy* (2002)

c. *Terms of Endearment* (1983)

d. *Throw Momma From the Train* (1987)

GAME 53 Q4 ANSWER d
Nicholson was a politician in *Carnal Knowledge*, a musician in *Five Easy Pieces*, and a publisher in *Wolf*. One of his real-life odd jobs was as an MGM office boy, answering fan mail for the cartoon cat-and-mouse duo Tom and Jerry. He had that job when he was discovered.

---

5. Which cigarette company had a radio ad with the pro-smoking tagline, "Experience is the best teacher"?

a. Lucky Strikes

b. Marlboro

c. Camel

d. Parliament

GAME 73 Q4 ANSWER b
Suspense ran some of the best radio chillers of its day, including Lucille Fletcher's terrifying radio plays *The Hitchhiker* and *Sorry, Wrong Number*. The show's unnerving music was written by Bernard Herrmann (famous for his score in *Psycho*) and featured a graveyard bell.

9. In the 1974 good cop/bad cop flick *Freebie and the Bean*, who played James Caan's harried and put-upon partner?

a. Ben Gazzara

b. Alan Arkin

c. Gene Wilder

d. Robert Blake

GAME 8 Q8 ANSWER c
The first and last films of this popular series were directed by John G. Avildsen. In the original ending of *Rocky V*, Rocky died after winning a street fight. Preview audiences didn't go for it, so the ending was changed and Rocky lived.

---

9. Which comic actor is the subject of the REM song "Man on the Moon"?

a. Jackie Gleason

b. Andy Kaufman

c. Jim Carrey

d. Jerry Lewis

GAME 28 Q8 ANSWER d
Coppola wrote and directed *The Conversation* during the period between *The Godfather* and *The Godfather Part II* (released in 1972 and 1974, respectively).

---

9. In *The Good, the Bad, and The Ugly* (1966), who played Tuco, the ornery bandit?

a. Donald Pleasence

b. Eli Wallach

c. Pat Hingle

d. Lee Van Cleef

GAME 48 Q8 ANSWER a
Born in 1927, Sahl was dubbed "Rebel Without a Pause" for the rapid-fire delivery of his stand-up routine. Primarily a political satirist, Sahl's trademark newspaper was where he turned for material. In the late '50s and early '60s, he made frequent appearances on *The Tonight Show*, *The Steve Allen Show*, and, oh yeah, *The Joe Franklin Show*.

---

9. Which film does *not* focus on a bank heist?

a. *Going in Style* (1979)

b. *Ocean's Eleven* (1960)

c. *Quick Change* (1990)

d. *A Fish Called Wanda* (1988)

GAME 68 Q8 ANSWER c
I guess I should say, *"No, What's the name of the guy on second,"* but Today's pitching and Tomorrow's catching, so . . .

GAME 13

4. Of these singers, who performed more Oscar-winning theme songs?

a. Doris Day

b. Celine Dion

c. Frank Sinatra

d. Madonna

GAME 13 Q3 ANSWER d
The theme song for *Sanford and Son* was written by Quincy Jones, while *Three's Company's* theme was co-written by *Sesame Street's* Joe Raposo. *The Partridge Family* theme song, "Come on Get Happy," was written by songwriters Danny Janssen and Wes Farrell.

GAME 33

4. Which Brooklyn movie is about a boxer?

a. *The Kid from Brooklyn*

b. *It Happened in Brooklyn*

c. *A Tree Grows in Brooklyn*

d. *Last Exit to Brooklyn*

GAME 33 Q3 ANSWER b
The Andersons, from the show *Father Knows Best,* lived in Springfield. The Cleavers lived in Mayfield, U.S.A. The Nelsons lived on Sycamore Road in Hillsdale in a replica of their actual Hollywood home. (*Dennis the Menace* also lived in Hillsdale.) And Shirley Partridge's brood lived in San Pueblo, California.

GAME 53

4. What was Jack Nicholson's role in *Terms of Endearment* (1983)?

a. Ex-politician

b. Ex-musician

c. Ex-publisher

d. Ex-astronaut

GAME 53 Q3 ANSWER c
Well before Regis Philbin got into the act, Tipton (the voice of Paul Frees) a.k.a. *The Millionaire* (1955 to 1960), would present his secretary, Michael Anthony (Marvin Miller), with a check for $1 million, to be given to an unsuspecting recipient. (This was back when a million dollars meant something.)

GAME 73

4. Which chilling radio show featured a host known only as "the man in black"?

a. *The Witching Hour*

b. *Suspense*

c. *Inner Sanctum*

d. *Arch Oboler's Lights Out, Everybody*

GAME 73 Q3 ANSWER d
Immensely popular, *The Kate Smith Show* had its radio debut in 1931, launching Smith as a top radio performer during the '30s and '40s. Perhaps her most famous hit was Irving Berlin's "God Bless America." In 1950, she pioneered daytime television with *The Kate Smith Hour,* which ran for four years.

10. Which motion picture marked Art Garfunkel's acting debut?

a. *Annie Hall*

b. *The King of Marvin Gardens*

c. *Carnal Knowledge*

d. *Catch-22*

GAME 8 Q9 ANSWER b
Arkin would later be paired with *Columbo* star Peter Falk in the very funny 1979 comedy, *The In-Laws.* They were paired again in 1986 in the not-so-funny *Big Trouble,* directed by the late cinema pioneer John Cassavetes.

10. Which director has *not* made a film based on a Stephen King novel?

a. Brian De Palma

b. Steven Spielberg

c. Rob Reiner

d. Stanley Kubrick

GAME 28 Q9 ANSWER b
Director Milos Forman borrowed the REM song for the title of his 1999 Andy Kaufman biopic, starring Jim Carrey as Andy.

10. What was the real name of TV's *Captain Kangaroo*?

a. Paul Reubens

b. Robert Zimmerman

c. Bob Keeshan

d. Allen Goorwitz

GAME 48 Q9 ANSWER b
Wallach played the "ugly" character of the film, Eastwood's character represented the "good," and Van Cleef played the "bad." Donald Pleasence played the heavy in Charlton Heston's *Will Penny* (1968), while Pat Hingle played a corrupt judge in Eastwood's *Hang 'em High,* released that same year.

10. Who was the undercover cop in *Reservoir Dogs*?

a. Steve Buscemi

b. Quentin Tarantino

c. Tim Roth

d. Harvey Keitel

GAME 68 Q9 ANSWER b
In the original 1960 Rat Pack *Ocean's Eleven,* Frank Sinatra plays Danny Ocean, who leads his gang to rob five Las Vegas casinos simultaneously. In the 2001 version, directed by Steven Soderbergh, George Clooney is Danny Ocean, and he and his gang have three casinos in their sights.

3. Jose Feliciano contributed the theme to what television sitcom?

a. *Sanford and Son*

b. *Three's Company*

c. *The Partridge Family*

d. *Chico and the Man*

GAME 13 Q2 ANSWER d
While his catchy themes for *Diff'rent Strokes* and *The Facts of Life* lasted the duration of each show, Alan Thicke's theme for *Wheel of Fortune* ("Big Wheels") was replaced in 1983 by Merv Griffin's "Changing Keys." The theme song from *Family Ties* ("Without Us") was written by Jeff Barry and Tom Scott.

3. Before *The Simpsons*, what other TV family lived in Springfield, U.S.A.?

a. The Cleavers

b. The Andersons

c. The Nelsons

d. The Partridges

GAME 33 Q2 ANSWER c
This 1968 police drama had Steve McQueen driving (more like "flying") his Ford Mustang over the hilly streets of San Francisco in a spectacular car chase. The film won the Academy Award for Film Editing. The incredible car chases in *The Seven Ups* and *The French Connection* were filmed on the streets of New York.

3. Which TV millionaire appeared first?

a. Blake Carrington

b. Thurston Howell, III

c. John Beresford Tipton

d. Maxwell Sheffield

GAME 53 Q2 ANSWER b
Willie Tanner (Max Wright) was a social worker, Steven Keaton (Michael Gross) was a public television programmer, and Cliff Huxtable (Bill Cosby) was a doctor. Mike Brady (Robert Reed) was an architect who lived with his wife, six kids, housekeeper, and dog in a house without enough bathrooms.

3. What was the theme song for *The Kate Smith Show*?

a. "God Bless America"

b. "Teddy Bears Picnic"

c. "Hello Everybody"

d. "When the Moon Comes Over the Mountain"

GAME 73 Q2 ANSWER c
Lux Presents Hollywood was sort of the audio book of its time. Its anthology of one-hour radio recreations of popular films often starred the films' leads. DeMille had no connection to the show other than as its paid host.

11. Who played the cute blonde in the white T-bird in *American Graffiti* (1973)?

a. Farrah Fawcett
b. Suzanne Somers
c. Tanya Roberts
d. Shelley Hack

GAME 8 Q10 ANSWER d
Carnal Knowledge (1971) was Garfunkel's second film, also directed by Mike Nichols. *The King of Marvin Gardens* (1972) was Jack Nicholson's second film with director Bob Rafelson after *Five Easy Pieces* (1970). Meanwhile, Woody Allen's Oscar-winning comedy *Annie Hall* (1977) marked the big-screen debut of Paul Simon.

---

11. Which of the following is not a Beck album?

a. *Odelay*
b. *Midnite Vultures*
c. *Mutations*
d. *Wired*

GAME 28 Q10 ANSWER b
Brian De Palma directed *Carrie* in 1976. In addition to *Stand By Me* (based on one of King's short stories), Rob Reiner also directed *Misery* (1990). Stanley Kubrick directed *The Shining* (1980).

---

11. Which of the following comedy groups was nominated for the Best Spoken Comedy Album Grammy in 2000?

a. Cheech & Chong
b. Bob & Ray
c. The Firesign Theatre
d. The Kids in the Hall

GAME 48 Q10 ANSWER c
Before he was the Captain, Keeshan was Clarabell the Clown on *Howdy Doody*. To date, *Captain Kangaroo* is the longest-running network show for children (1955 to 1984). As for the other real names listed in this question, Paul Reubens is Pee-wee Herman; Robert Zimmerman is Bob Dylan; and Allen Goorwitz is actor Allen Garfield.

---

11. What was the name of the 1995 Geena Davis swashbuckling money pit?

a. *Pirates*
b. *Anne of the Indies*
c. *Cutthroat Island*
d. *The Pirates of Penzance*

GAME 68 Q10 ANSWER c
Buscemi turned in a somewhat comic performance as "Mr. Pink" in this crime thriller about a botched diamond heist. Other gang members, known only by "color" code names, included Tim Roth, Harvey Keitel, Quentin Tarantino, Edmund Burke, and Michael Madsen. *Reservoir Dogs* marked the directorial debut of Tarantino, who also wrote the script.

2. *Growing Pains* star Alan Thicke composed the themes for all of the following TV shows *except*:

a. *Diff'rent Strokes*
b. *Wheel of Fortune*
c. *The Facts of Life*
d. *Family Ties*

GAME 13 Q1 ANSWER a

The song was "Best Friend." Nilsson is perhaps best-known for singing the Fred Neil theme "Everybody's Talkin'" from the movie *Midnight Cowboy* (1969). He had hoped that his song "I Guess the Lord Must Be in New York City" would become the film's main theme song, but Neil's was chosen instead.

---

2. Which film's classic car chase was filmed on location in San Francisco?

a. *The French Connection* (1971)
b. *The Seven-Ups* (1973)
c. *Bullitt* (1968)
d. *Streets of Fire* (1984)

GAME 33 Q1 ANSWER b

The fourteen-inch-tall bottle was a special smoked glass 1964 Holiday Edition decanter for the Kentucky bourbon. In the first season of the show, which ran on NBC from 1965 to 1970, Jeannie's black bottle had painted vines and gold leaves. After the first season, the bottle was bejeweled and, like Jeannie's wisp of smoke, colored purple.

---

2. Which TV dad was an architect?

a. Willy Tanner of *ALF*
b. Mike Brady of *The Brady Bunch*
c. Steven Keaton of *Family Ties*
d. Cliff Huxtable of *The Cosby Show*

GAME 53 Q1 ANSWER d

Ted Lange played bartender Isaac Washington on every voyage of the *Pacific Princess*. Sam Malone (Ted Danson) tended bar on *Cheers*, Joe the Bartender (Jackie Gleason) served 'em up on *Cavalcade of Stars/The Jackie Gleason Show*, and Archie (Ed Gardner) was the conniving bartender on radio's *Duffy's Tavern: Archie's Boy's Club*.

---

2. Who was the host of *Lux Presents Hollywood*?

a. Louis B. Mayer
b. Samuel Goldwyn
c. Cecil B. DeMille
d. Billy Wilder

GAME 73 Q1 ANSWER b

"Duffy's Tavern, where the elite meet to eat. Archie the manager speaking; Duffy ain't here." The setting for this weekly radio show was a Third Avenue bar in New York City. I've always wondered if it was a coincidence that Archie at *Duffy's Tavern* sounded just like Carroll O'Connor as Archie Bunker on TV's *All in the Family*.

12. Which of the following characters is *not* a Cunningham from ABC's *Happy Days*?

a. Richie Cunningham

b. Chuck Cunningham

c. Stretch Cunningham

d. Howard Cunningham

GAME 8 Q11 ANSWER b
Somers would go on to big fame as "airhead" Chrissie Snow on *Three's Company*. The remaining blondes were all *Charlie's Angels* at one point.

12. Who played the priest in John Boorman's *The Exorcist II: The Heretic* (1977)?

a. Nicol Williamson

b. Richard Burton

c. Jason Miller

d. James Earl Jones

GAME 28 Q11 ANSWER d
This is a bit tricky, because *Wired* is an album by Beck—*Jeff* Beck, that is. The recording artist known as Beck, whose name is Beck Hansen, first emerged on the pop scene with his hit single "Loser" in 1993. Since then, he has continued to make best-selling albums and popular videos while giving sold-out concerts.

12. When did my first TV show, *Joe Franklin— Disk Jockey*, go on the air?

a. 1950

b. 1951

c. 1952

d. 1953

GAME 48 Q11 ANSWER c
Since they first began doing radio shows together in Los Angeles in the mid-1960s, The Firesign Theatre have created some of the funniest, strangest, and most prophetic underground counterculture audio comedy this side of the album. They've released over twenty "comedy" albums and have received three Grammy nominations over the years.

12. Who starred with Bogart in *The Petrified Forest* (1936)?

a. Edward G. Robinson

b. Pat O'Brien

c. Leslie Howard

d. George Brent

GAME 68 Q11 ANSWER c
Davis's then-husband Renny Harlin (*Die Hard 2*, *Cliffhanger*) directed the pirate flop. The film, budgeted at over $92 million, took in under $11 million at the box office. I'll bet Michael Douglas is glad he dropped out of the project.

1. Which television show featured a theme song written and sung by Harry Nilsson?

a. *The Courtship of Eddie's Father*

b. *Green Acres*

c. *Love, American Style*

d. *Chico and the Man*

The answer to this question is on:

page 170, top frame, right side.

---

1. What was in the bottle before it became Barbara Eden's mobile home in *I Dream of Jeannie*?

a. Jean Nate Bubble Bath

b. Jim Beam Bourbon

c. Jelly Belly Jellybeans

d. Johnson's Baby Shampoo

The answer to this question is on:

page 170, second frame, right side.

---

1. Which of the following bartenders served on *The Love Boat*?

a. Sam

b. Joe

c. Archie

d. Isaac

The answer to this question is on:

page 170, third frame, right side.

---

1. Since Duffy was never there, who managed radio's *Duffy's Tavern*?

a. Finnegan

b. Archie

c. Sam

d. Miss Duffy

The answer to this question is on:

page 170, bottom frame, right side.

GAME 9

With a Little Help From

Friends . . .

*Turn to page 114
for the first question.*

GAME 8 Q12 ANSWER c
Stretch Cunningham was one of Archie Bunker's best friends on CBS's *All in the Family*. Stretch was played by acclaimed actor James Cromwell, who went on to star in 1995's *Babe* (for which he earned a Best Supporting Actor nomination) and *The Green Mile* (1999).

GAME 29

Young Stars

They Don't All Go to the "Time Out" Room

*Turn to page 114
for the first question.*

GAME 28 Q12 ANSWER b
Nicol Williamson was the exorcist in *The Exorcist III* (1990); James Earl Jones played an African shaman and warder of evil spirits in *Exorcist II;* and the late Jason Miller played the troubled Father Damian Karras in the first *Exorcist* in 1973. He also briefly appeared as the character in *Exorcist III*.

GAME 49

Crossing Over

What Became of What Was?

*Turn to page 114
for the first question.*

GAME 48 Q12 ANSWER b
My first show aired on ABC-TV weekdays from noon until 1 PM. We didn't tape back then, so there are no records of my programs until the late '60s. It's a shame. There were so many wonderful guests who joined me, and there's no record of their appearance.

GAME 69

Movies of the '40s

Bogey, Boyer, Bette, and Beyond

*Turn to page 114
for the first question.*

GAME 68 Q12 ANSWER c
Bogart has Leslie Howard to thank for his breakthrough movie role. Howard, who starred with Bogart in the Broadway production of *The Petrified Forest*, insisted the producers hire his Broadway co-star to play "Duke Mantee" in the film version. Bogey named his daughter Leslie after his old friend.

GAME 13

I Hear Music

Theme Songs and Soundtracks

Turn to page 169 for the first question.

GAME 12 Q12 ANSWER a

In an embarrassingly comical scene, Hoffman's son runs into a nude Williams in the middle of the night on his way to the bathroom. Williams went on to play a mother whose child is haunted by ghosts in *Poltergeist* (1982). Jane Alexander appeared in *Kramer vs. Kramer* as Hoffman's neighbor.

GAME 33

Location, Location, Location

On the Street Where You Live

Turn to page 169 for the first question.

GAME 32 Q12 ANSWER b

Horst Buchholz was the gunslinger wannabe of *The Magnificent Seven* and Leslie Caron's runaway sailor in *Fanny* (1937). In *Life Is Beautiful*, he shows up as Dr. Lessing, a German doctor who, with Benigni's character Guido, shares a love of riddles.

GAME 53

It's a Living

Odd Jobs

Turn to page 169 for the first question.

GAME 52 Q12 ANSWER c

A native Long Islander, Debbie (now *Deborah*) Gibson first hit stardom in 1986 at age sixteen. She was the youngest person to have a #1 single ("Foolish Beat"), which she wrote, produced, and performed herself. Gibson went beyond bubble-gum pop when she joined the Broadway cast of *Les Miserables* in 1992.

GAME 73

Tuning In

Old Time Radio

Turn to page 169 for the first question.

GAME 72 Q12 ANSWER c

As Jack's eccentric chef's assistant E. Z. Taylor, Alan Campbell had the lion's share of laughs on a show that would last only one season. Just as *Three's Company* was based on a British sitcom called *Man About the House*, *Three's a Crowd* was based on a British sitcom called *Robin's Nest*.

GAME 9

1. The *Friends* gang lives in which part of Manhattan?

a. Chelsea

b. Tribeca

c. Greenwich Village

d. Upper West Side

The answer to this question is on:

page 115, top frame, right side.

GAME 29

1. Who is the youngest actor to host *Saturday Night Live*?

a. Jodie Foster

b. Macaulay Culkin

c. Drew Barrymore

d. Fred Savage

The answer to this question is on:

page 115, second frame, right side.

GAME 49

1. *Sanford and Son* is to *Steptoe and Son* what *Three's Company* is to:

a. *Three's a Crowd*

b. *Robin's Nest*

c. *Man About the House*

d. *Two Girls and a Guy*

The answer to this question is on:

page 115, third frame, right side.

GAME 69

1. In 1949, Olivia de Havilland played a rich young woman disillusioned by Montgomery Clift in:

a. *The Ambassador's Daughter*

b. *The Well-Groomed Bride*

c. *The Heiress*

d. *Princess O'Rourke*

The answer to this question is on:

page 115, bottom frame, right side.

GAME 12

12. Which actress has a one-night stand with Dustin Hoffman's character in *Kramer vs. Kramer* (1979)?

a. JoBeth Williams

b. Kathleen Turner

c. Meg Tilly

d. Jane Alexander

GAME 12 Q11 ANSWER d
Though Aykroyd did play President Nixon on *Saturday Night Live*, he never played him in a film. Philip Baker Hall played Nixon in the Robert Altman film *Secret Honor* (1985). Dan Hedaya played a comically exaggerated Nixon in *Dick* (1999); he also played a government official who advises Anthony Hopkins' Nixon in *Nixon* (1995).

GAME 32

12. Which of *The Magnificent Seven* (1960) appeared in Roberto Benigni's *Life Is Beautiful* (1998)?

a. Robert Vaughn

b. Horst Buchholz

c. James Coburn

d. Yul Brynner

GAME 32 Q11 ANSWER b
The story of the middleweight boxing champ's life was intended as an inspirational story of a bad boy gone good. It was also the film that made Paul Newman a star. Other actors who made their film debut in this movie include Steve McQueen, Robert Loggia, and Angela Cartwright (all uncredited).

GAME 52

12. Which pop princess was *not* a Mouseketeer?

a. Annette Funicello

b. Britney Spears

c. Debbie Gibson

d. Christina Aguilera

GAME 52 Q11 ANSWER c
The "Boys" are A.J. McLean, Brian Littrell, Nick Carter, Howie Dorough, and Kevin Richardson. The group took its name from The Backstreet Market in Orlando, Florida, where the boys used to hang out.

GAME 72

12. On the *Three's Company* spinoff, *Three's a Crowd*, who was Jack's surfer-dude assistant?

a. Tyler

b. Biff

c. E. Z.

d. Frisbee Man

GAME 72 Q11 ANSWER d
On *Diff'rent Strokes*, Edna Garrett (Charlotte Rae) was the housekeeper for millionaire Phillip Drummond, his daughter Kimberly, and adopted sons Willis and Arnold Jackson. When she became *Facts of Life* headmistress at an all-girls school, NBC writers had Arnold Jackson (Gary Coleman) visit her in a few episodes.

2. To date, which of the following actors has *not* appeared on *Friends*?

a. Harry Connick, Jr.

b. Brad Pitt

c. Jon Lovitz

d. Robin Williams

GAME 9 Q1 ANSWER c
Central Perk, the café where the friends all meet and hang out, is very much based on the Manhattan Café in the West Village. As for me, I prefer staying close to the theatres on Times Square. That's where I've spent most of my life, and where I'm most comfortable.

---

2. How old was Mickey Rooney when he made his first film?

a. Six

b. Eight

c. Twelve

d. Fourteen

GAME 29 Q1 ANSWER c
Barrymore hosted the Thanksgiving episode back in 1982, when the *E.T.* star was just seven years old. Jodie Foster was fourteen when she hosted in November 1976. *The Wonder Years'* Fred Savage was thirteen for his February 1990 guest host stint. Macaulay Culkin was eleven when he hosted in 1991.

---

2. Which character appeared in *M*A*S*H* the movie, but *not* the TV series?

a. Capt. "Spearchucker" Jones

b. Capt. "Ugly John" Black

c. Lt. "Dish" Schneider

d. Capt. "Duke" Forrest

GAME 49 Q1 ANSWER c
Norman Lear based his *Sanford and Son* on the long-running British junkmen comedy *Steptoe and Son*. *Three's Company* was based on the British program *Man About the House*. In fact, the first episode of the American series was entitled "A Man About the House."

---

2. Humphrey Bogart's co-star in *Casablanca* was:

a. Ingrid Bergman

b. Katherine Hepburn

c. Lauren Bacall

d. Barbara Stanwyck

GAME 69 Q1 ANSWER c
In an interview with talk show host Charlie Rose, director Martin Scorsese said that it was the emotional violence of *The Heiress* that impressed him when he first saw the film as a young boy. He claimed the movie influenced his directorial style when filming the Edith Wharton novel *The Age of Innocence* (1993).

11. Which actor has *not* played President Richard Nixon in a film?

a. Sir Anthony Hopkins

b. Philip Baker Hall

c. Dan Hedaya

d. Dan Aykroyd

GAME 12 Q10 ANSWER d
Pacino was an Oscar-nominated Best Actor for both *Dog Day Afternoon* (1975) and *. . . And Justice for All* (1979). *Cruising* was released in 1980, and drew much controversy over its homosexual subject matter. Interestingly, Director William Friedkin had made another film in 1970—*The Boys in the Band*—that also dealt with this theme.

---

11. The 1956 film *Somebody Up There Likes Me* is based on the life of:

a. Father Flanagan

b. Rocky Marciano

c. Charles Lindbergh

d. Mickey Rooney

GAME 32 Q10 ANSWER c
The *Sorrow and the Pity* has a running time of over 4 hours. The others are between 3 and 4 hours each. The longest movie ever made is *The Cure for Insomnia* (1987) in which poet L.D. Groban reads one of his poems, interspliced with stock footage of pornography and heavymetal music videos. The film runs over 85 hours.

---

11. How many Backstreet Boys are there?

a. Three

b. Four

c. Five

d. Six

GAME 52 Q10 ANSWER b
Bing sang "Sweet Leilani" in the film *Waikiki Wedding* (1937), "White Christmas" in *Holiday Inn* (1942), and "Swinging on a Star" in *Going My Way* (1944). "Buttons and Bows" was performed by Bob Hope in *The Paleface* (1948).

---

11. Mrs. Garrett, the school mistress on *The Facts of Life*, was first a character on which other sitcom?

a. *Growing Pains*

b. *Family Matters*

c. *Silver Spoons*

d. *Diff'rent Strokes*

GAME 72 Q10 ANSWER b
Debuting in 1972, *Maude* was *All in the Family's* first spinoff, starring Bea Arthur as Maude, Edith Bunker's cousin. *The Jeffersons* first aired in 1975, when George and Louise—the Bunkers' black neighbors—"moved on up" and out of the neighborhood. In 1982, *Gloria* starred Archie's little girl, who became a veterinarian's assistant.

3. To date, which of the following actresses has *not* appeared on *Friends*?

a. Julia Roberts

b. Isabella Rossallini

c. Helen Hunt

d. Julia Louis-Dreyfus

GAME 9 Q2 ANSWER a

Although his wife, model Jill Goodacre, appeared in an early episode (she was stuck at an ATM machine with Matthew Perry's "Chandler"), Connick has never been on the show.

3. Who was the youngest entertainer to win a Best New Artist Grammy?

a. LeAnn Rimes

b. Debby Boone

c. Mariah Carey

d. Christina Aguilera

GAME 29 Q2 ANSWER a

Rooney, born Joe Yule, Jr. to vaudevillian parents, began acting on stage when he was fifteen months old. In his first film role at six years old, he played a midget in *Not to Be Trusted* (1926). The next year, he was cast as the lead in the Mickey McGuire silent film series—the foundation of his very long and successful career.

3. In which incarnation of *No Time for Sergeants* did Andy Griffith first play Pvt. Will Stockdale?

a. Film

b. Radio

c. Television

d. Play

GAME 49 Q2 ANSWER d

Forrest, played by Tom Skerritt in the 1970 movie, didn't make it to the TV series. "Spearchucker" was the football-playing doctor, "Ugly John" was the Aussie anesthesiologist, and Lieutenant "Dish" was one of the mobile hospital's nurses.

3. In which movie does Charles Boyer try to drive Ingrid Bergman mad?

a. *Gaslight* (1940)

b. *Double Indemnity* (1944)

c. *The 13th Letter* (1951)

d. *Algiers* (1938)

GAME 69 Q2 ANSWER a

Many consider 1942's *Casablanca* the most romantic movie ever made. The chemistry between Bogart and Bergman was undeniable. Here's a bit of trivia: Bogart's famous line "Here's lookin' at you, kid" was originally written as "Here's good luck to you." Bogie changed the line, which became one of the movie's most memorable.

10. All of the following Al Pacino films were released in the 1970s except:

a. *Dog Day Afternoon*

b. *Bobby Deerfield*

c. *. . . And Justice for All*

d. *Cruising*

Joining Roy Scheider in this sequel were Lorraine Gary as Ellen Brody and Murray Hamilton as Amity's skinflint mayor. Although Steven Spielberg did not return to direct the sequel, Academy Award-winning composer John Williams did return to write the score.

---

10. Which of these movies has the longest running time?

a. *Gone With the Wind* (1939)

b. *Apocalypse Now Redux* (2001)

c. *The Sorrow and the Pity* (1971)

d. *Dances With Wolves* (1990)

The estate of Elvis Presley has made as much as $35 million annually from licenses, merchandise, and record deals. And you wonder why there are over 35,000 Elvis impersonators and only two Orson Welles impersonators (that I'm aware of, anyway).

---

10. Bing Crosby performed all of these Oscar-winning songs *except:*

a. "White Christmas"

b. "Buttons and Bows"

c. "Swinging on a Star"

d. "Sweet Leilani"

Bing Crosby made 1,600 records during his fifty-one-year career as a crooner. He was the first singer to win an Academy Award for Best Actor for his performance in *Going My Way* (1944). One of my greatest honors as a talk show host was having Bing on my TV show as a guest.

---

10. Which of the following shows was *not* an *All in the Family* spinoff?

a. *Maude*

b. *Sanford and Son*

c. *The Jeffersons*

d. *Gloria*

The *Hill Street Blues* theme song was written in 1980 by Mike Post, a prolific composer and five-time Grammy winner to date, who has also created theme songs for TV shows such as *The Rockford Files, St. Elsewhere, The Greatest American Hero,* and *NYPD Blue.*

4. Which of the following has *not* been a character on *Friends*?

a. Mr. Heckles

b. Sammy

c. Paolo

d. Fun Bobby

GAME 9 Q3 ANSWER d
After deciding to remove Isabella Rossallini from his "fantasy" list of women, Ross actually ran into her at Central Perk. Helen Hunt showed up on *Friends* as her *Mad About You* character, Jamie Buchman. And Julia Roberts made a rare TV appearance on the show as Susan "Underpants" Moss.

4. Actress Christina Ricci debuted in which film?

a. *Mermaids*

b. *The Addams Family*

c. *Casper*

d. *Interview With the Vampire*

GAME 29 Q3 ANSWER a
LeAnn Rimes, the first country singer ever to win in this category, received the award in 1996 at age fourteen. Aguilera was eighteen when she won the award in 1999. Meanwhile, Mariah Carey won when she was twenty in 1990, and Pat Boone's daughter Debby won the award in 1977 at age twenty-one.

4. Which actor did *not* repeat his/her movie role on TV?

a. Dabney Coleman in *9 to 5*

b. Gary Burghoff in *M*A*S*H*

c. Vic Tayback in *Alice*

d. Carole Shelley in *The Odd Couple*

GAME 49 Q3 ANSWER c
Griffith's first role as the Air Force draftee was in the TV adaptation of Mac Hyman's novel, which aired in 1955. Later that year, Griffith reprised the role on Broadway, for which he received a Tony nomination. In 1958, he played the character once again in the movie version.

4. Who was the only actor ever nominated for Best Actor *and* Best Supporting Actor for the same performance?

a. John Wayne

b. Barry Fitzgerald

c. Joseph Cotton

d. Claude Rains

GAME 69 Q3 ANSWER a
The first version of *Gaslight* was directed by British director Thorold Dickinson and released in England in 1939, while the Charles Boyer and Ingrid Bergman version was directed by American director George Cukor in 1944. Both versions are excellent, but there is continued debate over which is the better. I prefer the American version myself.

9. How does the shark die in *Jaws II* (1978)?

a. Electrocuted
b. Blown up
c. Harpooned to death
d. Gets indigestion

Dylan never ended up singing the Bacharach-David song, which was sung by B.J. Thomas. When Thomas first recorded the song, he was said to be a bit hung over, and his scratchy-throat version is the one used in the film. A cleaner version was released shortly after, and shot to #1.

---

9. Which of the following departed celebrities has the richest estate?

a. Orson Welles
b. Fred Astaire
c. Elvis Presley
d. Frank Sinatra

The sleuth has been played by seventy-five actors in well over 200 films. John Barrymore, Basil Rathbone, Raymond Massey, Christopher Lee, Peter O'Toole, Christopher Plummer, Nigel Williamson, Peter Cushing, even Michael Caine, have all played the deductive detective.

---

9. Which of the following singers made the most recordings?

a. Andy Williams
b. Perry Como
c. Bing Crosby
d. Barbra Streisand

Torme, "the Velvet Fog," appreciated the reverence and appeared as himself on this sitcom nine times—at least once a season starting in 1986. He also appeared as Harry's guardian angel in the February 1991 episode, "Hey Harry, F'Crying Out Loud—It Is a Wonderful Life . . . Sorta."

---

9. Which of the following TV theme songs was *not* composed by Henry Mancini?

a. *Peter Gunn*
b. *What's Happening!!*
c. *Hill Street Blues*
d. *Remington Steele*

The Mary Tyler Moore Show spun off Mr. Grant (Ed Asner) to the dramatic series *Lou Grant*. In it, Grant becomes city editor for the *Los Angeles Tribune*. The Emmy Award-winning series ran on CBS from 1977 to 1982. *The MTM Show* also spun off sitcoms *Rhoda, Phyllis,* and *The Betty White Show*.

GAME 9

5. The *Friends* characters have been responsible for how many offspring?

a. Three
b. Four
c. Five
d. Six

GAME 9 Q4 ANSWER b

Mr. Heckles lived (and died) in an apartment on the floor below, Paolo was Rachel's Italian heartthrob (and sarcastically referred to by Ross as "Rigatoni"), and Monica once dated Fun Bobby (who turned out to be "fun" only when he had a few drinks).

GAME 29

5. Leonardo DiCaprio first appeared in which movie?

a. *Titanic*
b. *What's Eating Gilbert Grape?*
c. *This Boy's Life*
d. *Parenthood*

GAME 29 Q4 ANSWER a

The nine-year-old Ricci played younger sister to Winona Ryder in the 1990 Cher vehicle, *Mermaids*. She lost the role of young Claudia in *Interview With the Vampire* (1994) to Kirsten Dunst.

GAME 49

5. Which actor did *not* appear as Henry Aldrich?

a. Ezra Stone
b. Jackie Cooper
c. Jimmy Lydon
d. Paul Newman

GAME 49 Q4 ANSWER a

On the TV series *9 to 5*, chauvinistic boss Franklin Hart was played first by Jeffrey Tambor and later by actor/director Peter Bonerz. Dabney Coleman was starring in NBC's *Buffalo Bill* at the time.

GAME 69

5. How many screenwriters are given onscreen credit for *Casablanca* (1942)?

a. One
b. Two
c. Three
d. Four

GAME 69 Q4 ANSWER b

In *Going My Way* (1944), Fitzgerald's fine performance as Father Fitzgibbon earned him nominations for both lead actor and supporting actor. He won the supporting award, losing the other to co-star Bing Crosby.

8. "Raindrops Keep Fallin' on My Head" from the film *Butch Cassidy and the Sundance Kid* (1969) was written for:

a. Elvis Presley

b. Bob Dylan

c. Ricky Nelson

d. Dionne Warwick

GAME 12 Q7 ANSWER b
Vertigo is based on the novel *d'Entre les Morts* by French writer Pierre Boulle. A decade after *Vertigo* was released, Boulle's *Monkey Planet* served as the basis for another movie—*Planet of the Apes,* directed by Franklin J. Schaffner. Hitchcock's films *Rebecca* and *The Birds* were based on novels by Daphne du Maurier.

8. Which character has appeared in the most films?

a. Dracula

b. Sherlock Holmes

c. Tarzan

d. Charlie Chan

GAME 32 Q7 ANSWER d
Like Loretta Lynn, Bill Withers was the child of a coal miner. As a teen, he played professional baseball in the Negro League, and while traveling throughout the South, got his first real taste of the southern gospel music tradition that would lead him to write "Lean on Me."

8. Which singer did Judge Harry Stone of TV's *Night Court* idolize?

a. Frank Sinatra

b. Mel Torme

c. Perry Como

d. Paul Anka

GAME 52 Q7 ANSWER a
The Edge of Night was conceived as the TV version of the popular *Perry Mason* radio show. But the TV show's creator, Irving Vendig, wasn't granted the rights by Earle Stanley Gardner, the author of the Perry Mason books. Gardner had wanted assurances that his "Mason" and "Della Street" would not get romantically involved.

8. Which sitcom spun off one of its characters into a dramatic series?

a. *All in the Family*

b. *The Mary Tyler Moore Show*

c. *Happy Days*

d. *Cheers*

GAME 72 Q7 ANSWER d
DeNiro and Pesce first worked together in *Raging Bull* (1980), Martin Scorsese's film about middleweight boxer Jake LaMotta. They appeared together again in Scorsese's Las Vegas epic *Casino* (1995). In DeNiro's directorial debut, *A Bronx Tale* (1993), Pesce appears briefly alongside DeNiro's character at the end of the film.

6. On *Friends,* when talking about their unborn baby, how do Susan and Carol refer to Ross?

a. Mr. Donation

b. Helping Hand Man

c. BoBo the Sperm Guy

d. Mr. Useful

GAME 9 Q5 ANSWER d
Ross had two children with his first wife, Susan (one through artificial insemination); Phoebe was the surrogate mother for her brother's triplets; and Rachel gave birth to a daughter named Emma (also Ross's) at the end of the 2002 season.

6. At age twelve, whose first movie role was as the younger brother of Bing Crosby and Fred MacMurray?

a. Gene Kelly

b. Donald O'Connor

c. Bobby Driscoll

d. Robert Blake

GAME 29 Q5 ANSWER c
DiCaprio's got his industry start on TV (most notably as Luke in the 1991/92 season of *Growing Pains*). His breakthrough film appearance was as Robert DeNiro's stepson in *This Boy's Life* (1993). Later that year, he appeared in *What's Eating Gilbert Grape,* for which he received a Best Supporting Actor nomination.

6. Which of the following films was *not* based on the play *The Front Page*?

a. *His Girl Friday* (1940)

b. *The Front Page* (1931)

c. *Broadcast News* (1987)

d. *Switching Channels* (1988)

GAME 49 Q5 ANSWER d
Although Jimmy Lydon is the best-known Henry, the original was Ezra Stone, who played Henry on stage in *What a Life* and on the radio's "The Aldrich Family." Child star Jackie Cooper played the role in the first two films. In one of his earliest TV roles, Newman appeared as an occasional cast member on *The Aldrich Family* during the 1952/53 season.

6. In the 1945 film *The Enchanted Cottage*, a cottage helps a couple:

a. Forget their son's death

b. Forget World War II

c. Deal with adultery

d. Look beautiful to each other

GAME 69 Q5 ANSWER c
In the film's opening credits, Julius and Philip Epstein are listed along with Howard Koch as *Casablanca's* screenwriters. This classic 1942 film began as a play by Murray Burnett and Joan Allison called *Everybody Comes to Rick's.*

7. Alfred Hitchcock's film *Vertigo* (1958) is based on a novel by which writer?

a. Daphne du Maurier
b. Pierre Boulle
c. Ray Bradbury
d. Joseph Bloch

GAME 12 Q6 ANSWER c
Hackman plays an ultra-conservative Senator whose daughter wants to marry a man who was raised by a gay couple (Robin Williams and Nathan Lane). This was not the first time Hackman had dressed up for a part. When going undercover in *The French Connection*, he dressed up as Santa Claus.

7. Which song was *not* a hit for singer/songwriter Bill Withers?

a. "Just the Two of Us"
b. "Lean on Me"
c. "Ain't No Sunshine"
d. "Give Me the Night"

GAME 32 Q6 ANSWER d
"It was beauty killed the beast." Despite her many other appearances (including those on my show over the years), it was Wray's combination of sex appeal, vulnerability, and sheer lung capacity in *King Kong* that guaranteed her lasting fame as one of the original "scream queens."

7. Which daytime TV drama originally focused on crime stories and courtroom drama?

a. *The Edge of Night*
b. *As the World Turns*
c. *Days of our Lives*
d. *Search for Tomorrow*

GAME 52 Q6 ANSWER b
Although CBS aired *As the World Turns*, it turned down the spinoff *Another World*. NBC picked up the new program, but was not allowed crossovers of any major characters from *As the World Turns*. One minor character, Geoffrey Lum (played by Mitchell Dru), appeared on both shows.

7. Which film does *not* feature Robert DeNiro and Joe Pesce together onscreen?

a. *Raging Bull*
b. *A Bronx Tale*
c. *Casino*
d. *The Godfather Part II*

GAME 72 Q6 ANSWER c
The soundtrack also includes the duo's "April, Come She Will." Although a few lines of "Mrs. Robinson" do appear in the movie, Paul Simon did not finish writing the song until after the movie was released. The album swept the 1968 Grammys.

Why I Love Silent Movies

There are many reasons why I was so bowled over by silent films. Even though the "talkies" were the big thing in the early- to mid-1930s when I was a kid, I once went to a theatre where they were they doing a Lillian Gish retrospective. She was a wonderful actress, and the heroine of many classic films directed by D.W. Griffith, including *The Birth of a Nation, Intolerance, Orphans of the Storm, Broken Blossoms, Way Down East,* and many more. I later became very friendly with Lillian Gish. She took me to her house several times, and she showed me some of her older films. I became intrigued by silent films as a viewing experience and as an art form.

Then I began collecting photographs. I've got an immense collection of 8 x 10-inch film stills from the heyday of forgotten Hollywood. I won't pretend to contend with the archives of some of the world's museums in this department. But it's safe to say that I could trace a trail from my office on 43rd Street and Times Square to my restaurant over on 45th Street using only a third of my collection as memorabilia bread crumbs.

I've always been fascinated by the names of the women in the silent films—names like Bessie Love and Jean Darling, Beatrice Joy, Clara Bow, Mary Miles Minter, Priscilla Dean. They all had such gorgeous, beautiful names in those days and there were so many of them acting at that time.

In my early days as a radio announcer and budding memorabilia collector, I was lucky enough to meet a great actor named Monte Blue. Monte Blue and a certain dog named Rin Tin Tin had been the two big stars that saved Warner Brothers. Their movies always helped keep the studio in the black—for every expensive John Barrymore extravaganza, a modestly budgeted Monte Blue or Rin Tin Tin feature would keep Warner Brothers in the moviemaking business. Rin Tin Tin was a great dog. There was a film that came out in 1976 called *Won Ton Ton, the Dog Who Saved Hollywood*—that movie was really about Rin Tin Tin.

Not too many people know about this, but I was also close to Buster Keaton from a very young age. I was about fourteen years old when I first met him. I thought he was just a wonderful film star, a great guy. In fact, he starred with Jimmy Durante in the first movie I ever saw—*What, No Beer?* Even though the movie was a "talkie," I could tell just by watching him that he was a comic genius. Nobody did a deadpan better than Keaton—it was the key to his Everyman persona. When I knew him, he was very soft-spoken, very quiet, but I thought he was just the best. He was one of my first guests when I started on TV. He gave me the hat he wore during his appearance on the show.

It's funny—nowadays, we've got guys like Jim Carrey and Adam Sandler making more than $20 million a movie, and a guy like Buster Keaton was making only $500 a week in his prime. Some of it's inflation, but it's also the fact that Keaton was never really treated as well as he could have and should have been. In fact, he spent years in poverty before the film *The Buster Keaton Story* starring Donald O'Connor was released in 1957. Buster received a pretty modest fee for the rights to his life story, but it helped him pay the bills and even manage a bit of comfort for a while. It also kept him comfortably fed.

Keaton was one of silent film's great geniuses. He knew exactly where to put the camera every time. Keaton was a great craftsman and every bit Chaplin's equal in terms of film comedy. They had different styles but they each knew how to make people both laugh and think. Most of all, they made people feel. That's ultimately what has kept me so enamored of silent movies all these years. It's the feelings that I get watching them. Good feelings.

7. What physical secret does Chandler reveal about himself to the *Friends* gang?

a. He has no sense of smell

b. He's missing the baby toe on his left foot

c. He wears dentures

d. He has three nipples

GAME 9 Q6 ANSWER c

Ross, played by David Schwimmer, is the show's resident sensitive guy. He has been married once to lesbian ex-wife Carol, a second time briefly to British beauty Emily, and even more briefly to Rachel (Jennifer Aniston) after a wacky night in Las Vegas.

---

7. Who played Marsha Mason's young daughter in *The Goodbye Girl* (1977)?

a. Kristy McNichol

b. Quinn Cummings

c. Danielle Brisbois

d. Trini Alvarado

GAME 29 Q6 ANSWER b

Sing You Sinners launched O'Connor's career in 1938 as a child actor. He made eleven films in two years, including *Beau Geste* (1939) in which he played a young Gary Cooper. He then went back to the family vaudeville act. O'Connor returned to the screen a decade later, making his mark in *Francis, the Talking Mule* (1949) and *Singin' in the Rain* (1952).

---

7. Which of the following films was *not* based on the book *To Have and Have Not*?

a. *To Have and Have Not* (1944)

b. *The Breaking Point* (1950)

c. *The Gun Runners* (1958)

d. *The Killers* (1946)

GAME 49 Q6 ANSWER c

The play by Ben Hecht and Charles Macarthur became a film with the same name in 1931, starring Pat O'Brien and Adolphe Menjou. The 1974 film version starred Jack Lemmon and Walter Matthau. In *His Girl Friday*, a male character was changed to a female, while *Switching Channels* took the story to a TV newsroom.

---

7. Which 1940s film musical paired Gene Kelly with Rita Hayworth?

a. *Anchors Aweigh* (1945)

b. *On the Town* (1949)

c. *For Me and My Gal* (1942)

d. *Cover Girl* (1944)

GAME 69 Q6 ANSWER d

Although Robert Young's character was disfigured in the war and Dorothy McGuire's character is plain, the two suddenly find that the cottage has made them both whole and beautiful. Ultimately, they realize that their love has only made them *appear* beautiful to each other. But the strength of their love allows them to face the world together.

6. In which movie does Gene Hackman dress up in drag?

a. *The French Connection* (1971)

b. *Superman: The Movie* (1978)

c. *The Birdcage* (1996)

d. *Narrow Margin* (1990)

GAME 12 Q5 ANSWER b
If you carefully watch this film, you'll notice two small cameos by two important men—Ronald Reagan, who plays Alec, Davis's perpetually drunk cousin, and a pre-WWII Humphrey Bogart, who plays Michael, the embittered stable hand with an on-again, off-again Irish brogue. (Bogey admitted he was never too good with accents!)

6. In *King Kong* (1933), what was the name of Fay Wray's character?

a. Lucy Weston

b. Dawn Prescott

c. Jill Young

d. Ann Darrow

GAME 32 Q5 ANSWER b
The song "White Christmas" by Irving Berlin was so popular following the release of *Holiday Inn* that Paramount decided to name a film after the song. The studios planned to reunite Crosby with *Holiday Inn* co-star Fred Astaire, but Astaire declined the project after reading the script. Danny Kaye took the role.

6. The daytime TV drama *Another World* was a spinoff of which other soap?

a. *Love of Life*

b. *As the World Turns*

c. *Guiding Light*

d. *Search for Tomorrow*

GAME 52 Q5 ANSWER b
ELO (Electric Light Orchestra) went to #4 on the charts with its song "Telephone Line," which is the same slot that The Orlons' "Don't Hang Up" reached in 1962. Jim Croce's 1972 classic "Operator (That's Not the Way It Feels)" climbed to #17. The Five Americans' hit, "Western Union," went to #6 in 1967.

6. Which Simon and Garfunkel song is *not* featured in *The Graduate* (1967)?

a. "Scarborough Fair"

b. "The Sound of Silence"

c. "Homeward Bound"

d. "Mrs. Robinson"

GAME 72 Q5 ANSWER b
Born Marie McDonald McLaughlin Lawrie, her manager renamed her, saying that she was a "lulu of a kid." The number one song of 1967, *To Sir, With Love* was written by Lulu's friend Mark London.

8. Which *Friends* character has never been married?

a. Phoebe
b. Joey
c. Chandler
d. Rachel

This physical characteristic is referred to as his "nubbin." Interestingly, James Bond's nemesis Francisco Scaramanga (played by Christopher Lee) also had three nipples in *The Man With the Golden Gun* (1974).

---

8. Ron Howard's directorial film debut starred:

a. Ron Howard
b. Michael Keaton
c. Tom Hanks
d. Steve Guttenberg

Cummings received a Best Supporting Actress Academy Award nomination for her performance in this movie. She then went on to co-star as Kristy McNichol's orphaned cousin Annie in the aptly-named ABC-TV drama *Family*.

---

8. After *Seinfield*, which sitcom did Jerry Stiller find himself in?

a. *The King of Queens*
b. *Everybody Loves Raymond*
c. *Frazier*
d. *Friends*

Based on the 1937 Hemingway novel, the film *To Have and Have Not* starred Humphrey Bogart. *The Breaking Point* starred John Garfield, while *The Gun Runners* starred Audie Murphy. It's no surprise that Bogart's film is the best of the bunch—novelist William Faulkner wrote much of the dialogue.

---

8. What is Bette Davis's hobby in the early portion of the 1942 film *Now, Voyager*?

a. Painting still lifes
b. Making dolls
c. Carving ivory boxes
d. Writing poetry

Cover Girl was also the first film Kelly choreographed. He co-starred with Judy Garland in *For Me and My Gal*, his first Hollywood film. Kathryn Grayson and Frank Sinatra joined him in *Anchors Aweigh*, while Vera-Ellen was his romantic interest in *On the Town*.

5. Who played the caring doctor and eventual husband of doomed heiress Bette Davis in 1939's *Dark Victory*?

a. Robert Donat
b. George Brent
c. Cary Grant
d. Gregory Peck

GAME 12 Q4 ANSWER b
Because of a heart condition, Robinson decided the extensive make-up and extreme heat of shooting outdoors in the summer months would be too much for his health, and he bowed out of the film. He was replaced by Shakespearean actor Maurice Evans.

5. Who starred in both *Holiday Inn* (1942) and *White Christmas* (1954)?

a. Danny Kaye
b. Bing Crosby
c. Fred Astaire
d. Walter Abel

GAME 32 Q4 ANSWER c
When the Oscars were traditionally broadcast on Monday nights, Woody Allen usually missed them. That's the night he plays clarinet at Michael's Pub in Manhattan. Although Steve Allen portrayed clarinet player Benny Goodman in the movies, he was actually a piano player. George Segal plays banjo, and Jack Lemmon was an accomplished pianist.

5. Who did *not* have a hit with a telephone-related song?

a. ELO
b. The Five Americans
c. The Orlons
d. Jim Croce

GAME 52 Q4 ANSWER c
"Chef-of-the-future" Ralph brings down the TV studio while demonstrating how to "core a apple." Always looking to get rich quick, he also made glow-in-the-dark shoe polish, managed a boxer, bought a hotel in New Jersey, and dug for Captain Kidd's treasure on Long Island. One of his ideas actually became a reality. It was frozen pizza.

5. Lulu sang the title song for which movie?

a. *The Blackboard Jungle*
b. *To Sir, With Love*
c. *American Graffiti*
d. *Porky's*

GAME 72 Q4 ANSWER a
This motto is located on the base of the statue of the founder of Faber College. The tagline for this 1978 film was "It was the Deltas against the rules. The rules lost!" *National Lampoon's Animal House* was John Belushi's first motion picture.

9. Which of the following actors plays Phoebe's brother?

a. John Cusack

b. Giovanni Ribisi

c. Crispin Glover

d. Ben Stiller

GAME 9 Q8 ANSWER b
Chandler married Monica, Rachel and Ross "unknowingly" tied the knot one night in Las Vegas, and Phoebe, in order to help him get a green card, married a Canadian ice dancer named Duncan.

---

9. Who holds the record as the highest paid entertainer under the age of eighteen?

a. Shirley Temple

b. Michael Jackson

c. Macaulay Culkin

d. Drew Barrymore

GAME 29 Q8 ANSWER a
Grand Theft Auto (1977) was the film that kicked off Howard's career as a director. Howard also starred in this movie, which he co-wrote with his father. Michael Keaton appeared in Howard's *Night Shift* (1982), Tom Hanks had his first starring role in *Splash* (1984), and Steve Guttenberg appeared in *Cocoon* (1985).

---

9. Which of the following people was *not* one of the original five VJs on MTV?

a. Martha Quinn

b. Mark Goodman

c. "Downtown" Julie Brown

d. JJ Jackson

GAME 49 Q8 ANSWER a
Stiller plays Arthur Spooner, the cantankerous and oddly eccentric father-in-law to "everyman" Doug Heffernan, played by actor/comedian Kevin James. I love Jerry Stiller. He and his wife, Anne Meara, were on my show plenty of times in the 1960s, when they gained national attention as the comedy duo Stiller & Meara.

---

9. Which 1940s Alfred Hitchcock thriller features a dream sequence designed by surrealist Salvador Dali?

a. *Spellbound* (1945)

b. *Notorious* (1946)

c. *Rope* (1948)

d. *Suspicion* (1941)

GAME 69 Q8 ANSWER c
As the depressed, lonely spinster Charlotte Vale, Davis seeks refuge in the elaborate carving of ivory boxes. Later in the film, after she is helped by psychiatrist Claude Rains, the character acquires less solitary interests. Although Davis starred in many tearjerkers, she had a real problem with being able to cry in a scene.

4. Who was originally supposed to play Dr. Zaius in *Planet of the Apes* (1967)?

a. Sir John Gielgud

b. Edward G. Robinson

c. James Mason

d. Martin Balsam

GAME 12 Q3 ANSWER d
Coppola's winery is run from his own Napa Valley estate, which he purchased in the 1970s at the height of his success with the first two *Godfather* films.

---

4. Many actors are also musicians. Which of these actors plays the clarinet?

a. George Segal

b. Steve Allen

c. Woody Allen

d. Jack Lemmon

GAME 32 Q3 ANSWER c
Laughton won the Best Actor Oscar for *The Private Life of Henry VIII* (1933). He was nominated twice more for *Mutiny on the Bounty* (1935) and *Witness for the Prosecution* (1958).

---

4. On *The Honeymooners*, what did Ralph and Norton try to sell in a commercial?

a. Kram-Mar's Delicious Mystery Appetizer

b. Old Gold Cigarettes

c. Happy Housewife Helper

d. Vitameatavegimin

GAME 52 Q3 ANSWER c
Cronkite hosted *It's News to Me* in 1954. He was also a "Quiz Authority" on the show *Two For the Money* during its 1955/56 season.

---

4. What is the motto of the college in *National Lampoon's Animal House*?

a. Knowledge is Good

b. Fat, Drunk, and Stupid is No Way to Go Through Life

c. Always Eat Your Vegetables

d. Tuck In Those Pajamas

GAME 72 Q3 ANSWER d
The original 1927 film starred Al Jolson as Jakie Rabinowitz (Jack Robin), the son of a Jewish cantor who defies his father to pursue the dream of becoming a jazz singer. Danny Thomas played the role in 1952, and Neil Diamond was Jakie in the 1980 remake.

10. Which Hollywood legend finds Joey taking a shower in his dressing room during a film shoot?

a. Lloyd Bridges

b. Robert Vaughn

c. Charlton Heston

d. Al Pacino

Giovanni Ribisi earned critical praise for his portrayal of a mildly retarded young man who finds love in Garry Marshall's film *The Other Sister* (1999). He was also one of the soldiers in *Saving Private Ryan* (1998) and the leading character in *Boiler Room* (2000).

---

10. Both Tatum O'Neal and Anna Paquin picked up their Best Supporting Actress Oscars at the age of:

a. Nine

b. Eleven

c. Thirteen

d. Fifteen

Although Barrymore and Jackson are multi-million dollar entertainers who have been in the spotlight since childhood, it was Culkin who, when barely a teenager, managed an $8 million payday for each of his two 1994 films—*Richie Rich* and *Getting Even With Dad*.

---

10. Which British rock band gave the Los Angeles metal group Quiet Riot not one but two big hits in the early 1980s?

a. Deep Purple

b. Emerson, Lake & Palmer

c. Slade

d. Spinal Tap

Of the five original MTV-VJs, only Jackson and Goodman had worked as radio DJs. Martha Quinn was a broadcasting major at NYU, Nina Blackwood was an aspiring actress and classically-trained musician, and Alan Hunter was an actor who had appeared in a David Bowie video. Julie Brown, who started as a VJ in the UK, became an MTV-VJ in 1986.

---

10. In which movie does Cary Grant play an ad executive?

a. *Bringing Up Baby*

b. *Arsenic and Old Lace*

c. *Mr. Blandings Builds His Dream House*

d. *The Talk of the Town*

In this wartime thriller starring Ingrid Bergman and Gregory Peck, Hitchcock and producer David Selznick wanted to draw on Dali's unique vision to help portray the world of the subconscious. Although the dream sequence was supposed to be about twenty minutes long, it lasted only a few minutes.

3. Which acclaimed film director also owns a winery?

a. Martin Scorsese
b. Steven Spielberg
c. Sydney Pollack
d. Francis Ford Coppola

GAME 12 Q2 ANSWER a

The made-for-TV movie aired in 1976, more than twenty years before novelist Ira Levin wrote his sequel to the story called *Son of Rosemary*. Even with Ruth Gordon reprising her Oscar-winning role as Minnie Castevet from the 1968 film, this TV movie was a disappointment.

---

3. Who was the first Brit to win an Academy Award?

a. Alfred Hitchcock
b. Leslie Howard
c. Charles Laughton
d. Arthur Treacher

GAME 32 Q2 ANSWER c

Page also performed lead on Joe Cocker's rendition of "A Little Help From My Friends," and "Sea of Love" by The Honey drippers.

---

3. Which newscaster is a former game show host?

a. Mike Wallace
b. Peter Jennings
c. Walter Cronkite
d. Eric Sevareid

GAME 52 Q2 ANSWER a

Although this 1961 film had a number of bankable stars, a great director, and an Arthur Miller original screenplay, it proved to be a box office disappointment. A few days after the movie's final filming, Gable died from a massive heart attack. Monroe died a year and a half later from an overdose of sedatives.

---

3. Who did *not* star in a version of *The Jazz Singer*?

a. Al Jolson
b. Danny Thomas
c. Neil Diamond
d. Adam Sandler

GAME 72 Q2 ANSWER d

My Favorite Wife was originally written by husband-and-wife team Bella and Sam Spewack. The 1940 film starred Cary Grant and Irene Dunne. A 1962 remake of the film, *Something's Got to Give*, was never completed after Marilyn Monroe was fired from the project. *Move Over, Darling* is the 1963 remake starring Doris Day and James Garner.

11. What classic TV show did Chandler watch late at night during the *Friends* 1994 season?

a. *Star Trek*

b. *The Honeymooners*

c. *The Outer Limits*

d. *The Ernie Kovacs Show*

Although he's often characterized as gruff and macho, Heston actually has one of the more sophisticated wits in the business. His deadpan line delivery upon finding a naked Joey in his shower made for classic TV. By the way, Joey, an aspiring actor, also had the distinction of playing Al Pacino's naked buttocks in another episode.

---

11. All of these young actors appeared in *Parenthood* except:

a. Martha Plimpton

b. Christian Slater

c. Joaquin Phoenix

d. Keanu Reeves

O'Neal won for *Paper Moon* (1973), in which she co-starred with her dad, Ryan. Paquin won twenty years later for her role in *The Piano*.

---

11. Who sang an unlikely duet with David Bowie on the 1977 single, "Peace on Earth/Little Drummer Boy"?

a. Perry Como

b. Bing Crosby

c. Mel Torme

d. Andy Williams

Quiet Riot went straight to the top when it adapted Slade's early 1970s hit "Cum on Feel the Noize" on its first album, *Metal Health*. On the second album, *Condition Critical*, the band again scored a hit with Slade's song "Mama Weer All Crazee Now." Slade itself had a big hit around this time with the song "Run Runaway."

---

11. In *Rebecca,* starring Joan Fontaine and Sir Laurence Olivier, "Rebecca" is the name of:

a. Olivier's first wife

b. Fontaine's sister

c. Olivier's evil housekeeper

d. Olivier's dead mother

In this 1948 comedy, Grant is so distracted by the difficulties of building a house in the country that he gives little time and attention to his job with a New York advertising firm. Yet in the final scene of the movie, we find that Grant has (with the unwitting help of his maid) devised a great advertising slogan for his key account.

2. Mia Farrow played the part of Rosemary in *Rosemary's Baby*. Who played the part in the made-for-TV sequel?

a. Patty Duke
b. Blythe Danner
c. Sondra Locke
d. Twiggy

GAME 12 Q1 ANSWER b
Stephen King produced a TV version of *The Shining* in 1997. *Salem's Lot* was initially shown in 1979 as a four-hour made-for-TV movie. *Pet Sematary* (1989) spawned a mediocre sequel, and *Misery* (1990) was made only once—and that was enough for me!

---

2. Which future member of Led Zeppelin performed on The Who's first record in 1965, "I Can't Explain"?

a. Robert Plant
b. John Paul Jones
c. Jimmy Page
d. John Bonham

GAME 32 Q1 ANSWER c
This pop duo must be the most famous lip-synchers of the late 1980s, if not the history of audio dubbing. Losing the Grammy they had been awarded for Best New Artist ended the careers of the two, a former German break dancer and a French gymnast.

---

2. Who directed *The Misfits*, the last movie for both Marilyn Monroe and Clark Gable?

a. John Huston
b. Elia Kazan
c. George Cukor
d. Billy Wilder

GAME 52 Q1 ANSWER d
Passions debuted on NBC in 1999, and centers on the natural and supernatural happenings in the picturesque New England town of Harmony, Maine. *Dark Shadows*, which aired on ABC from 1966 to 1971, was the first daytime serial to feature vampires, witches, and things that go bump in the night.

---

2. Which of these films was *not* based on the same story?

a. *My Favorite Wife*
b. *Something's Got to Give*
c. *Move Over, Darling*
d. *The Lady Eve*

GAME 72 Q1 ANSWER a
Chinatown was produced in 1974 by Robert Evans, directed by Roman Polanski, and starred Jack Nicholson and Faye Dunaway in an Oscar-winning script by Robert Towne. The 1990 sequel was again a Robert Towne script produced by Robert Evans and starring Jack Nicholson, who also directed the film.

12. Who plays Jack Geller, father of Ross and Monica on *Friends*?

a. Elliott Gould

b. Ron Leibman

c. Robert Culp

d. Kathleen Turner

GAME 9 Q11 ANSWER d
Chandler is my kind of guy—he has an obsession with Kovacs' classic Nairobi Trio, featuring the seemingly mechanized monkeys that clowned around in rhythm to "Solfeggio." He also had a pet duck for a while . . .

---

12. In which film musical does Donald O'Connor play Ethel Merman's son?

a. *Yankee Doodle Dandy* (1942)

b. *There's No Business Like Show Business* (1954)

c. *Call Me Madam* (1950)

d. *Anything Goes* (1956)

GAME 29 Q11 ANSWER b
Martha Plimpton played the older sister of Joachin Phoenix in this 1989 film. (Ironically, she was dating his older brother River at the time.) Keanu played Plimpton's on-screen boyfriend.

---

12. What was actor Michael Keaton's real name before he changed it?

a. Michael Redgrave

b. Michael Douglas

c. Michael Maggiore

d. Michael Murphy

GAME 49 Q11 ANSWER b
Though a bit unusual, the pairing of these singers made for wonderful music, all that ever really mattered to a singer like Bing Crosby. I was fortunate enough to have Bing on my show in the early 1970s. He was a wonderful man and is sorely missed.

---

12. In which '40s film did Rita Hayworth remove only one silk glove in a famous striptease?

a. *The Lady From Shanghai*

b. *Down to Earth*

c. *Tonight and Every Night*

d. *Gilda*

GAME 69 Q11 ANSWER a
The mystery of Rebecca's death and her true nature is central to this 1940 film, and Rebecca's name is mentioned quite often in the movie. In contrast, Fontaine, who plays Olivier's second wife, has no first name in the movie, just as her character has no first name in the Daphne du Maurier novel on which the film was based.

GAME 12

1. Which Stephen King novel was made into a movie twice?

a. *Salem's Lot*

b. *The Shining*

c. *Misery*

d. *Pet Sematary*

The answer to this question is on:

page 156, top frame, right side.

GAME 32

1. Fake pop duo Milli Vanilli included Fabrice "Fab" Morvan and:

a. Robert Cray

b. Robert Palmer

c. Rob Pilatus

d. Rob Zombie

The answer to this question is on:

page 156, second frame, right side.

GAME 52

1. Which daytime TV drama includes a regular character who is a witch?

a. *Guilding Light*

b. *Port Charles*

c. *One Life to Live*

d. *Passions*

The answer to this question is on:

page 156, third frame, right side.

GAME 72

1. Which of the following films is the sequel to *Chinatown*?

a. *The Two Jakes*

b. *The Big Sleep*

c. *Jake and the Fatman*

d. *Raging Bull*

The answer to this question is on:

page 156, bottom frame, right side.

GAME 10

Auteur, Auteur

The Great Directors

*Turn to page 128
for the first question.*

GAME 9 Q12 ANSWER a
Ron Leibman plays Rachel's dad, while Kathleen Turner plays Chandler's *father* after a sex-change operation (his mother is played by Morgan Fairchild). Meanwhile, Robert Culp plays Patricia Heaton's father on the CBS sitcom *Everybody Loves Raymond.*

GAME 30

Attention-Getting Females

Divas and Leading Ladies

*Turn to page 128
for the first question.*

GAME 29 Q12 ANSWER b
Basically a musical travelogue, *There's No Business . . .* was 20th Century Fox's answer to MGM's splashy big budget musicals of the '50s. The cast included Dan Dailey as the father, Johnnie Ray and Mitzi Gaynor as O'Connor's siblings, and a wonderfully sexy Marilyn Monroe.

GAME 50

Horror House

From Vincent Price to Freddy Krueger

*Turn to page 128
for the first question.*

GAME 49 Q12 ANSWER b
In the mid-1970s, Keaton decided to change his name so he wouldn't be confused with Kirk Douglas's son Michael. He chose the last name Keaton after reading an article about actress Diane Keaton. Interestingly, Keaton's real name is Hall, but she changed it in honor of my good friend Buster Keaton.

GAME 70

Superheroes

Here They Come to Save the Day!

*Turn to page 128
for the first question.*

GAME 69 Q12 ANSWER d
Hayworth's provocative performance of "Put the Blame on Mame" in this 1946 film definitely earned her the term "love goddess."

GAME 12

Memory Lane Grab Bag

Turn to page 155 for the first question.

GAME 11 Q12 ANSWER b
Lewis was one of the guest hosts before Johnny Carson took over for Jack Paar. Here's the memory test he taught Paar's announcer/sidekick Hugh Downs: One hen; two ducks; three squawking geese; and so on, up to ten lyrical, spherical, diabolical denizens of the deep who quiver and shiver and shake around a corner all at the same time.

GAME 32

Memory Lane Grab Bag

Turn to page 155 for the first question.

GAME 31 Q12 ANSWER a
Still hot from her starring role on CBS's *Mary Hartman, Mary Hartman,* Lasser was apparently thrown by the realities of "live" television. She retreated to her dressing room for nearly the entire show and was never invited back.

GAME 52

Memory Lane Grab Bag

Turn to page 155 for the first question.

GAME 51 Q12 ANSWER a
Candace Cameron, who played D.J., was joined on this ABC sitcom by the Olsen twins, Mary Kate and Ashley, who shared the role of sister Michelle. The show's third sister, Stephanie, was never mentioned, so I'm going to let her share the spotlight here—she was played by Jodie Sweetin.

GAME 72

Memory Lane Grab Bag

Turn to page 155 for the first question.

GAME 71 Q12 ANSWER c
This lighthearted tale of a good-natured witch and the spell she casts on the man she loves must have been a relief after the intensity of appearing in Alfred Hitchcock's *Vertigo* that same year. In 1995, the actors were onscreen again when director Terry Gilliam used a scene from *Vertigo* in his film *Twelve Monkeys.*

1. Which movie was *not* directed by Stanley Kubrick?

a. *A Clockwork Orange* (1971)

b. *Eyes Wide Shut* (1999)

c. *Tom Jones* (1963)

d. *Full Metal Jacket* (1987)

The answer to this question is on:

page 129, top frame, right side.

1. The cast of *Steel Magnolias* included all of these actors *except:*

a. Shirley MacLaine

b. Debra Winger

c. Sally Field

d. Daryl Hannah

The answer to this question is on:

page 129, second frame, right side.

1. Before his television success on *21 Jump Street*, Johnny Depp appeared in which film?

a. *From Hell*

b. *A Nightmare on Elm Street*

c. *Edward Scissorhands*

d. *Sleepy Hollow*

The answer to this question is on:

page 129, third frame, right side.

1. On TV's *Batman*, the hidden button to the Batcave was inside a bust of:

a. Bruce Wayne

b. Ludwig van Beethoven

c. William Shakespeare

d. Alfred Lord Tennyson

The answer to this question is on:

page 129, bottom frame, right side.

12. Jerry Lewis taught which *Tonight Show* regular his famous "one hen, two ducks" memory test in 1962?

a. Ed McMahon
b. Hugh Downs
c. Ed Herlihy
d. Jack Paar

GAME 11 Q11 ANSWER c
Set in the suburban basement of host Ken Ober's parents' house, the TV-and-pop-music-trivia game show was co-hosted by Colin Quinn. It was on *Remote Control* that Adam Sandler created the type of characters he would later play on *Saturday Night Live*.

12. Which *Saturday Night Live* host had an attack of stage fright during the show's opening?

a. Louise Lasser
b. Frank Zappa
c. William S. Burroughs
d. Rob Reiner

GAME 31 Q11 ANSWER b
John Belushi was the first of NBC's "Not Ready for Prime Time Players" to appear in an *SNL* skit along with head *SNL* writer Michael O'Donohue. O'Donohue played a remedial English tutor, who was teaching foreigner Belushi how to say, "I would like to feed your fingertips to the wolverines."

12. Candace Cameron, Kirk's sister, starred in which sitcom?

a. *Full House*
b. *Empty Nest*
c. *My Two Dads*
d. *Blossom*

GAME 51 Q11 ANSWER d
The movie was *Scrooged* (1988), a decidedly modern and often caustic retelling of Dickens' *A Christmas Carol*. Brian-Doyle Murray played Bill's father during the Ghost of Christmas Past segment. Bill's other brother, John Murray, also appeared in the film as (what else?) Bill's brother. A family affair if ever there was one . . .

12. After *Vertigo* in 1958, what other film starred Jimmy Stewart and Kim Novak?

a. *Winchester '73*
b. *Pal Joey*
c. *Bell, Book and Candle*
d. *Rear Window*

GAME 71 Q11 ANSWER d
John Michael Hayes enjoyed a steady burst of work with Alfred Hitchcock in the 1950s, working on such successful pictures as *Rear Window* (1954), *To Catch a Thief* (1955), and the 1956 remake of *The Man Who Knew Too Much*.

2. Which film's screenplay was co-written by Steven Spielberg's sister Anne?

a. *American Beauty* (1999)

b. *Rain Man* (1988)

c. *Big* (1988)

d. *Harry Potter and the Sorcerer's Stone* (2001)

GAME 10 Q1 ANSWER c

Tony Richardson's *Tom Jones*, based on the novel by Henry Fielding, stars Albert Finney as an 18th-century rascal trying to make his fortune. It is not to be confused with Kubrick's 1975 film *Barry Lyndon*, starring Ryan O'Neal. Based on the novel by William Makepeace Thackeray, it is also about an 18th-century rogue determined to make his fortune.

2. Which of these movies did *not* star Julia Roberts?

a. *Mystic Pizza* (1988)

b. *Pretty Woman* (1990)

c. *Shakespeare in Love* (1998)

d. *America's Sweethearts* (2001)

GAME 30 Q1 ANSWER b

The cast of this beloved 1989 James L. Brooks film also included Olympia Dukakis, Dolly Parton, and Oscar nominee Julia Roberts, as well as Dylan McDermott, Tom Skerritt, and Sam Shephard.

2. Which classic horror movie actor has never appeared as Dracula, Dr. Frankenstein, or his monster?

a. Christopher Lee

b. Peter Cushing

c. Vincent Price

d. John Carradine

GAME 50 Q1 ANSWER b

Depp may have pruned many a bush in *Edward Scissorhands* (1990) before staving off the Headless Horseman in *Sleepy Hollow* (1999) and Jack the Ripper in *From Hell* (2001), but it was his role as one of Freddy Krueger's victims in the original *A Nightmare on Elm Street* (1984) that gave us our first look at him.

2. Which crime-fighting actor is the *Lone Ranger's* grandnephew?

a. Bruce Wayne (Batman)

b. Dick Grayson (Robin)

c. Lamont Cranston (The Shadow)

d. Britt Reid (The Green Hornet)

GAME 70 Q1 ANSWER c

After pushing the hidden button, a library wall would slide open to reveal the Batpoles. Bruce Wayne and Dick Grayson would slide down the poles, and in the next shot, would suddenly be in their costumes in the Batcave.

11. Which comic did *not* get his start on the MTV game show *Remote Control*?

a. Dennis Leary

b. Adam Sandler

c. David Spade

d. Colin Quinn

GAME 11 Q10 ANSWER c
Don Knotts was nominated for and won five Emmys for his portrayal of Deputy Barney Fife. Frances Bavier won a 1967 Supporting Actress Emmy for playing Aunt Bea. Ron Howard won his first Emmy for producing the HBO mini-series *From the Earth to the Moon* (1998). Andy Griffith has never won an Emmy.

11. Which *Saturday Night Live* cast member was in the first skit of the first show in 1975?

a. Dan Aykroyd

b. Gilda Radner

c. John Belushi

d. Garrett Morris

GAME 31 Q10 ANSWER c
Although producer Lorne Michaels offered The Beatles $3,000 to perform on the show in 1976, Harrison was the only one to appear that year. McCartney was first on the show in 1980, while Starr first hosted in 1984. At the time of his death in 1980, John Lennon had never been on the show.

11. Which of the following actors starred in a movie in which his brother played his father?

a. Sylvester Stallone

b. Dan Aykroyd

c. Groucho Marx

d. Bill Murray

GAME 51 Q10 ANSWER c
The four brothers are Alec, William (sometimes called Billy), Stephen, and Daniel. All four brothers hail from Long Island, New York. Alec is the most well known and politically outspoken Baldwin. Who knows, maybe they'll band together and do a remake of a Marx Brothers movie someday.

11. Which of the following Hollywood screenwriters was *not* blacklisted in the 1950s?

a. Ring Lardner, Jr.

b. Dalton Trumbo

c. Michael Wilson

d. John Michael Hayes

GAME 71 Q10 ANSWER d
Edward G. Robinson starred in an earlier Welles' film called *The Stranger* (1945). In *Touch of Evil*, Joseph Cotten appears briefly as a witness to a car bombing; Zsa Zsa Gabor does a cameo as a stripper; and Marlene Dietrich plays Tanya, the mysterious Mexican bar owner who utters the film's last word: "Adios."

3. Which famous director appeared as a county clerk in John Landis's *The Blues Brothers* (1980)?

a. Robert Altman
b. Stanley Kubrick
c. Martin Scorsese
d. Steven Spielberg

GAME 10 Q2 ANSWER c
Anne Spielberg and Gary Ross co-wrote and co-produced the movie *Big*, for which they received an Academy Award nomination for Best Original Screenplay. The movie was directed by Penny Marshall and starred Tom Hanks, whose performance earned him an Oscar nomination for Best Actor.

3. Julie Andrews appeared topless in which film?

a. *The Man Who Loved Women* (1983)
b. *Victor/Victoria* (1982)
c. *S.O.B.* (1982)
d. *10* (1979)

GAME 30 Q2 ANSWER c
Julia was offered the lead in *Shakespeare in Love,* but turned it down. This turned out to be a good break for Gwyneth Paltrow, who won an Academy Award for the role.

3. *The Return of the Texas Chainsaw Massacre* (1994) provided early lead roles for Renee Zellweger and:

a. Matthew McConaughey
b. Skeet Ulrich
c. David Arquette
d. Mike Myers

GAME 50 Q2 ANSWER c
Oh, the horror of it all. Price *did* play the vampire Count Sfoza on an episode of *F-Troop.* Otherwise, the closest he came to these characters was as the voice of the Invisible Man in *Abbott and Costello Meet Frankenstein* (1948).

3. On TV's *Batman*, what kind of car was the *Batmobile*?

a. Lincoln
b. Cadillac
c. Oldsmobile
d. Corvette

GAME 70 Q2 ANSWER d
Texas Ranger John Reid, the lone survivor of an ambush by the Cavendish gang, became *The Lone Ranger* in 1933, when he was created by George Trendle for radio. Reid's only living relative was nephew Dan, editor of *The Daily Sentinel.* Dan's son, Britt Reid, played *The Green Hornet,* who was created in 1936, also by Trendle.

10. Which cast member from *The Andy Griffith Show* has won the most Emmys?

a. Andy Griffith
b. Ron Howard
c. Don Knotts
d. Frances Bavier

GAME 11 Q9 ANSWER c
Jerry and Jason have both been guest hosts, and Julia was a cast member from 1982 to 1985. Richards and *Seinfeld* co-creator Larry David were cast members of *Fridays*, ABC's answer to *SNL*, from 1980 to 1982.

---

10. Which Beatle was the only one to appear on *Saturday Night Live* in the 1970s?

a. John Lennon
b. Paul McCartney
c. George Harrison
d. Ringo Starr

GAME 31 Q9 ANSWER c
Chevy Chase has hosted the show more than any other ex-cast member. Bill Murray has been host over five times. Chris Farley hosted in October 1997, two months before his death. To date, none of *SNL's* thirty-six female ex-cast members/featured players has hosted the show.

---

10. How many "actor" Baldwin brothers are there?

a. Six
b. Five
c. Four
d. Three

GAME 51 Q9 ANSWER b
Bruce Willis first won fame as Cybil Shepherd's detective partner on *Moonlighting*. Jim Carrey caused a sensation with his crazy high jinks on *In Living Color*. Early in his career, Brad Pitt played a small role on a 1989 episode of *Growing Pains*. In 2001, he played a hilarious cameo opposite real-life wife Jennifer Aniston on *Friends*.

---

10. All of the following actors make a brief appearance in Orson Welles' 1958 film *Touch of Evil* except:

a. Zsa Zsa Gabor
b. Joseph Cotten
c. Marlene Dietrich
d. Edward G. Robinson

GAME 71 Q9 ANSWER b
Directed by Fred Zimmerman, *The Men* (1950) features Brando playing Ken Wilozek, an embittered wheelchair-bound World War II veteran. Although he was nominated for an Oscar in this role, Brando did not win a Best Actor Oscar until 1955, when he played down-and-out ex-boxer Terry Malloy in Elia Kazan's film *On the Waterfront*.

4. Which famous director has *not* directed a Michael Jackson music video?

a. Martin Scorsese

b. John Landis

c. Brian De Palma

d. Spike Lee

GAME 10 Q3 ANSWER d

Others with small roles in the film included Carrie Fisher, Twiggy, Paul "Pee-wee Herman" Reubens, and musicians Joe Walsh, Ray Charles, James Brown, Cab Calloway, and Aretha Franklin.

4. Which *Baywatch* regular got her start as one of the models on CBS's *The Price Is Right*?

a. Pam Anderson

b. Gena Lee Nolin

c. Erika Eleniak

d. Donna D'Errico

GAME 30 Q3 ANSWER c

In *Victor/Victoria*, Andrews played a woman playing a man and appeared wigless, but not topless. *S.O.B.* was Andrews' director/husband Blake Edwards' attack on the hypocrisies of the Hollywood studio system.

4. Which screen monster has appeared in the most films to date?

a. The Mummy

b. Frankenstein's Monster

c. The Wolfman

d. Dracula

GAME 50 Q3 ANSWER a

The two both first appeared in small roles in the 1993 teen flick *My Boyfriend's Back* (also known as *Johnny Zombie*). McConaughey also appeared in *Dazed and Confused* that same year, playing one of a group of young potheads trying to make sense out of the '70s—that, and bell bottoms.

4. Who was the Green Hornet's sidekick?

a. Speedy

b. Robin

c. Kato

d. Tonto

GAME 70 Q3 ANSWER a

TV's Batman drove a modified 1955 Lincoln Futura. Batman was also named television's worst driver by the Automobile Legal Association. In just one episode, he managed to make a U-turn on a busy street, cross over road dividers, turn without signaling, and crash through safety barriers. At least he wore a seatbelt.

9. Which *Seinfeld* cast member has never appeared on *Saturday Night Live*?

a. Jerry Seinfeld

b. Jason Alexander

c. Michael Richards

d. Julia Louis-Dreyfus

GAME 11 Q8 ANSWER d
This sequel to the mini-series *The Winds of War* starred Robert Mitchum and Jane Seymour. It cost over $110 million to produce and took over three years to complete. The show's fourteen episodes aired in two parts during November 1988 and March 1989.

---

9. Which of these ex-*Saturday Night Live* cast members has *not* returned as guest host?

a. Chevy Chase

b. Chris Farley

c. Joan Cusack

d. Bill Murray

GAME 31 Q8 ANSWER c
Kaufman appeared on *SNL* in October 1975, lip-synching the theme song to the old *Mighty Mouse* cartoon show. He made another dozen appearances on the show, wrestling women, playing the bongos, and impersonating Elvis. In a typically zany stunt, he was "voted off" the show forever by viewers in 1982.

---

9. Who played Elise's alcoholic brother, Ned, on NBC's *Family Ties*?

a. Bruce Willis

b. Tom Hanks

c. Jim Carrey

d. Brad Pitt

GAME 51 Q8 ANSWER a
The Cusacks had small parts as geeks in this classic '80s Brat Pack comedy. The brother and sister duo has appeared in a number of movies together, including *Class* (1983), *Say Anything* (1989), *Grosse Pointe Blank* (1997), *Cradle Will Rock* (1999), and *High Fidelity* (2000).

---

9. What was Marlon Brando's first film?

a. *I Remember Mama*

b. *The Men*

c. *The Wild One*

d. *A Streetcar Named Desire*

GAME 71 Q8 ANSWER a
MacLaine made her debut in this wonderfully offbeat 1955 Hitchcock black comedy. She appeared in *Can-Can* and *The Apartment* in 1960, and in *Irma La Douce* in 1963.

5. Which film was *not* directed by Herbert Ross?

a. *Steel Magnolias* (1989)

b. *Funny Girl* (1968)

c. *Play it Again, Sam* (1972)

d. *The Odd Couple* (1968)

GAME 10 Q4 ANSWER c
Scorsese directed "Bad" in 1987. Landis directed the 1983 breakthrough video for "Thriller," as well as the 1991 "Black or White" video with its innovative morphing technique. Spike Lee directed two versions of "They Don't Care About Us" from *HIStory: Past, Present and Future, Book I.*

---

5. Which pinup girl had no eyebrows?

a. Betty Grable

b. Lana Turner

c. Rita Hayworth

d. Marilyn Monroe

GAME 30 Q4 ANSWER b
In 1995, Gena Lee Nolan went directly from being one of "Barker's Beauties" to playing Neely Capshaw on UPN's *Baywatch.* Erika Eleniak, Pam Anderson, and Donna D'Errico were all Playboy Playmates of the Month.

---

5. Which movie about *Frankenstein* author, Mary Shelley, featured Natasha Richardson?

a. *Frankenstein Unbound* (1990)

b. *Gothic* (1986)

c. *Haunted Summer* (1988)

d. *Rowing in the Wind* (1987)

GAME 50 Q4 ANSWER d
The Count has made an appearance in over 160 films. That's an average of three movies every two years since Bram Stoker first published his book back in the 1890s! As far as Hollywood is concerned, Dracula is one monster you can always "Count" on.

---

5. Lynda Carter played TV's Wonder Woman. Who played her sister, Wonder Girl?

a. Debra Winger

b. Margaux Hemingway

c. Margot Kidder

d. Cathy Lee Crosby

GAME 70 Q4 ANSWER c
The secret identity of Britt Reid, editor and publisher of the *Daily Sentinel,* was known only by Kato, his houseboy; Lenore Case, his secretary; and Frank Scanlon, the district attorney. Kato was played by the legendary Bruce Lee.

8. Which was the most expensive television mini-series to produce?

a. *Roots*

b. *Shoah*

c. *The Thorn Birds*

d. *War and Remembrance*

NBC's *Mary Kay and Johnny* (1947 to 1950), played by Mary Kay and Johnny Stearns, was one of TV's first sitcoms. The show's plotline revolved around a newlywed couple that lived in Greenwich Village. Later, Johnny Stearns became the producer of NBC's *The Tonight Show*, starring Steve Allen.

---

8. Which comedian appeared on the first episode of *Saturday Night Live*?

a. Lily Tomlin

b. Richard Pryor

c. Andy Kaufman

d. Steve Martin

Rowan & Martin's Laugh-In ran from 1968 to 1973. The only other cast members who rode out the show were hosts Dan Rowan and Dick Martin, and announcer Gary Owens.

---

8. Which John Hughes comedy featured siblings John and Joan Cusack?

a. *Sixteen Candles* (1984)

b. *Weird Science* (1985)

c. *Pretty in Pink* (1986)

d. *Ferris Bueller's Day Off* (1986)

Yes, there were brothers in The Beach Boys (leader Brian Wilson and his brothers Carl and Dennis), but the group was led by Brian and first cousin Mike Love. Nowadays, Mike Love "gets around" with a new Beach Boys group, and Brian Wilson "gets around" on his own.

---

8. Which film was Shirley MacLaine's first?

a. *The Trouble With Harry*

b. *Can-Can*

c. *The Apartment*

d. *Irma La Douce*

Shot in glorious Technicolor, the famous dance sequence required the use of milk in place of water because its thicker, more opaque quality showed up far better on film than water did. The wonderful title song from this film was later used by maverick director Stanley Kubrick in his disturbing 1971 masterpiece, *A Clockwork Orange*.

6. In the 1992 biopic *Chaplin*, Dan Aykroyd played director Mack Sennett. Who played Mabel Normand?

a. Geraldine Chaplin
b. Marisa Tomei
c. Diane Lane
d. Moira Kelly

GAME 10 Q5 ANSWER d
Ross also directed the popular 1984 dance film *Footloose,* and received a Best Director Oscar nomination for *The Turning Point* (1977). Although *The Odd Couple* was directed by Gene Saks, Ross did direct five other Neil Simon scripts, including *The Sunshine Boys* (1975) and *The Goodbye Girl* (1977).

6. Which film features Gwyneth Paltrow as the daughter of the President?

a. *Nixon* (1995)
b. *JFK* (1991)
c. *Dick* (1999)
d. *Jefferson in Paris* (1995)

GAME 30 Q5 ANSWER b
Producer Samuel Goldwyn didn't think Turner's eyebrows were exotic enough for her role in the 1938 film *The Adventures of Marco Polo.* At his insistence, they were shaved off and straight black brows were penciled in. Her eyebrows never grew back. Thereafter, Turner either wore false brows or drew them in.

6. Who played the head vampire, Max, in *The Lost Boys* (1987)?

a. John Lithgow
b. Edward Herrmann
c. James Widdoes
d. Donald Sutherland

GAME 50 Q5 ANSWER b
Natasha Richardson played Shelley in Ken Russell's *Gothic* opposite Julian Sands. *Frankenstein Unbound* featured Bridget Fonda as the author. *Rowing in the Wind* (*Remando al Viento*), an English-language film from Spain, included performances by future (and now past) couple Elizabeth Hurley and Hugh Grant.

6. Toby Maguire played Spider-Man in the 2002 movie. Who played the role in the live-action TV series?

a. Dean Cain
b. Lou Ferrigno
c. Nicholas Hammond
d. Pat Paulsen

GAME 70 Q5 ANSWER a
Winger played Drusilla, younger sister to Diana Prince, in a dozen episodes of the World War II-era superhero series. In later episodes, the action switched to the present day. Debra Winger started making movies, leaving her costumed crusader days behind.

7. Which was the first TV couple shown together in bed?

a. Mary Kay and Johnny Stearns

b. Fred and Wilma Flintstone

c. Lucy and Ricky Ricardo

d. Ozzie and Harriet Nelson

The 1980 episode that answered this question had the highest all-time ratings (until the *M*•*A*•*S*•*H* finale). Texas oilman J.R. Ewing (Larry Hagman) was pure scoundrel with lots of enemies. His wife, Sue Ellen (Linda Gray), was the prime suspect, but the guilty one turned out to be her sister Kristen (Mary Crosby), who had been having an affair with J.R.

---

7. Which original cast member of *Rowan & Martin's Laugh-In* stayed with the show for its entire run?

a. Ruth Buzzi

b. Arte Johnson

c. Henry Gibson

d. Alan Sues

Chase officially left the show soon after the first season and was replaced by Bill Murray. Chase's first hosting gig was in February of 1978; Bill Murray's was in 1981. Steve Martin has been a frequent host on the show, but never a cast member.

---

7. Which rock group is *not* led by two brothers?

a. The Kinks

b. Oasis

c. Van Halen

d. The Beach Boys

Peter Aykroyd joined *SNL* in 1979 for one season after big brother Dan left the show. Jim Belushi joined the cast from 1983 through 1985. Bill Murray's older sibling Brian Doyle-Murray, already a contributor to the show, joined the cast for the 1981/82 season.

---

7. In the 1952 film classic *Singin' in the Rain*, what was the rain that Gene Kelly danced around in actually made of?

a. Water

b. Seltzer

c. Milk

d. Cold coffee

Winkler co-starred with Sylvester Stallone and Perry King as members of a gang of Brooklyn youths trying to deal with growing up in Brooklyn. It wasn't until Winkler appeared in TV's *Happy Days* that Arthur "The Fonz" Fonzarelli was born.

7. Alfred Hitchcock directed a remake of which of his own films?

a. *The 39 Steps* (1937)

b. *The Lady Vanishes* (1938)

c. *The Man Who Knew Too Much* (1934)

d. *Sabotage* (1936)

GAME 10 Q6 ANSWER b
1992 was a banner year for Tomei, who won a Best Suporting Actress Oscar for her role in *My Cousin Vinny* and then received good reviews for her performance in Sir Richard Attenborough's *Chaplin*.

---

7. Julia Roberts' first major film role was in:

a. *Steel Magnolias*

b. *Satisfaction*

c. *Sweet Lorraine*

d. *Pretty Woman*

GAME 30 Q6 ANSWER d
Paltrow played daughter Patsy Jefferson in this Merchant-Ivory production. Interestingly, Paltrow's mother, Blythe Danner, played Jefferson's wife in the film *1776*, which was released just weeks after Gwyneth was born in 1972.

---

7. Which actor has played Dracula in the most films?

a. Bela Lugosi

b. Peter Cushing

c. John Carradine

d. Christopher Lee

GAME 50 Q6 ANSWER b
Joel Schumacher directed this teen vampire flick, which featured the two Coreys—Haim and Feldman—together for the first time. Dianne Wiest played the mother of Haim and Jason Patric. Unknowingly, Wiest's character dates the town's answer to Dracula.

---

7. Which film is about a starving actor who becomes a costumed superhero?

a. *Hero at Large* (1980)

b. *A Hero Ain't Nothin' But a Sandwich* (1978)

c. *Some Kind of Hero* (1982)

d. *Hero* (1992)

GAME 70 Q6 ANSWER c
Before taking on the role of Peter Parker in *The Amazing Spider-Man,* which ran from 1977 to 1979, Hammond was best known for playing Freidrich, one of the Von Trapp children in *The Sound of Music* (1965).

6. Who shot J.R. on CBS's *Dallas*?

a. Sue Ellen Ewing

b. Cliff Barnes

c. Kristen Shepard

d. Jock Ewing

GAME 11 Q5 ANSWER b
Who Wants to Be a Millionaire? has daily editions. Wednesday night's cliffhanger on *Batman* (1966 to 1968) was resolved on Thursday at the "same Bat time, same Bat channel." *Peyton Place* (1964 to 1969) ran two, then three episodes a week for the first two seasons.

6. Who was the first ex-*Saturday Night Live* cast member to host the show?

a. Bill Murray

b. Gilda Radner

c. Chevy Chase

d. Steve Martin

GAME 31 Q5 ANSWER b
From 1967 to 1978, Burnett established herself as TV's comedy queen with her Emmy Award-winning *The Carol Burnett Show*. The CBS variety program's cast of regulars included Vicki Lawrence, Harvey Korman, and Lyle Wagonner. Burnett's tug on her ear at the end of each show was a signal to her Grandmother, who raised her.

6. Which Not Ready for Prime Time Player did *not* have a sibling join the cast of *Saturday Night Live*?

a. Dan Aykroyd

b. John Belushi

c. Jane Curtin

d. Bill Murray

GAME 51 Q5 ANSWER c
Jennifer, the Tilly sister who usually plays the part of a ditsy airhead, received an Oscar nomination for doing just that in *Bullets Over Broadway*. This hilarious Woody Allen film has her cast as Olive, a gangster's girlfriend who wants to be an actress (in spite of her very obvious lack of talent).

6. In what movie did Henry Winkler portray a leather-coated greaser?

a. *The Wanderers* (1979)

b. *The Lords of Flatbush* (1974)

c. *American Graffiti* (1973)

d. *Night Shift* (1982)

GAME 71 Q5 ANSWER b
O'Connor played the bumbling Peter Stirling in six films, but explained that "the mule still gets more fan mail." So after *Francis Joins the Navy* (1955), he passed the mule's reins to former child star Mickey Rooney. Chill Wills then handed over the voice work to Paul Frees, and director Arthur Lubin moved on to TV with *Mr. Ed.*

GAME 10

8. Director Chris Columbus wrote the screenplays for all of the following movies *except*:

a. *The Goonies* (1985)

b. *Gremlins* (1984)

c. *Young Sherlock Holmes* (1985)

d. *Back to the Future* (1985)

GAME 10 Q7 ANSWER c
The 1934 British version starred Leslie Banks and Edna Best as the couple whose daughter is kidnapped while on a winter holiday. The 1956 American version, which starred Jimmy Stewart and Doris Day, featured the Oscar-winning song, "Que Sera Sera."

GAME 30

8. Which actress made her feature film debut in the 1976 remake of *King Kong*?

a. Farrah Fawcett

b. Bo Derek

c. Jessica Lange

d. Cheryl Ladd

GAME 30 Q7 ANSWER b
Along with Julia, this 1988 film starred Justine Bateman and Trini Alvarado as members of a teen band. Roberts appeared later that year in *Mystic Pizza*, but it was *Steel Magnolias* in 1989 that made audiences sit up and take notice of her.

GAME 50

8. To date, which horror film has spawned the most sequels?

a. *Psycho* (1960)

b. *Poltergeist* (1982)

c. *Friday the 13th* (1980)

d. *Halloween* (1978)

GAME 50 Q7 ANSWER d
Since 1948, Lee has made over two hundred films—twelve of them as the Count. Lee's most current roles include Master Dooku in *Star Wars II: Attack of the Clones* (2002) and Saruman in the "Lord of the Rings" movies.

GAME 70

8. Which group wrote the soundtrack for the 1980 film *Flash Gordon*?

a. ELO

b. Queen

c. The Alan Parsons Project

d. Survivor

GAME 70 Q7 ANSWER a
This 1980 comedy has John Ritter as a starving actor who is hired to promote a superhero movie. On his way home, he foils a robbery while still in costume. Anne Archer co-stars as the woman who protects Ritter from danger and then falls in love with him.

5. Which show never aired new episodes more than once a week?

a. *Who Wants to Be a Millionaire?*

b. *That's Incredible!*

c. *Batman*

d. *Peyton Place*

GAME 11 Q4 ANSWER b

Actor/producer/director Sheldon Leonard produced the Emmy Award-winning *The Danny Thomas Show*, as well as *The Andy Griffith Show*, *The Dick Van Dyke Show*, *I Spy*, and *My World and Welcome to It*, for which he also won an Emmy.

---

5. Carol Burnett ended her shows by singing "I'm So Glad We Had This Time Together" and by:

a. Blowing a kiss

b. Tugging her ear

c. Giving a peace sign

d. Giving a Tarzan yell

GAME 31 Q4 ANSWER a

Woody Allen, born Allan Konigsberg, began his comedy career while still in high school writing jokes for Jack Paar. He also wrote for Sid Caesar's *Your Show of Shows* with Neil Simon, Mel Brooks, and Carl Reiner. Simon's play *Laughter on the 23rd Floor* is based on the experiences of this four-man team of comedy writers.

---

5. Which film starred Jennifer Tilly (not her sister Meg)?

a. *The Big Chill* (1983)

b. *Agnes of God* (1985)

c. *Bullets Over Broadway* (1994)

d. *Leaving Normal* (1992)

GAME 51 Q4 ANSWER c

"For All We Know" was the love theme from the 1970 film *Lovers and Other Strangers,* based on the play by Joe Bologna and Renee Taylor. For the soundtrack, the song was performed by Larry Meredith. Diane Keaton made her film debut in this movie.

---

5. Which "Francis" movie does *not* star Donald O'Connor?

a. *Francis Goes to West Point*

b. *Francis in the Haunted House*

c. *Francis Joins the WACS*

d. *Francis Goes to the Races*

GAME 71 Q4 ANSWER d

After losing out to James Dean in *East of Eden*, Newman won the lead in *The Silver Chalice* (1954) co-starring Virginia Mayo, Natalie Wood, E.G. Marshall, and Jack Palance. Newman despised the movie so much that he took out an ad "apologizing" to his fans when it was later aired on TV.

9. Which film was *not* directed by Alfred Hitchcock?

a. *Saboteur* (1941)

b. *The Third Man* (1949)

c. *The Lady Vanishes* (1938)

d. *To Catch a Thief* (1955)

GAME 10 Q8 ANSWER d

Columbus was working in a comic book store when he sold his *Gremlins* script to Steven Spielberg. Columbus came into his own as a director with *Adventures in Babysitting* (1987), *Home Alone* (1990), and *Harry Potter and the Sorcerer's Stone* (2001). The writing credits for *Back to the Future* go to Robert Zemeckis and Bob Gale.

---

9. Which leggy singer was born Annie Mae Bullock?

a. Tina Turner

b. Diana Ross

c. Whitney Houston

d. Paula Abdul

GAME 30 Q8 ANSWER c

Lange had been a model before landing the role in *King Kong* opposite co-star Jeff Bridges. Bridges later appeared with Farrah Fawcett at the height of her *Charlie's Angels* fame in *Somebody Killed Her Husband* (1978). Meanwhile, Bo Derek had her leg bitten off by a killer whale in her 1977 film debut, *Orca*.

---

9. In the 1979 sci-fi horror *Alien,* who is the first member of the *Nostromo* space crew to be killed?

a. Yaphet Kotto

b. Harry Dean Stanton

c. Veronica Cartwright

d. John Hurt

GAME 50 Q8 ANSWER c

With the release of *Jason X* in 2002, the *Friday the 13th* film series is in the lead, with a total of ten movies. Following close behind with eight installments is the *Halloween* series. Both *Psycho* and *Poltergeist* have spawned two theatrically released sequels and one made-for-cable film to date.

---

9. What was Luke Skywalker first called in George Lucas's screenplay for *Star Wars*?

a. Luke Starkiller

b. Zack Skyglider

c. Brett Starwalker

d. Matt Starblaze

GAME 70 Q8 ANSWER b

ELO wrote the soundtrack for the Olivia Newton-John film *Xanadu* (1980). Alan Parsons was the music supervisor of Andrew Powell's score for the Michelle Pfeiffer film *Ladyhawke* (1985). And Survivor's #1 hit single "Eye of the Tiger" was played throughout Sylvester Stallone's *Rocky III* (1982).

4. Which *Guys and Dolls* actor produced some of the most popular TV shows of the late '50s and '60s?

a. Marlon Brando

b. Sheldon Leonard

c. Stubby Kaye

d. Frank Sinatra

It's said that Richard Nixon's inordinate amount of "flop sweat" during his televised debates with John F. Kennedy cost him the election. I had both men on my show, and President Kennedy clearly was more at ease in front of the camera.

---

4. Which of these TV shows had Woody Allen as a writer?

a. *Your Show of Shows*

b. *The Smothers Brothers Comedy Hour*

c. *Texaco Star Theatre*

d. *You Bet Your Life*

After a five-year absence, Lorne Michaels came back to produce *SNL* for NBC in 1985 with an entirely new cast. Hall was only seventeen when he joined Joan Cusack, Robert Downey, Jr., Nora Dunn, Jon Lovitz, Randy Quaid, Terry Sweeney, and Danitra Vance.

---

4. Which Oscar-winning song was a 1971 hit for the Carpenters?

a. "Moon River"

b. "Raindrops Keep Fallin' on My Head"

c. "For All We Know"

d. "All the Way"

Led by Wilson sisters Ann and Nancy, Heart's first album contained the hits "Crazy on You" and "Magic Man." Nancy, the guitarist, is married to writer/director Cameron Crowe. She has either appeared in or written music for nearly all of his films.

---

4. What was Paul Newman's first movie?

a. *Somebody Up There Likes Me*

b. *The Long, Hot Summer*

c. *Exodus*

d. *The Silver Chalice*

Although Dean started with an uncredited bit part in the Martin and Lewis comedy *Sailor Beware* (1951), it wasn't until four years later that he burst onto the screen in Elia Kazan's *East of Eden,* a powerful adaptation of John Steinbeck's novel.

10. Who directed Robin Williams' film debut?

a. Steven Spielberg

b. Francis Ford Coppola

c. Barry Levinson

d. Robert Altman

GAME 10 Q9 ANSWER b

Carol Reed directed Orson Welles and Joseph Cotten in *The Third Man*—probably the best suspense film that was *not* directed by Alfred Hitchcock.

---

10. Which actress did *not* appear in the film *Thoroughly Modern Millie* (1967)?

a. Julie Andrews

b. Carol Burnett

c. Mary Tyler Moore

d. Carol Channing

GAME 30 Q9 ANSWER a

The ex-wife of musician Ike Turner was born in 1939. Her story was told in the 1993 movie *What's Love Got to Do With It* starring Angela Bassett as Tina and Laurence Fishburne as abusive husband Ike.

---

10. What is the name of the bartender who gives Jack Nicholson shots of bourbon in *The Shining* (1980)?

a. Grady

b. Lloyd

c. Mr. Ullman

d. Joe

GAME 50 Q9 ANSWER d

John Hurt's character comes to a violent end when a newborn alien explodes from his stomach. The British actor later parodied this death scene in the Mel Brooks sci-fi comedy *Spaceballs*. When the alien pops from his stomach, Hurt exclaims, "Oh, no. Not again!"

---

10. All of the following people did a cameo on the *Batman* TV series except:

a. Jerry Lewis

b. Bruce Lee

c. Sammy Davis, Jr.

d. Robert Kennedy

GAME 70 Q9 ANSWER a

The name Starkiller was ultimately considered too militaristic by Lucas, who had read Joseph Campbell's work on mythology when coming up with his notion of "The Force."

3. What was televised in 1960 for the first time?

a. World Series

b. Commercial advertisement

c. Presidential debate

d. Lunar landing

GAME 11 Q2 ANSWER c
The Columbia Broadcasting System was founded in 1927, and its eye logo was unveiled in October 1951, two days after the premiere of *I Love Lucy.* Designer Bill Golden conceived it while driving through Pennsylvania Dutch country, where he noticed eye-like Shaker hex symbols, which were meant to ward off the "evil eye."

---

3. Who was the youngest *Saturday Night Live* cast member?

a. Anthony Michael Hall

b. Eddie Murphy

c. Joan Cusack

d. Adam Sandler

GAME 31 Q2 ANSWER a
Garrett Morris said the opening phrase that season for the December show with guest host Richard Pryor. President Gerald Ford said the line for the April show that was hosted by his former press secretary Ron Nessen.

---

3. The 1975 debut album of hard-rock band Heart was:

a. *Little Queen*

b. *Dreamboat Annie*

c. *Heart*

d. *Brigade*

GAME 51 Q2 ANSWER c
These sisters are probably best known for their renditions of the World War II-era favorites "Don't Sit Under the Apple Tree" and "Boogie Woogie Bugle Boy" (made popular again by Bette Midler in the early '70s).

---

3. James Dean's first lead role was in:

a. *Rebel Without a Cause*

b. *Giant*

c. *East of Eden*

d. *Sailor Beware*

GAME 71 Q2 ANSWER a
In this 1950 film, Bette Davis plays aging stage actress Margo Channing, and Anne Baxter plays would-be actress Eve Harrington, who wants to steal Channing's roles. Holm plays Channing's best friend, and Marilyn Monroe has a small part as an aspiring actress.

11. Boris Karloff took his last bow in *Targets* (1968), which was the feature debut of which director?

a. Francis Ford Coppola

b. Brian De Palma

c. Peter Bogdanovich

d. Sydney Pollack

GAME 10 Q10 ANSWER d
Williams played the title character in Altman's live-action film *Popeye* (1980). Spielberg directed Williams in *Hook* (1991); Coppola directed him in *Jack* (1996); and Levinson directed him in *Good Morning, Vietnam* (1987) and *Toys* (1992).

---

11. In which film does Judy Garland sing "Be a Clown"?

a. *The Pirate* (1948)

b. *Easter Parade* (1948)

c. *Words and Music* (1948)

d. *Girl Crazy* (1943)

GAME 30 Q10 ANSWER b
Burnett has never appeared in a movie with any of these actresses, but she has performed often with her friend Julie Andrews. In fact, Burnett is godmother to Andrews' daughter, Emma Kate Walton.

---

11. What was the number of the hotel room that houses very evil things in Stanley Kubrick's film *The Shining* (1980)?

a. 217

b. 227

c. 237

d. 247

GAME 50 Q10 ANSWER b
Grady is the waiter who tries to convince Jack to kill his family. Mr. Ullman is the man who owns the Overlook Hotel and hires Jack to be the caretaker. My name is Joe—I've never been a bartender.

---

11. Which well-known film critic made a brief cameo in *Superman: The Movie* (1978)?

a. Gene Siskel

b. Rex Reed

c. Roger Ebert

d. Gene Shalit

GAME 70 Q10 ANSWER d
According to Adam "Batman" West, the producers always wanted the young Senator to appear on the show, but he was never able to. West, however, had the honor of knowing that his framed picture as Batman hung in the Senator's office.

2. ABC uses letters. NBC uses a peacock. WB is a frog. What does CBS use as a logo?

a. A mountain

b. A woman with a torch

c. An eye

d. A clock

GAME 11 Q1 ANSWER b
Miyoshi Umeki played the role in this sitcom, which aired from 1969 to 1972. She was also the first Asian actor to win an Oscar—Best Supporting Actress for *Sayonara* (1957). Mr. French kept house on *Family Affair;* Mrs. Figalilly was the governess on *Nanny and the Professor;* and Mrs. Robinson seduced *The Graduate* (1967).

2. Who said "Live from New York, it's Saturday Night" in all but two shows during *SNL's* first season?

a. Chevy Chase

b. Garrett Morris

c. John Belushi

d. Dan Aykroyd

GAME 31 Q1 ANSWER b
Aykroyd received a Best Supporting Actor nomination for *Driving Miss Daisy* (1989); Downey was nominated for Best Actor for *Chaplin* (1992); Cusack received two nods for Best Supporting Actress—for *Working Girl* (1988) and *In and Out* (1997).

2. Which sister act includes Patti, Maxine, and Laverne?

a. The Lennon Sisters

b. Sister Sledge

c. The Andrews Sisters

d. The McGuire Sisters

GAME 51 Q1 ANSWER a
The Pointer Sisters began as backup singers for artists such as Dave Mason, Grace Slick, and Boz Scaggs. In the early '70s, they formed their own act, wearing clothes from the forties and performing songs that covered a wide range of musical styles. They have won Grammys for "Fairytale," "Jump," and "Automatic."

2. In *All About Eve*, who played Eve?

a. Anne Baxter

b. Bette Davis

c. Celeste Holm

d. Marilyn Monroe

GAME 71 Q1 ANSWER c
First released in spring of 1954, "Rock Around the Clock" didn't rise to #1 until after it was featured in 1955's *The Blackboard Jungle,* and then re-released. The song was also used to open George Lucas's 1973 film *American Graffiti,* and was heard for a while as the theme to TV's *Happy Days.*

12. Ron Howard received his first Oscar for directing:

a. *Apollo 13* (1995)

b. *A Beautiful Mind* (2001)

c. *Splash* (1984)

d. *Cocoon* (1985)

GAME 10 Q11 ANSWER c

Long before he became a well-known director, Bogdanovich worked for me, writing my program notes. He later had Cybill Shepherd cancel an appearance on my show to promote *At Long Last Love,* which did *not* do well at the box office.

12. Which pop diva starred in the movie with the most disappointing box office results?

a. Diana Ross in *Lady Sings the Blues*

b. Mariah Carey in *Glitter*

c. Olivia Newton-John in *Xanadu*

d. Bette Midler in *The Rose*

GAME 30 Q11 ANSWER a

Garland sings the song with Gene Kelly in this film (her last project with director-husband Vincente Minnelli). *The Pirate* spotlighted the songs of Cole Porter; *Easter Parade* featured the music of Irving Berlin; Rogers and Hart's music was heard in *Words and Music;* and *Girl Crazy* featured the music of George and Ira Gershwin.

12. In *Rosemary's Baby* (1968), how does Rosemary learn her neighbor's real name?

a. In a dream

b. Her friend Hutch tells her

c. By playing Scrabble

d. Her doctor tells her

GAME 50 Q11 ANSWER c

In Stephen King's novel, the room number is 217. When filming, Kubrick shot exteriors of a real hotel, but its owners worried that the movie would scare people away from room 217, so they asked that the number be changed to 237—a room the hotel didn't have. Now I never stay in room number 237.

12. Damon Wayans played a silly would-be superhero in which 1994 comedy?

a. *Stupidman*

b. *Fartman*

c. *Blankman*

d. *Geekman*

GAME 70 Q11 ANSWER b

As Lois Lane (Margot Kidder) and Clark Kent (Christopher Reeve) leave *The Daily Planet* offices for lunch early in the film, Lois says "Hi" to Rex as they walk through a set of revolving doors. Clark tries to say hello to Reed as well, but Rex must have been too busy trying to get up to his office to write a good review of the film.

1. Who was the Japanese housekeeper on ABC's *The Courtship of Eddie's Father*?

a. Mrs. Robinson

b. Mrs. Livingston

c. Mrs. Figalilly

d. Mr. French

The answer to this question is on:

page 143, top frame, right side.

1. Which of the following *Saturday Night Live* alumni has *not* received an Oscar nomination?

a. Dan Aykroyd

b. Bill Murray

c. Joan Cusack

d. Robert Downey, Jr.

The answer to this question is on:

page 143, second frame, right side.

1. Bonnie, Anita, and June make up the core of which sister act?

a. The Pointer Sisters

b. Sister Sledge

c. The Andrews Sisters

d. The McGuire Sisters

The answer to this question is on:

page 143, third frame, right side.

1. Which Bill Haley and the Comets song was featured in *The Blackboard Jungle* (1955)?

a. "See You Later, Alligator"

b. "Shake, Rattle, and Roll"

c. "Rock Around the Clock"

d. "Rock the Joint"

The answer to this question is on:

page 143, bottom frame, right side.

GAME 11

Calling All
Couch Potatoes

TV Trivia Tidbits

Turn to page 142
for the first question.

Turn to page 142
for the first question.

GAME 31

Make 'em Laugh

Saturday Night Live and
Other Sketch Comedies

Turn to page 142
for the first question.

GAME 51

Brothers and Sisters

Sibling World

Turn to page 142
for the first question.

GAME 71

Shake, Rattle,
and Roll

Movies of the '50s

Turn to page 142
for the first question.

ABOUT
THE AUTHOR

Joe Franklin began his remarkable show business career as a New York talk-and-variety show host in 1951. His show's format set the standard for many talk shows that followed. Over the years, his extraordinary guest list has read like a who's who of celebrity royalty, including such entertainment greats as Rudy Vallee, George Jessel, Barbra Streisand, Joan Rivers, Liza Minnelli, and Bill Cosby—and that's just for starters. Joe holds the Guinness Book of World Records for hosting the most TV shows—31,015 in all!

Joe has also appeared in such movies as *29th Street*, *Ghostbusters*, and *Broadway Danny Rose*. His Memory Lane theme restaurant, located in the Broadway District of Manhattan, continues to receive rave reviews. Currently, he can be heard on Bloomberg Radio, and in New York on WOR-AM.